The Political Economy of U.S. Monetary Policy

Mainstream economists explain the Federal Reserve's behavior over its one hundred years of existence as (usually failed) attempts to stabilize the economy on a non-inflationary growth path. The most important monetary event during those first one hundred years was the replacement of fixed exchange rates, based on a gold-exchange standard, with flexible exchange rates.

In this book, Dickens explains how flexible exchange rates became necessary to accommodate the Federal Reserve's relentless efforts to prevent progressive social change. It is argued that the Federal Reserve is an institutionalized alliance of the large New York banks and the large regional banks. When these two groups of banks are united, they constitute an unassailable force in the class conflict. However, when the large regional banks are at loggerheads with the large New York banks, over the proper role of bank clearinghouses during the populist period, along with the proper role of the Eurodollar market during the social democratic period, there is an opening for progressive social reforms.

This book builds upon Hyman Minsky's financial instability hypothesis as well as the Marxian model constructed by Thomas Piketty. It follows Piketty's historical method of deepening our understanding of the current Neoliberal Era (1980–2014) of global financial capitalism by comparing and contrasting it with the first era of global financial capitalism—the Gilded Age (1880–1914). In contrast with Piketty, however, this book incorporates monetary factors, including monetary policy, into the set of determinants of the long-run rate of economic growth. This book is suitable for those who study political economy and banking as well as macroeconomics.

Edwin Dickens is Professor and Chair at the Department of Economics and Finance at Saint Peter's University, New Jersey, U.S.

The Political Economy of U.S. Monetary Policy

How the Federal Reserve Gained Control and Uses It

Edwin Dickens

Routledge
Taylor & Francis Group

LONDON AND NEW YORK

First published 2016
by Routledge
2 Park Square, Milton Park, Abingdon, Oxon OX14 4RN

and Routledge
711 Third Avenue, New York, NY 100172016

First issued in paperback 2017

Routledge is an imprint of the Taylor & Francis Group, an informa business

British Library Cataloguing in Publication Data
A catalogue record for this book is available from the British Library

Library of Congress Cataloging in Publication Data
Names: Dickens, Edwin T., author. Title: The political economy of U.S. monetary policy: how the Federal Reserve gained control and uses it / Edwin Dickens. Description: Abingdon, Oxon; New York, NY: Routledge, 2016. Identifiers: LCCN 2015040846 (print) | LCCN 2015043377 (ebook) | ISBN 9781138909311 (hardback) | ISBN 9781315694030 (ebook) Subjects: LCSH: United States. Federal Reserve Board. | Monetary policy– United States. | Banks and banking, Central–United States. Classification: LCC HG2563.D53 2016 (print) | LCC HG2563 (ebook) | DDC 339.5/3– dc23LC record available at http://lccn.loc.gov/2015040846

ISBN 13: 978-1-138-49546-3 (pbk)
ISBN 13: 978-1-138-90931-1 (hbk)

Typeset in Times New Roman
by Sunrise Setting Ltd, Paignton, UK

For Karen

Content

List of Illustrations   ix
Foreword by Gerald Epstein   x
Acknowledgments   xiii
Introduction   xiv

1 The Theoretical Framework   **1**

1.1 The Orthodox Theory of Monetary Policy   2
1.2 Keynes's Theory of Monetary Policy   8
1.3 Summary and Conclusions   19

**2 The Origin of the Federal Reserve System:
the Institutionalization of the Alliance between the Large
New York Banks and the Large Regional Banks**   **27**

*2.1 The Origin of the Federal Reserve System as Lender
of Last Resort*   28
*2.2 The Origin of the Federal Reserve System as Controller
of the Money Supply*   29
*2.3 Stabilizing the Economy at Full Employment with
Price Stability*   33
2.4 Summary and Conclusions   34

**3 Democratic Control versus Banker Control of the
Federal Reserve System**   **37**

3.1 The Mainstream Literature   39
*3.2 Banker Influence and the Use of Monetary Policy to Stabilize
the Economy at Full Employment with Price Stability*   42
*3.3 Banker Influence and U.S. Monetary Policy during
the 1953–4 Recession*   51
3.4 Summary and Conclusions   55

4   The Federal Reserve's Implacable Opposition to Social Democracy   62

4.1 From a Penalty-rate Policy to Quantity Restraints   63
4.2 The Federal Reserve's Low-interest-rate Policy of 1970–2: Determinants and Constraints   84
4.3 The Federal Reserve's Tight Monetary Policy during the 1973–5 Recession   90
4.4 Summary and Conclusions   96

5   The End of the Golden Age of Relatively Stable Capitalist Development   108

5.1 The Financial Instability Hypothesis   109
5.2 Critique of the Financial Instability Hypothesis   110
5.3 The Intra-class Conflict Underlying the 1966 Financial Crisis   111
5.4 The 1966 Financial Crisis   113
5.5 Summary and Conclusions   121

6   The Eurodollar Market and Flexible Exchange Rates: the Linchpins of the Current Neoliberal Era of Global Financial Capitalism   130

6.1 The Origins of the Eurodollar Market   132
6.2 The U.S. Bank Cartel and the Eurodollar Market   133
6.3 The Endogeneity of the U.S. Money Supply   136
6.4 The End of the Movement toward Social Democracy in the U.S.   142
6.5 The Denouement   149
6.6 Summary and Conclusions   153

7   Summary and Conclusions   160

Appendix   164
Index   172

Illustrations

Figures

4.1	Phillips-curve analyses of the effects of monetary policy, in both the short-run and the long-run	92
5.1	Prime rate, market yield on three-month CDs, and the discount rate, 1964–70	114

Tables

3.1	Yields on short-term U.S. government securities, 1920–54	38
3.2	The cyclical movement of free reserves and the stock of money, 1953–60	40
3.3	The ratio of bank loans outstanding to banks' holdings of government securities	44
3.4	The ratio of the weekly reporting banks' holdings of treasury bills to their holdings of government securities	47
3.5	F-Test on four geometrical distributed lags	54
3.6	Monetary policy preferences of the Federal Advisory Council, 1951–88	58
4.1	The Federal Reserve's control variable during the last eight recessions	91
4.2	Targeted and estimated M_1 growth rates	94
6.1	Net size of the Eurodollar market and the U.K. share of it	133
6.2	Financing the costs of empire	134
6.3	Results from estimating the May 1967 U.S. bank cartel reunification with the Sept. 1969 imposition of reserve requirements	138
6.4	Creation of a Eurodollar deposit	139
6.5	U.S. bank borrowing of Eurodollars	140
6.6	The mitigation of tight U.S. monetary policy by U.S. bank Eurodollar borrowings	140
6.7	An underlying deterioration of the balance of payments	145

Foreword

The Federal Reserve is in the spotlight again, with investors and politicians hanging on every word about what its next policy move will be. This raises several key questions in economics, politics and history: How did the Federal Reserve get to be so powerful? Who gains and who loses from this power? What SHOULD the Federal Reserve do with its power and authority?

In *The Political Economy of U.S. Monetary Policy: How the Federal Reserve Gained Control and Uses It*, Edwin Dickens addresses these questions head-on. And they are not easy to answer. For questions about economic and political power – who has it, how do they get it, and in whose interest do they wield it? – are questions that many, and especially the powerful themselves, expend a lot of effort and resources to obscure.

To draw back the curtain on the power of the Fed and get to the root of the history, Dickens has to use a whole battery of techniques. He uses rigorous economic theory, archival material, publicly available data, econometric analysis, and a good dose of historical research to place Federal Reserve monetary policy in a rich, fascinating—and controversial—political economy context. In doing so, Dickens makes one point crystal clear and compelling: The Federal Reserve is an intensely political institution. It is not a marble hall filled with technocrats trying to fine tune the dials of the economy in the public interest.

This point might seem obvious to most observers of Federal Reserve behavior, but it goes squarely against the dominant view of mainstream macroeconomics. This view, incorporated in most standard macro textbooks and in much policy discussion, is that, left to their own devices, central banks, the Federal Reserve included, are neutral technicians trying to steer the economy toward its optimal path for all. It is only when governments try to interfere and tell the central banks what to do that monetary policy gets disoriented and leads to excessive inflation or recession. This view of the political economy of monetary policy lies behind the popular and still dominant view in mainstream policy and economic circles that central banks should be "independent" of governments. The most prevalent current version of this idea is that central banks should be independent to "target inflation." They argue that this would lead to politically neutral and optimal policy from society's point of view.

Dickens argues that there is no such thing as a politically neutral, technocratic Federal Reserve. He shows that, for good structural reasons, the Federal Reserve has been—apart from exceptional moments—strongly influenced by, if not under the control, of various segments of the financial community and especially the large Wall Street Banks and large regional banks. The exceptional moments have come in times of massive social, political, and economic crisis. Dickens shows that following the Great Depression of the 1930s and especially during the Second World War, the Federal Reserve was under more democratic control. During this period, it was oriented toward pursuing the broad goals set out by the government: namely, winning the war and implementing the New Deal and more "social democratic" oriented policies. But by 1951, with the famous "Federal Reserve–Treasury Accord," the Federal Reserve was able to begin reasserting its relative political independence from government and to do the bidding, once again, of various key segments of the capitalist class, especially the big Wall Street and (sometimes) big regional banks.

This connection to the banks is outlined by Dickens with interesting use of archival and statistical evidence based on the minutes of meetings by the Federal Reserve and the Advisory Committee (FAC), made up of bankers. Connecting these FAC minutes to actual monetary policy decisions by the Fed is an important contribution of the book.

In some ways, Dickens provides evidence for an idea that has become more popular in recent years. Especially since the Great Financial Crisis of 2008, it has become more acceptable, and even fashionable, to argue in some circles that the Federal Reserve has the best interests of Wall Street at heart.

But Dickens's argument is not so simple. Indeed, one of the distinctive and fascinating aspects of Dickens's argument is that, especially in the 1950s and 1960s, the Federal Reserve's main preoccupation was not just to support the banks but to try to undermine the power of the working class. To be sure, this determination by the Fed—illustrated with important quotes from Federal Reserve minutes—was often couched in terms of the Federal Reserve's concern with inflation. But the intensity of discussion concerning union wage negotiations and the desire to help capitalists resist these wage demands makes quite clear which side the Federal Reserve was on. This should be a welcome antidote for pundits who regularly claim that only "liberals" engage in "class warfare", or for economists who claim that the Federal Reserve is a bunch of neutral technocrats. Indeed, Dickens uses this evidence to argue that that the Federal Reserve was fighting against an entire social program—social democracy— and not just trying to control inflation or even simply maximizing bank profits.

In this far-ranging book, Dickens also introduces us to the monetary theory underlying an appropriate understanding of monetary policy from a Keynesian perspective. So this is a book not just about the political economy of Federal Reserve policy, but also about deep issues in policy-relevant economic theory. Dickens well explains Keynes's little understood analysis as to why the appropriate monetary policy is one where the Federal Reserve holds interest rates low in the long run, and acts as a lender of last resort when necessary. He contrasts this to the common view of Fed Policy by U.S. Keynesians and, indeed, most Keynesians in much of the world, that the Federal Reserve should pursue counter-cyclical monetary policy, including trying to pre-empt inflationary forces by raising interest rates. This interesting discussion of Keynes's approach helps the reader understand Dickens's argument that the decisions by the Fed to raise interest rates to oppose the wage increases of labor unions was politically and economically mistaken.

One does not have to agree with all of Dickens's arguments and interpretations to agree that this is a book filled with insight, evidence, and arguments that will make us think more deeply and more intelligently about one of the most powerful institutions in the American Political Economy. To know "the Fed", it is important to know this book.

Gerald Epstein
Professor of Economics and Co-Director
Political Economy Research Institute (PERI)
University of Massachusetts, Amherst, U.S.

Acknowledgments

It was my good fortune to learn how to do economics from Nilufur Cagatay, John Eatwell, Gerald Epstein, David Gordon, Robert Heilbroner, Edward Nell, Willi Semmler, Anwar Shaikh, and Ross Thomson at the New School for Social Research in the 1980s. I am particularly grateful to Gerald Epstein, who has remained a constant source of inspiration and support.

I am also grateful for permission to use in this book material from my following publications: "Financial Crises, Innovations and Federal Reserve Control of the Stock of Money," *Contributions to Political Economy*, 1990, Vol. 9: 1–23; "U.S. Monetary Policy in the 1950s: A Radical Political Economic Approach," *Review of Radical Political Economics*, 1995, Vol. 27, No. 4: 83–111; "The Great Inflation and U.S. Monetary Policy in the Late 1960s: A Political Economic Approach," *Social Concept*, 1995, Vol. 9, No. 1, 49–81; "The Federal Reserve's Low Interest Rate Policy of 1970–72: Determinants and Constraints," *Review of Radical Political Economics*, 1996, Vol. 28, No. 3: 115–25; "The Federal Reserve's Tight Monetary Policy During the 1973–75 Recession: A Survey of Possible Interpretations," *Review of Radical Political Economics*, 1997, Vol. 29, No. 3: 79–91; "Bank Influence and the Failure of U.S. Monetary Policy During the 1953–54 Recession," *International Review of Applied Economics*, 1998, Vol. 12, No. 2: 221–40; "A Political-Economic Critique of Minsky's Financial Instability Hypothesis: The Case of the 1966 Financial Crisis," *Review of Political Economy*, 1999, Vol. 11, No. 4: 379–98; "The Eurodollar Market and the New Era of Global Financialization," in *Financialization In the World Economy*, Gerald Epstein (ed.), 2005, New York, Edward Elgar; "Keynes's Theory of Probability, Investment Behavior, and Behavioral Finance," in *Keynes and Macroeconomics after 70 Years: Critical Assessments of the General Theory*, Wray, L. R. and Forstater, M. (eds), 2008, Aldershot, Edward Elgar, pp. 223–33; "Keynes's Theory of Monetary Policy: An Essay in Historical Reconstruction," *Contributions to Political Economy*, 2011, Vol. 30, 1–11; and "The Political Economy of U.S. Monetary Policy: How the Federal Reserve Gained Control and Uses It," *International Journal of Political Economy*, 2013, Vol. 42, No. 3, pp. 24–43.

Introduction

In this book, I explain the Federal Reserve's behavior in terms of class and intra-class conflicts, with the class conflict taking the form of a populist movement prior to the New Deal then a movement toward social democracy, while the intra-class conflict at issue here is between the large regional banks and the large New York banks. I show that when these two groups of banks are united, they constitute an unassailable force in the class conflict. However, when the large regional banks are at loggerheads with the large New York banks, over the proper role of bank clearinghouses during the populist period, and the proper role of fixed-interest-rate rules during the social-democratic period, there is an opening for progressive economic reforms.

In contrast, orthodox economists explain the Federal Reserve's behavior as (usually failed) attempts to stabilize the economy on a non-inflationary growth path. However, they are divided over how the Federal Reserve should accomplish this goal. Some argue that the Federal Reserve should concern itself exclusively with inflation, decreasing and increasing the money supply according to whether inflation is above or below a target rate of about 2 percent (see, for example, Bernanke, 1999). Others argue that the Federal Reserve should also concern itself with unemployment, decreasing or increasing the money supply according to whether the economy is growing above or below a rate that corresponds to a non-accelerating inflation rate of unemployment, although this argument is somewhat mitigated by the fact that orthodox economists cannot agree on what the non-accelerating inflation rate of unemployment is (see, for example, Blinder, 1999).

In this book, I show that both normative arguments are misleading. Practically speaking, propaganda about the Federal Reserve's role in stabilizing the economy on a non-inflationary growth path is key to undermining the movement toward social democracy (Chapter 4). Theoretically speaking, it is based on a fallacious belief that inflation is caused by excessive growth of the money supply (for a demonstration of the fallacy, see Chapter 1). In fact, long-term inflationary pressures are caused by average real wages increasing more rapidly than labor productivity (Chapter 4), and the appropriate response is an incomes policy (Chapter 5). There are also short-term inflationary pressures caused by excess aggregate demand during cyclical expansions, which lends some credence to the notion of a non-accelerating inflation rate of unemployment. But the appropriate response is government interventions to remove bottlenecks in the pipelines of supply, once again leaving no role for the Federal Reserve (see, for example, Keynes, 1936, pp. 320–4; Robinson, 1956, pp. 198–216).

The Federal Reserve's only legitimate role is to act as lender of last resort to the banking system since private-sector profit-maximizing banks cannot be relied upon to carry out this necessary function (Chapter 2). I show that, for the period between the New Deal of 1933–5 and the Treasury–Federal Reserve Accord of 1951, and again in the early 1960s, the Federal Reserve acted as lender of last resort while adhering to fixed-interest-rate rules (for the importance of imposing fixed-interest-rate rules on the Federal Reserve, see Chapter 1). Fixed-interest-rate rules are essential components of the movement toward social democracy, the other essential components being an incomes policy and capital controls (Chapter 5).

When establishing the Federal Reserve as a lender of last resort in 1913, it was an egregious error to also give it control of the money supply. My thesis is that the Federal Reserve is an institutional alliance of the large New York banks and the large regional banks. By giving the Federal Reserve control of the money supply, these banks were empowered to beat back the populist movement toward a more equitable institutional structure for a central bank (Chapter 2). And the history of the Federal Reserve since the Accord of 1951 is the story of how it uses its control of the money supply to beat back the even more progressive movement toward social democracy. In fact, the Federal Reserve is the principal institutional obstacle to progressive economic reforms today.

To speak more schematically, I proceed as follows. In Chapter 1, I make the theoretical case for imposing fixed-interest-rate rules on central banks. My argument takes the form of a reconstruction of John Maynard Keynes's theory of monetary policy, as presented in *The General Theory of Employment, Interest, and Money* (1936). I counterpose Keynes's theory with the orthodox one for independent central banks capable of attempting to stabilize the economy on a non-inflationary growth path, and show that fixed-interest-rate rules tend to bring about more aggregate output and less unemployment in the long period.

In Chapter 2, I explain the origins of the Federal Reserve in terms of class and intra-class conflicts, with the class conflict taking the form of a populist movement and the intra-class conflict at issue here being between the large New York banks and the large regional banks. I show that, when the large regional banks were at loggerheads with the large New York banks over the proper role of bank clearinghouses, there was an opening for progressive economic reforms—in particular, the establishment of a democratically accountable central bank. However, when these two groups of banks united over the terms for establishing an independent Federal Reserve System as essentially a cartel manager to preserve and enhance their profit margins by limiting the supply of their output (i.e. money), they constituted an unassailable force in the class conflict.

In Chapter 3, I demonstrate that to the degree the Federal Reserve is independent of democratic control it is dependent on the large banks. Consequently, it is incapable of stabilizing the economy on a non-inflationary growth path because its dependence on the large banks creates a bias in favor of high interest rates, regardless of the state of the economy. This bias became a political issue in the depths of the Great Depression in 1932, which prompted the New Deal financial reforms of 1933–5, which increased democratic control and thus reduced banker influence on monetary policy. However, when the large banks regained control of monetary policy with the Federal Reserve–Treasury Accord of 1951 this bias re-emerged, and has not been seriously challenged since.

In Chapter 4, I demonstrate the Federal Reserve's implacable opposition to social democracy, which I define as a strong and organized labor movement aligned with the interests of the unemployed. Whenever the labor movement made demands, principally during tri-annual rounds of wage negotiations in the automobile and steel industries during the 1951–75 period, the Federal Reserve set itself the task of defeating it by using high interest rates to precipitate then sustain recessions. I show that the Federal Reserve finally achieved its goal during the 1974–5 recession.

In Chapters 5 and 6, I offer an explanation of the structural transformation from the postwar Golden Age of capitalism to the current Neoliberal Era. In a straightforward application of my theoretical framework, I counterpose these two long-period positions as being defined by fixed-interest-rate rules and Federal Reserve independence to change interest rates respectively. And, in Chapter 5, in an equally straightforward application of my thesis concerning the nature of the Federal Reserve as an institutional alliance of the large New York banks and the large regional banks, I characterize the last moment of the Golden Age as an effort by the Johnson administration to extend the movement toward social democracy by means of an incomes policy, made possible by the fact that the large regional banks were at loggerheads with the large New York banks over the proper role of the fixed-interest-rate rules. In Chapter 6, I then characterize the founding moment of the Neoliberal Era as these two groups of banks overcoming their differences over fixed-interest-rate rules, thereby uniting as an unassailable force in the class conflict.[1]

In Chapter 7, I provide a summary and conclusions.

Note

1 If the long-period position we call the Golden Age of capitalism is defined by fixed-interest-rate rules imposed on the Federal Reserve, then its founding moment was the New Deal financial reforms of 1933–5. This fits perfectly with my thesis since the essence of the New Deal financial reforms was breaking the unity of the large banks as an unassailable force in the class conflict (see, for example, Ferguson, 1995, pp. 145–50).

Bibliography

Bernanke, Ben S. 1999. *Inflation Targeting: Lessons from the International Experience*. Princeton, NJ: Princeton University Press.

Blinder, Alan. 1999. *Central Banking in Theory and Practice*. Cambridge, MA: MIT Press.

Ferguson, Thomas. 1995. *Golden Rule: The Investment Theory of Party Competition and the Logic of Money-driven Political Systems*. Chicago, IL: University of Chicago Press.
Keynes, John Maynard. 1936 [1964]. *The General Theory of Employment, Interest, and Money*. New York: Harcourt Brace Jovanovich.
Robinson, Joan. 1956. *The Accumulation of Capital*. Philadelphia, PA: Porcupine Press.

1   The Theoretical Framework

> Perhaps a complex offer by the central bank to buy and sell at stated prices gilt-edged bonds of all maturities, in place of a single bank rate for short-term bills, is the most important practical improvement which can be made in the technique of monetary management.
>
> (Keynes, 1936, p. 206)

Introduction

The purpose of this chapter is to reconstruct Keynes's theory of monetary policy, as stated in *The General Theory of Employment, Interest and Money* (1936). Keynes's theory is composed of three concepts—namely, the investment multiplier, the marginal efficiency of capital, and the interest rate. By analyzing how these three concepts interact in the short period, Keynes explains why he is opposed to efforts by the Federal Reserve to stabilize the economy on a non-inflationary growth path, or countercyclical monetary policies. And by analyzing how they interact in the long period, he explains why the economy tends to fluctuate around a long-period equilibrium position that is characterized by unemployment. Keynes concludes that central banks should "buy and sell at stated prices gilt-edged bonds of all maturities" to dislodge the economy from its tendency toward a long-period equilibrium position that is characterized by unemployment and propel it toward a long-period equilibrium position that is characterized by full employment.

This is not what orthodox economists believe central banks should do. Some orthodox economists argue that central banks should concern themselves exclusively with inflation (or the rate of change of the price level), decreasing and increasing the stock of money according to whether inflation is above or below a target rate of about 2 percent (see, for example, Bernanke *et al.*, 1999). Others argue that central banks should also concern themselves with unemployment, decreasing and increasing the stock of money according to whether the economy is growing above or below a rate that corresponds to a non-inflationary rate of unemployment, which is estimated to be somewhere between 4 percent and 6.5 percent (see, for example, Blinder, 1999).

In this chapter, I argue that the difference between Keynes's theory of monetary policy and the orthodox one results from the fact that they characterize the persistent and systematic forces at work in the economy differently. In other words, the long-period equilibrium position is not a fixed point, a stationary state, or even a steady state. It is simply the position toward which the persistent and systematic forces at work in the economy, at any given moment, are tending. When these persistent and systematic forces change, so does the long-run equilibrium position (see, for example, Halevi *et al.*, 2013).

In orthodox theory, monetary policy is not one of the persistent and systematic forces at work in the economy, nor are any other financial or monetary variables. Financial markets and institutions only cause short-period fluctuations of the economy around an equilibrium position determined by other forces in such a way that it is characterized by full employment. In contrast, for Keynes (1936, p. 254), monetary policy, and financial markets and institutions in general, are persistent and systematic forces that contribute to the determination of the economy's long-period equilibrium position is such a way that

> we oscillate, avoiding the gravest extremes of fluctuation in employment … in both directions, round an intermediate position appreciably below full employment and appreciably above the minimum employment a decline below which would endanger life.

In Section 1.1, I explain the persistent and systematic forces that propel the economy in the orthodox theory of monetary policy. In Section 1.2, I then counterpose the long-period equilibrium position of the economy as determined in orthodox theory with the one determined in Keynes's theory. In Section 1.3, I provide a summary and conclusions.

Section 1.1 The Orthodox Theory of Monetary Policy

The orthodox theory of monetary policy is derived from the Quantity Equation, which can be written as follows:

$$MV = PY \tag{1.1}$$

where M is the stock of money; V is the velocity of money; P is the price level; and Y is the equilibrium level of aggregate output. It follows that PY is the equilibrium level of nominal income.

Equation 1.1 is an identity. That is to say, nominal income (PY) is defined as the monetary value of all final goods and services produced and *sold* within a country within a given time period. Consequently, it must be exchanged for money. But each unit of the stock of money (M) may be used in more than one transaction during the time period in question. The number of such transactions is what is meant by the velocity of money (V). Therefore, PY must, by definition, equal MV.

Orthodox economists transform the Quantity Equation into a theory of monetary policy by making two assumptions and one causal claim—namely, that the equilibrium level of aggregate output (Y) and the velocity of money (V) are constant and causality runs from changes in the stock of money (M) on the left side of Equation 1.1 to changes in the price level (P) on the right side.

Given this theory, orthodox economists need only introduce the money multiplier to explain how the Federal Reserve determines inflation (i.e. changes in the price level), which can be derived as follows:

$$H = C + R \tag{1.2}$$

$$M = C + D \tag{1.3}$$

where H is the monetary base, or high-powered money, which can take the form of either currency in circulation (C) or bank reserves (R); and M is the stock of money, which can take the form of either currency in circulation (C) or demand deposits at banks (D). If we divide Equation 1.3 by Equation 1.2 and rearrange terms,[1] we obtain:

$$M/H = [(C/D) + 1]/[(C/D) + (R/D)]$$

or:

$$M = \{[(C/D) + 1]/[(C/D) + (R/D)]\}H$$
$$M = mH \tag{1.4}$$

where the parenthetical term m is the money multiplier, or the ratio of the stock of money (M) to the monetary base (H).

On the basis of Equation 1.4, orthodox economists argue that the stock of money (M) is determined by:

a   the public's decisions to hold currency as a proportion of demand deposits (C/D);
b   the banks' decisions to hold reserves as a proportion of demand deposits (R/D); and
c   the monetary base (H).

Studies by Milton Friedman and Anna J. Schwartz (1963), Phillip Cagan (1965), and Allan Meltzer (1969, 1982, 2003, 2009), among others, suggest that in long-period equilibrium changes in the monetary base (H) account for 90 percent of change in the stock of money, with changes in the reserve-deposit ratio (R/D) and currency-deposit ratio (C/D) accounting for the rest.

About 70 percent of the monetary base is supplied through central-bank open-market purchases of securities or direct lending to banks (see, for example, Burger, 1971, p. 19). Since the Federal Reserve has reliable information on the other factors supplying the monetary base,[2] it appears that the Federal Reserve can control the monetary base and thereby control the stock of money (the money multiplier itself can be forecast with a small margin of error (see, for example, Rasche, 1972; Johannes and Rasche, 1981)).

However, I present evidence in Chapter 3 that this appearance is false. These orthodox economists assume that the banks passively accept the discipline implied by the Federal Reserve's alleged control the stock of money because they are unwilling to risk insolvency by overextending themselves and granting more loans than can be sustained by the reserves the Federal Reserve supplies. But the banks are not passive in this way. They are dynamic economic agents, aggressively pursuing profitable lending opportunities, creating bank deposits in the process, and only looking for reserves later (see, for example, Holmes, 1969, p. 74). If the Federal Reserve refuses to supply the required reserves under these circumstances, it will precipitate a financial crisis. As Thomas Palley (1987–8, pp. 382–3; also see Moore, 1979, 1988, 1989; Wray, 1998, 1999) puts it:

> Though the monetary authority may deny [discount] window access to any single bank, in the event of generalized reserve shortages arising from collective overlending by banks, it cannot deny access to the banking system as a whole without generating financial crises. As a consequence, the money supply is endogenously determined by the demand for bank credit.

Of course, the Federal Reserve is also an active economic agent, willing to risk pushing the economy to the brink of financial crises in order to exercise control over the supply of bank reserves at the same time that private banks are willing to risk insolvency in order to pursue profitable lending opportunities. After all, financial crises do occur. This is why Charles Kindleberger (1978) defines the 'art of central banking' as the ability to exercise monetary control over the supply of bank reserves during periods of calm between financial crises despite the fact that the central banks must intervene, and financial-market participants know they must intervene, as lender of last resort when financial crises do occur. Or, as Andrew S. Carron (1982, pp. 416–18; also see Wojnilower, 1980) puts it:

> The Federal Reserve has been seen to play two roles in the development and resolution of financial market difficulties. As an inflation fighter, it has the power to induce stresses in the real sector that can lead to a financial crisis. As central banker the [Federal Reserve] Board can prevent illiquidity and restore lost confidence that comes with a crisis. These two activities may at times be inconsistent with each other. ... It appears that monetary policy has been controlled so as to force the economy through a financial crunch, into the early stages of a crisis. But that is as far as the Federal Reserve is willing to go.

It follows that, even though financial crises force the Federal Reserve to abandon control over the supply of bank reserves, for periods of time prior to financial crises, changes in the supply of bank reserves cause changes in the stock of money. In Chapter 3, I show how the "art of central banking" thus played out in the early 1950s.

Nonetheless, it does not follow from the fact that changes in the supply of bank reserves (i.e. in the monetary base) cause changes in the stock of money during periods of calm in financial markets that the orthodox theory of monetary policy is correct. For changes in the stock of money do not necessarily cause changes in the price level. This is for two reasons. First, the orthodox assumption of a constant velocity of money does not hold when the banks respond to the Federal Reserve's control of the supply of bank reserves not by foregoing profitable lending opportunities, but by undertaking financial innovations. For example, in Chapter 6, I demonstrate that when the Federal Reserve attempted to fight the Great Inflation from 1966 to 1979 by restricting the supply of reserves, and thus the domestic stock of money, the banks responded by developing the Eurodollar market as a source of funds for their domestic lending operations. Consequently, although the Federal Reserve decreased the domestic supply of money in the late 1960s and 1970s, this decrease was offset, not by a decrease the price level, but an increase in the velocity of the domestic supply of money (see, for example, Hester, 1981, especially p. 183; Rousseas, 1989, p. 477; and Kaldor, 1970).[3]

The second reason why changes in the stock of money do not necessarily cause changes in the price level is because the level of aggregate income (or output) is not constant. Orthodox economists argue that aggregate income is constant in the sense that the forces of demand and supply in the markets for capital and labor cause it to always tend toward the full-employment level. So far as the forces of demand and supply in the capital market are concerned, orthodox economists assume that firms demand capital in order to undertake investments and that households supply capital in the form of savings. If the volume of investments undertaken results in a rate of capital accumulation greater than the savings rate, then increases in the interest rate reduce it, and vice versa. Therefore, when the capital market is in equilibrium, the interest rate is such that savings automatically coagulate as an augmented stock of means of production; the rate of capital accumulation equals the savings rate; and causality runs from changes in the savings rate to changes in the rate of capital accumulation (see, for example, Michl and Foley, 2004, p. 39; Foley and Michl, 1999, p. 256).

So far as the forces of demand and supply in the labor market are concerned, orthodox economists assume that this rate of capital accumulation cum savings rate constitutes the demand for labor (i.e. the demand for the labor required to operate the means of production). And they assume that the supply of labor is given by the rate of population growth plus the rate of growth of labor productivity (understood as a proxy for the rate of technological progress). If the rate of growth of the demand for labor (i.e. the rate of capital accumulation) is greater than the rate of growth of the technologically augmented supply of labor, then wages rise, which is the same thing as saying profits fall, since the portion of aggregate income (or output) that does not take the form of wages takes the form of profits. On the assumption that profits are saved at a greater rate than wages, the rise in wages reduces the savings rate (i.e. the rate of capital accumulation). Contrariwise, if the rate of growth of the demand for labor (i.e. the rate of capital accumulation) is less than the rate of growth of the technologically augmented supply of labor, then wages fall and profits increase, with the result that the savings rate (i.e. the rate of capital accumulation) rises to the rate of growth of the technologically augmented supply of labor (see, for example, Flaschel and Greiner, 2011).

In short, in the same way that orthodox economists claim that the interest rate adjusts the demand for capital (i.e. the volume of investments) to the supply of it (i.e. savings) in the capital market, they claim that the wage adjusts the demand for labor (i.e. the rate of capital accumulation) to the supply of it (i.e. the rate of population growth plus the rate of technological progress) in the labor market. The equilibrium level of aggregate income (or output) is the volume that can be produced when the forces of demand and supply have established the equilibrium levels of the interest rate and the wage in the capital and labor markets. Therefore, in orthodox theory, equilibrium aggregate income (or output) is ultimately determined by the full utilization of the available savings for capital formation, given the rate of population growth and the rate of technological progress. In such a world, there is no role for financial markets and institutions, including the Federal Reserve, in the long period. All financial markets and institutions can do is cause short-period fluctuations of the economy around a tendency toward a long-period equilibrium position given by the savings rate, the rate of population growth, and the rate of technological progress.

Given that the persistent and systematic forces at work in the economy cause it to thus tend toward an equilibrium level of income (or output) characterized by full employment, orthodox economists complete their theory of monetary policy by calling the equilibrium interest rate, as determined by the forces of demand and supply in the capital market, the real interest rate, or the rate of profit. They then define the money (or nominal) interest rate as the real interest rate plus an inflation premium, given by the expected rate of inflation. The expected rate of inflation, in turn, is given by the rate of growth of the money supply relative to the equilibrium level of income (or output). If the money supply is growing at a more rapid rate than the economy is tending toward the full-employment level of output, then the inflation premium is positive, making the money interest rate greater than the real interest rate, and vice versa. In short, monetary policy does not affect the equilibrium position toward which the economy is tending, only the level of the money interest rate relative to the real interest rate (see, for example, Goodhart, 1991, pp. 222–6).

It is against this characterization of the persistent and systematic forces at work in the economy in terms of demand and supply in the markets for capital and labor that Keynes (1936, chapter 2) directs his critique of orthodox monetary theory. His basic point is that financial markets and institutions are not adequately represented as intermediaries between firms who demand capital in order to undertake investments and households who supply capital in the form of savings. Instead, banks in particular are active economic agents, actively pursuing profitable lending opportunities and in doing so they act in such a way that the rate of capital accumulation is independent of the savings rate.

For example, assume that workers receive wages in the form of monthly, bi-weekly, and weekly paychecks, which they then deposit at the banks. Also assume that over the period between paychecks, workers gradually withdraw all their income from the banks (i.e. there are no savings out of wages). It follows that, on average, workers hold one half of their wage income at banks (e.g. if their paychecks are for X dollars, which they deposit on the day they get paid, and they gradually spend the X dollars so that they have 0 dollars on deposit the day before they get their next paycheck, then on average workers have on deposit: [x dollars + 0 dollars/2] = 0.5 X dollars). Banks can finance investments up to this average amount of deposits with them, so long as the Federal Reserve supplies them with reserves, thereby making the rate of capital accumulation independent of the savings rate. The rate of capital accumulation depends, instead, on the prospective profits of banks from granting loans, and the volume of reserves supplied by the Federal Reserve.

In other words, banks, including central banks, constitute persistent and systematic forces at work in the economy determining the long-period equilibrium position it tends toward. In particular, rather than there being a real interest rate determined by the forces of demand and supply in the capital market, banks, as well as other financial markets and institutions, use their relative autonomy to make loans independently of the savings rate to impose a required rate of return on investments by industrial capitalists. Following Keynes (1936, pp. 144–5, 222–9 and 240), I will call this required rate of return the "safe" interest rate.

In industries with expected profit rates less than the safe interest rate, banks and other financial institutions use hostile takeovers, leveraged buyouts, and other tools of their trade to compel industrial capitalists to disgorge their capital to the financial markets, which financial institutions then invest by setting up new firms in industries with expected profit rates greater than the safe interest rate. The lack of reinvestment in mature industries causes them to shrink, and thus improves the prospects for a higher rate of profit for the industrial capitalists continuing to operate in them. At the same time, the flood of new investments into industries with the highest expected profit rates causes a tendency toward overbuilding, and thus dampens the prospective rates of profit for the industrial capitalists already engaged in them. In this way, financial markets and institutions constitute a persistent and systematic force at work in the economy which causes expected rates of profit to tend toward a uniform rate that equals the safe rate (see, for example, Marx, 1894, pp. 435, 173, 365, and *passim*).

In short, it is by substituting the concept of the safe interest rate for the orthodox concept of the real interest rate that Keynes is able to argue that financial markets and institutions, including central banks, constitute persistent and systematic forces determining the equilibrium level of income (or output) that the economy tends toward in the long period, only now that equilibrium is given not by the forces of demand and supply in the markets for capital and labor, but by the equality of the uniform rate of profit with the safe interest rate. In fact, as I show in the next section, this equilibrium level of output tends to correspond with unemployment. Keynes 1936, pp. 142–3; 1937a, pp. 113–14; 1937b, 1937c) drives the nail into the coffin of the orthodox theory of monetary policy by arguing that the expected rate of inflation, far from serving to differentiate the money interest rate from the real interest rate, is just a factor that goes into the determination of the expected rates of profit, not the safe interest rate. As the expected prices at which firms can sell their output rise, so do their expected profits, and vice versa.

Section 1.2   Keynes's Theory of Monetary Policy

David Ricardo (1817) first developed the concept of the persistent and systematic forces at work in the economy as tending toward an equilibrium characterized by full employment. Consequently, it was with reference to Ricardo that Keynes (1936, p. 191) laid out his own theoretical project:

> Ricardo and his successors overlook the fact that even in the long period the volume of employment is not necessarily full but is capable of varying, and that to every banking policy there corresponds a different long-period level of employment, so that there are a number of positions of long-period equilibrium corresponding to different conceivable interest policies on the part of the monetary authority.

My purpose in this section is to concretize this passage.[4] First, I use Keynes's concepts of the investment multiplier and the marginal efficiency of capital to specify the long-period equilibrium that the economy tends toward as characterized by unemployment. Second, to explain why the economy fluctuates around this equilibrium position, I specify the difference, as well as the relationship, between Keynes's concepts of probability (or uncertainty) and risk and their orthodox counterparts. Last, I use Keynes's concept of the interest rate to explain the effects of monetary policy in both the short period and the long period.

Let N^s be the supply of labor and N^d the demand for labor, or the actual volume of employment (n). We can then define full employment (n_o) as $N^d/N^s = 1$, unemployment (n_k) as $N^d/N^s < 1$, and the unemployment rate as $1 - n_k$.

For Keynes (1936, pp. 25–9*ff*.), n is determined by the aggregate level of output (Y) and the productivity of labor (β). That is to say, by definition $\beta = Y/N^d$. Rearranging terms, $N^d = Y/\beta$. Substituting into our definition of n, we thus get $n = Y/\beta\, N^s$.

For Keynes (1936, p. 96*ff*.), Y is determined, via the investment multiplier (defined as the reciprocal of the marginal propensity to save (s)), by the aggregate rate of investment (I). Consequently, we can derive the determination of the unemployment rate ($1 - n_k$) by building upon the following counterposing of the effects of an aggregate rate of investment that is insufficient to generate full employment (I_k) with the effects of an aggregate rate of investment that is sufficient to generate full employment (I_o) (see Shaikh, 2004 for a similar formalization):

$$Y_K = I_K/s; \quad Y_O = I_O/s \tag{1.5}$$

or:

$$n_k = I_k/s\beta N^s; \quad n_o = I_O/s\beta N^s \tag{1.6}$$

where, *ceteris paribus*, $1 - n_k$ is determined by $I_k < I_o$.

For Keynes (1936, pp. 135–7), I is determined by the net present value of prospective investment projects (NPV):[5]

$$NPV = -Sp + E_1/1 + r_s + E_2/(1 + r_s)^2 + \cdots + E_t/(1 + r_s)^t \qquad (1.7)$$

where Sp is the supply price of prospective investment projects; E is the profit expected from operating them for t periods; and r_s is the 'safe' interest rate (I define the safe interest rate below). If $NPV > 0$, I increases. If $NPV < O$, I decreases. If $NPV = O$, I is in equilibrium.

Assume that $t = 1$ and Sp and r_s are given. Then the expected profit (E_o) in equilibrium that induces investors to undertake the full-employment aggregate rate of investment (I_o) and the expected profit (E_k) that induces them to undertake the less-than-full-employment aggregate rate of investment (I_k) can be distinguished as follows:

$$NPV = -Sp + E_k/1 + r_s = 0; \quad NPV = -Sp + E_O/1 + r_s = 0. \qquad (1.8)$$

Equations 1.5–1.8 apply to both the long period and the short period, depending upon whether E_k and E_o denote long-term expectations or short-term expectations. *Ceteris paribus*, long-term expectations determine the volume of investment projects undertaken and short-term expectations determine the pace of their implementation.

In Section 1.1, I distinguished Keynes's theory of monetary policy from its orthodox counterpart in terms of this difference between the short period and the long period. I argued that, whereas monetary policy only has short-period effects in orthodox theory, it also has long-period effects in Keynes's theory. With Equation 1.8, I add a dimension to this distinction, showing that it comes down to different specifications of the concept of expected profits, as either E_o or E_k. In both cases, the issue is how to project long-period trends into the future. The whole point of identifying the persistent and systematic forces in the economy is to discern these trends. As explained in Section 1.1, orthodox economists identify them with the forces of demand and supply in the markets for capital and labor and Keynes identifies them with the tendency toward a uniform rate of profit which equals the safe interest rate.

The new dimension to be added in this section has to do with the nature of historical time. As we will now see, orthodox economists perceive time as an unbroken continuum. The only difference between past, present, and future is that they occupy different places on this continuum. In principle, if we can discern the current mass and velocity of the persistent and systematic forces at work in the economy, we can predict the future. For example, for orthodox economists, future events—the long-period tendency of the economy—can be deduced with certainty by simply ascertaining if there are excess demands or supplies in the markets for capital and labor, then projecting the long-period direction of the economy in terms of the changes in the real interest rate and the wage required to rectify these imbalances. In contrast, for Keynes (1937a, 1937b, 1937c; also see Robinson, 1956, pp. 179–81) we are immersed in historical time, which is not an unbroken continuum but a discontinuous path in which the present moment constitutes a fundamental break between an irrevocable past and an unknown future. The point of ascertaining the long-period equilibrium position of the economy is to form long-term expectations about where the economy is tending. But this long-period equilibrium changes with every change in the persistent and systematic forces at work in the economy, such as monetary policy (see, for example, Halevi *et al.*, 2013).

Since aggregate output and employment are ultimately determined by the rate of capital accumulation (i.e. the rate of investment), the fundamental move that allows orthodox economists to perceive of time as an unbroken continuum is the reduction of the concept of expected profits to a certainty equivalent—namely, actual profits (see, for example, Goldstein, 2009, p. 42; Sardoni, 2013, pp. 235–8). If actual profits are used as a proxy for expected profits, then the future movements of the economy are predictable, just as the future movements of celestial bodies or subatomic particles are predictable; we need only ascertain the current state of the underlying forces of demand and supply in the markets for capital and labor. In contrast, Keynes's concept of expected profits leaves the future fundamentally uncertain because it depends on historically contingent moods of bankers and entrepreneurs. Therefore, unlike the movements of celestial bodies or subatomic particles, the overall movements of the economy follow a unique path, determined by singular events. History matters; actual profits are not a proxy for expected profits.

In this section, I show that this difference between time conceived as an unbroken continuum and as an historical process means that, for a given investment project, Keynes's estimate of the possibility of the pay-off, and thus of the expected profit, is less than the estimates of orthodox economists. Moreover, if the monetary authority—the Federal Reserve System in the U.S.—maintains a fixed-interest-rate structure, Keynes's estimates can be brought closer to the orthodox ones. I leave the history of how this has played out in practice for subsequent chapters.

The question of the formation of expectations is the topic of probability theory. For Keynes, the major problem with orthodox probability theory is the concept of risk that it implies. The orthodox concept of risk is derived from the definition of probability in terms of the principle of non-sufficient reason. However, orthodox economists assume, often implicitly, that it is also implied by the definition of probability in terms of the law of large numbers.[6]

In contrast, Keynes derives his concept of risk from the definition of probability in terms of the logical relationship between propositions, which opens the way for him to introduce the concept of the weight of arguments. Consequently, I will first derive the orthodox concept of risk from the definition of probability in terms of the principle of non-sufficient reason then explain why it is invalid, insofar as explanations of investment behavior are concerned. Second, I will show how the orthodox concept of risk appears to follow from the definition of probability in terms of the law of large numbers then explain why it is invalid, again insofar as investment behavior (not the movements of celestial bodies or subatomic particles) is concerned. Third, I will use the definition of probability as a logical relationship between propositions to explain Keynes's concepts of risk and the weight of arguments then demonstrate their validity in the case of investment behavior. Finally, to explain why the monetary authority should maintain a fixed-interest-rate structure, rather than pursuing a countercyclical monetary policy, I will connect the results of this analysis of the difference between Keynes's concepts of probability and risk and the orthodox ones to Equations 1.5–1.8.

According to the principle of non-sufficient reason, if we do not have a reason to assign different probabilities to a set of possible outcomes or events or propositions, then we must assign them equal probabilities. Starting with Markowitz (1959), this principle has become the basis for the paradigmatic explanation of investment behavior among orthodox economists. We are asked to assume that investors ascertain all possible outcomes of an investment project (measured in terms of dollars of return). Investors are able to use the principle of non-sufficient reason to assign a probability to each possible outcome of an investment project, with the sum of assigned probabilities equal to one. The expected profit from the investment project is then taken to be a mathematical mean of the sum of the products of each outcome and its probability.

The orthodox concept of risk is derived from the principle of non-sufficient reason as thus applied to investment decisions. That is to say, orthodox economists define the risk of an investment project as the variability (or standard deviation) of the products of each possible outcome and its probability, around its mathematical mean.

Following Capen *et al.* (1971), the refutation of this explanation of investor behavior has come to be called the "winner's curse."[7] Capen *et al.* examined the bids made by companies for oil-drilling rights on parcels of land in the Gulf of Mexico and the North Slope of Alaska in the 1950s and 1960s. Each bid for the rights was unbiased and equally likely to be correct. Therefore, the principle of non-sufficient reason implies that the mathematical mean of the amounts bid by different companies for oil-drilling rights on each parcel of land represented the true value of those rights. But of course it was the highest bidder who received the rights in each case. Therefore, the winning bid was invariably higher than the true value of the rights, prompting Capen *et al.* (1971, pp. 652–3) to conclude as follows: "He who bids on a parcel what he thinks it is worth, will, in the long run, be taken for a cleaning" (also see Bazerman and Samuelson, 1983; Kagel and Levin, 1986).

In other words, instead of explaining investment decisions, the application of the principle of non-sufficient reason to them implies that no rational person would ever undertake an investment project. As Keynes (1921, p. 152) points out, this is clearly absurd. Consequently, the orthodox concept of expected profit is refuted by means of *reductio ad absurdam*.[8]

The orthodox concept of risk as derived from the principle of non-sufficient reason is identical to the one derived from the law of large numbers. According to the law of large numbers, or statistical frequency, we can define probability (p_o) as follows:

$$p_o = m/z \tag{1.9}$$

where m is the number of occurrences of an outcome and z is the number of possible occasions for the outcome or event to occur.

The law of large numbers applies to games of chance, such as coin tosses or wheels of fortune. On the assumption that investment projects resemble games of chance, orthodox economists follow Markowitz (1959, p. 39*ff.*) and define expected profits (E_o) as follows:

$$E_o = p_o A \tag{1.10}$$

where A is the pay-off from the investment project, if it is successful.

Since p_o implies a value derived from a large number of instances, E_o appears to still be the mathematical mean of the sum of the products of each outcome and its probability. Consequently, orthodox economists assume that the risk of an investment project has been taken into account by the variability (or standard deviation) of the products of each possible outcome and its probability, around E_o.

For example, assume that people are asked the following question: how much are you willing to pay in order to receive \$1 in the event of the next toss of a coin turning up heads, but nothing in the event of the next coin toss turning up tails? The answers that people give to this question give their betting quotients, and orthodox economists assume that a rational investor will use Equations 1.9 and 1.10 to calculate them. That is to say, if z_1 is the number of coin tosses and m_1 is the number of times that heads occurs, then, according to Equation 1.9, $p_o = m_1/z_1 = 0.5$. It thus follows from Equation 1.10 that the expected profit (E_o) from an investment in the next coin toss is $E_o = 0.5\,(\$1) = \$0.50$. In other words, orthodox economists assume that rational investors will calculate a betting quotient of \$0.50 in this case (that is, they will be willing to pay \$0.50 for the right to receive \$1 in the event of the next coin toss turning up heads but nothing in the event of it turning up tails).

Unfortunately for orthodox economists, Hershey and Schomaker (1985) found that, in this case, people typically calculate a betting quotient of \$0.40. I will now argue that this is because people weigh Equation 1.9 not as the determinant of the probability of the pay-off from an investment project, but as one argument among others which must be considered in determining that probability. I then show how this case can be extended to explain Keynes's concept of liquidity preference.

The third meaning of probability (p_k), as a logical relationship between propositions, and the modified meaning of expected profits implied by it, was first formulated by Keynes (1921, pp. 3–9; also see Rottenstreich and Tversky, 1997) as follows:

$$p_k = a \mid h \tag{1.11}$$

$$E_k = p_k A \tag{1.12}$$

where h is a set of propositions which constitutes the premises of an argument; a is a set of propositions (or more often the proposition) which constitutes its conclusion; A is still the pay-off, if the investment project is successful, but the probability assigned to A in order to estimate the expected profit (E_k) is now obtained from Equation 1.11 rather than Equation 1.9.

Equation 1.11 can be read as "proposition a on the hypothesis h has a probability of p_k." Alternatively, it can be read as "the conclusion a can be inferred from the evidence h with a probability of p_k."

If $a \mid h = 1$, then the hypothesis h implies the conclusion a with certainty. If $a \mid h = 0$, then hypothesis h implies that the conclusion a is impossible. If $0 < p_k < 1$, then there is a probability relation of degree p_k between a and h.

For Keynes, the concepts of the weight of arguments and of risk are the factors determining our degree of belief (p_k) in a conclusion (a) following from its premises (h). Following Keynes (1921, pp. 77–80), the concept of the weight of arguments (w) can be formulated as follows:[9]

$$p_k = w(a \mid h \cdot p_o) \tag{1.13}$$

where $0 < w < 1$; and p_o is the proposition that dominants h.

For example, the data on betting quotients above can be explained as follows:

$$p_{o1} = a_1 \mid h_1 = 0.5; \quad E_{o1} = p_{o1}(A_1) = \$0.50 \tag{1.14}$$

$$p_{k1} = w_1(a_1 \mid h_1) = 0.4; \quad E_{k1} = P_{k1}(A_1) = \$0.40 \tag{1.15}$$

where a_1 is $A_1 = \$1$, or the proposition that "the pay-off will be \$1 if the next coin toss turns up heads"; h_1 is the set of propositions that people weigh as they contemplate the next coin toss, including $m_1/z_1 = 0.5$; and $w_1 = 0.8$. In Equation 1.14, the proposition $m_1/z_1 = 0.5$ is dominant, but in Equation 1.15, other propositions weigh against it. As I explain below, one such proposition weighing against the dominant one in this case can be formulated in terms of Keynes's concept of liquidity preference.

In Equations 1.14 and 1.15, the underlying causal structure, which determines the pay-off from the investment project, is both knowable and known. It was thus possible to compare the estimates obtained from Equations 1.9 and 1.10 with those obtained from Equations 1.13 and 1.12 in terms of numerical values.

Unlike Equations 1.9 and 1.10, Equations 1.11 and 1.12 apply to classes of cases which cannot be evaluated in terms of numerical values. Nonetheless, I show below that a formal relationship of inequality can still be ascertained between the estimates obtained from Equations 1.9 and 1.10 and those obtained from Equations 1.11 and 1.12.

The two classes of cases in which numerical values cannot be obtained are those in which the underlying causal structure is knowable but unknown[10] and those in which it is unknowable.[11] For example, suppose that, while waiting to board an airplane, I consider investing in an insurance policy which costs \$1 and will pay \$250,000 if I die in an airplane crash. At first glance, the problem confronting me is as follows:

$$p_{k2} = a_2 \,|\, h_2 = 1/250,000 \tag{1.16}$$

where a_2 is "I will die in an airplane crash" and h_2 is a set of propositions of which "I can buy a \$250,000 flight-insurance policy for \$1" is dominant.

However, there are other propositions in h_2 which may weigh against the dominant one. On the one hand, I may interpret my investment opportunity as a member of the class of cases with a knowable causal structure which is unknown to me. Consequently, I may reformulate the problem as follows:

$$p_{k3} = w_2(a_2 \,|\, h_2) < 1/250,000 \tag{1.17}$$

where w_2 reflects the fact that the proposition in h_2—"the insurance company knows the statistical frequency of airplane crashes and expects to profit by offering flight insurance"—weighs against the dominant one. In other words, I suspect that:

$$a_2 \,|\, h_2 > a_2 \,|\, h_2 \cdot m_2/z_2 \tag{1.18}$$

where m_2 is the number of people who have died in airplane crashes and z_2 is the number of people who have flown on airplanes. As a result, I assign a weight (w_2) to the argument for a_2 in such a way that it becomes less probable (p_{k3}) than the probability implicit in the offer of the flight insurance (p_{k2}). In short, I will not buy the flight insurance.

On the other hand, I may interpret my investment opportunity as a member of the class of cases with an unknowable causal structure. Perhaps the growing threat of blowback from conflict in West Asia in the form of terrorist attacks implies that the statistical frequency (m_2/z_2) of airplane crashes in the past no longer represents the causal structure which will determine the truth of a_2. I may thus reformulate the problem as follows:

$$p_{k4} = w_3(a_2 \,|\, h_2) > 1/250,000 \tag{1.19}$$

where w_3 reflects the fact that the proposition in h_2—"the insurance company has failed to take into account the fundamental uncertainty of the current situation"—weighs against the dominant one. In short, I will buy the flight insurance.

In addition to the concept of the weight of arguments, Keynes also reformulates the concept of risk as a factor determining our degree of belief (p_k) in a conclusion (a) following from its premises (h). For Keynes, the problem with the orthodox concept of risk as the variance (or standard deviation) of the products of each possible outcome of an investment project and its probability, around the expected profit (E_o), is that it includes the possibility that the actual profit of an investment project will exceed the expected profit. Risk (R) only results from the possibility that the actual profit will fall short of the expected profit. For this reason, Keynes (1921, p. 348) defines it as follows:

$$R = (1 - p_o)E_o$$

or:

$$R = q\,E_o \tag{1.20}$$

where $q = 1 - p_o$.

Equation 1.20 is formulated in such a way that risk (R) represents the cost of insurance against the loss of the money wagered on an investment project. The cost of re-insurance of the insurer (R_1) would then be $q\,R = q^2\,E_0$. If the re-insurance company buys re-insurance (R_2), and that re-insurance company buys re-insurance and so on, then the risk of loss is eliminated, but so is the expected profit (that is, $E_0 + R_1 + R_2 + \ldots = E_o\,(1 + q + q^2 + \ldots) = E_o/1 - q = E_o/p_o = A$). In short, Equation 1.20 is formulated in such a way that it is only by bearing some risk of loss that potential investors can expect to profit.

Equation 1.20 can be used to show how risk, like the weight of arguments, is a factor determining the degree of belief (p_k) in a conclusion (a) following from its premises (h). That is to say, we can write (Keynes, 1921, p. 348):

$$p_k = [2w/(1 + q)(1 + w)]\,p_o \tag{1.21}$$

Equation 1.21 is formulated in such a way that two conditions are met: if $p_o = 1$ and $w = 1$, then $p_k = 1$; and if $p_o = 0$ and $w = 0$, then $p_k = 0$. It follows that, for any values of p_o and/or w between 0 and 1, $p_k < p_o$.

Whereas Keynes (1936, p. 240) calls p_o "the risk premium," "risk proper," or "the best estimates we can make of probabilities," he calls p_k "the liquidity premium," "liquidity proper," or "the confidence with which we make" our best estimates of probabilities. As such, the bracketed expression in Equation 1.21, or the difference between p_o and p_k, provides us with a measure of the difference in perspectives of the entrepreneurs who own investment projects and the owners of wealth contemplating an investment in them—for the former are exclusively concerned with the risk premium, while the latter are also concerned with the liquidity premium.

For example, Thaler and Tversky (1992) conducted an experiment based on the following two bets:

$$
\begin{aligned}
&\text{Bet One}: a \text{ is } `A = \$4\text{' and } p_o = 8/9; \\
&\text{Bet Two}: a \text{ is } `A = \$40\text{' and } p_o = 1/9.
\end{aligned}
\tag{1.22}
$$

What they found was a "preference reversal." That is to say, Thaler and Tversky found that people who owned the bets valued Bet Two more highly than Bet One; but when the same people owned cash and were offered the opportunity to invest in the bets, they valued Bet One more highly than Bet Two.

The entrepreneurs who own the bets prefer Bet Two to Bet One because they are exclusively concerned with the risk premium (p_o), as calculated by means of Equation 1.9. That is to say, they simply plug the numbers from Equations 1.22 into Equation 1.10 and get:

$$\text{Bet One}: E_o = p_o A = 8/9(4) = \$3.56;$$
$$\text{Bet Two}: E_o = p_o A = 1/9(40) = \$4.44. \tag{1.23}$$

In short, for the entrepreneurs who own the bets, Bet Two has more value than Bet One (that is, the expected profit from owning Bet Two is \$4.44, as opposed to an expected profit of \$3.56 from owning Bet One).

In contrast, the owners of wealth contemplating an investment in the bets are not only concerned with the risk premium, but also with the liquidity premium. Their preference for Bet One rather than Bet Two is thus explained by plugging the numbers from Equations 1.22 into Equations 1.21 and 1.12. Since the weight of arguments (w) is not an issue in this case, $w = 1$. Therefore, Equation 1.21 becomes: $p_k = p_o/1 + q$ and we get:

$$\text{Bet One}: p_k = p_o/1 + q = 8/9/1 + 1/9 = 0.8;$$
$$\text{Bet Two}: p_k = p_o/1 + q = 1/9/1 + 8/9 = 0.06. \tag{1.24}$$

$$\text{Bet One}: E_k = p_k(A) = 0.8(4) = \$3.20;$$
$$\text{Bet Two}: E_k = p_k(A) = 0.06(40) = \$2.40. \tag{1.25}$$

In short, for the owners of wealth contemplating an investment in the bets, Bet One has more value than Bet Two (that is, an investment in Bet One has an expected profit of \$3.20, as opposed to an expected profit of \$2.40 for Bet Two).[12]

Even in this case, where $w = 1$, p_k is still less than p_o because Keynes's concept of risk differs from the orthodox one. If $p_k < p_o$, we know from comparing Equations 1.12 and 1.10 that $E_k < E_o$. Then from Equations 1.8, 1.5 and 1.6 respectively, we know that $I_k < I_o \rightarrow Y_k < Y_o \rightarrow 1 - n_k > 0$. In other words, if Keynes's concepts of probability and risk are correct, then the long-period equilibrium that the economy tends toward is characterized by unemployment.

The fundamental proposition of Keynes's theory of monetary policy is that, by eschewing countercyclical actions in favor of maintaining a fixed-interest-rate structure, central banks can dislodge the economy from its long-period equilibrium position that is characterized by unemployment and propel it toward a long-period equilibrium position that is characterized by full employment. To explain why, first note that central banks directly control the short-term interest rate.[13] With "a modest measure of persistence and consistency of purpose," Keynes (1936, p. 204) asserts that the monetary authority can also influence the long-term interest rate.[14] Orthodox economists (see, for example, Ingersoll, 1989, pp. 172–8) have accepted Keynes's assertion, taking it to mean that the long-term interest rate is the mathematical mean of the sum of the products of all possible outcomes of the short-term interest rate and their probability. For example, the yield on the 10-year bond allegedly equals the mathematical mean of the expected yields on 3-month securities for the next ten years, plus an illiquidity premium which reflects the orthodox concept of risk. Unfortunately, orthodox economists ignore the difference between Keynes's concepts of probability and risk and the orthodox ones. To reconstruct Keynes's theory of monetary policy, this oversight must be rectified.[15]

As I explained in my analysis of Equations 1.22–1.25, the difference between Keynes's concept of probability (p_k) and the orthodox one (p_o), as formulated in Equation 1.21, is best understood as a liquidity premium that people place on their holdings of money, over and above the risk premium calculated by people who own investment projects. If we transform this liquidity premium into an illiquidity premium, i.e. $1 - [2 w/(1 + q) (1 + w)]$, then it is the key to explaining Keynes's concept of the long-period equilibrium value of the long-term interest rate, or what Keynes (1936, pp. 144–5, 222–9, 240) calls the safe interest rate (r_s). We need only note that Keynes also explains the safe interest rate as "a duplication of a proportion of entrepreneur's risk," so that it can be formulated as follows:

$$r_s = g \ \{1 - [2w/(1 + q)(1 + w)]\} \tag{1.26}$$

where g has a value between 0 and 1 and measures the proportion of the entrepreneur's risk that is duplicated.

As Keynes famously explains in chapter 12 of *The General Theory*, the actual expected profits (E_a) from investment projects are determined in the stock market, just as the actual long-term interest rate (r_a) is determined in the bond market. Consequently, we can reformulate Equation 1.8 to specify the relationship between r_s and r_a as follows:[16]

$$NPV = -S_p + E_k/1 + r_s = 0; \ NPV = -S_P + E_a/1 + r_a = 0 \tag{1.27}$$

In the same way, Equations 1.5 and 1.6 can be reformulated as follows to specify the relationship between the long-period equilibrium aggregate rate of investment (I_k) and the actual aggregate rate of investment (I_a) and thus the relationships between the long-period aggregate level of output (Y_k) and the actual aggregate level of output (Y_a), and between the long-period equilibrium employment (n_k) and the actual employment (n_a) respectively:

$$Y_k = I_k/s; \ Y_a = I_a/s \tag{1.28}$$

$$n_k = I_k/s \ PN^s; \ n_a = I_a/s \ PN^s \tag{1.29}$$

In Equation 1.27, r_a tends toward r_s in the same way that, in Equations 1.28 and 1.29, I_a, Y_a, and n_a tend toward I_k, Y_k, and n_k respectively.

For Keynes (1936, pp. 202, 206, 313–20), the short-period fluctuations of r_a around r_s are strictly limited to "the difference between the[ir] squares."[17]

In contrast, since the stock market determines the actual expected profits (E_a) in the short period, the short-period fluctuations of I_a and Y_a around I_k and Y_k are unlimited.[18] Therefore, efforts by the monetary authority to stabilize the short-period fluctuations of the economy are futile for two reasons. First, any drastic changes that the monetary authority makes in the short-term interest rate simply cause a more steeply sloped yield curve as r_a reaches the limits of its variability around r_s. Second, such drastic changes in the short-term interest rate threaten to shatter the confidence of investors in their calculations of E_a. If drastic enough, such changes may cause a severe recession as investors contemplate trillions of dollars of losses on their bets in the stock market.

More importantly, Keynes (1936, pp. 119, 206, 301–4, 321–2) argues that the monetary authority, rather than attempting to stabilize the short-period fluctuations of the economy around its long-period equilibrium position characterized by unemployment, should attempt to reduce the amount of unemployment that characterizes the long-period equilibrium position, which can be done by making a credible commitment "to buy and sell at stated prices gilt-edged bonds of all maturities." To see why, Equations 1.13, 1.12, and 1.26 can be reformulated as follows:

$$p_{k1} = w_1(a_1 \mid h_1 \cdot p_o) > p_{k2} = w_2(a_2 \mid h_2 \cdot p_o) \tag{1.30}$$

$$E_{k1} = p_{k1}A > E_{k2} = p_{k2}A \tag{1.31}$$

$$r_{s1} = g\{1 - [2w_1/(1+q)(1+w_1)]\} < r_{s2}$$
$$= g\{1 - [2w_2/(1+q)(1+w_2)]\} \tag{1.32}$$

where, in Equation 1.30, h_1 includes the proposition that "the monetary authority has made a credible commitment to buy and sell at stated prices gilt-edged bonds of all maturities" and h_2 includes the proposition that "the monetary authority is committed to changing the short-term interest rate in an effort to stabilize short-period fluctuations of the economy."

If the monetary authority has the discretion to change the short-term interest rate, investors must take into account the possibility that future investment projects, with lower financing costs, will compete against investment projects undertaken today at higher financing costs. As a result, h_2 weighs more heavily than does h_1 against the dominate proposition for undertaking investment projects (p_o). That is to say, $w_1 > w_2$. It follows from Equation 1.31 that $p_{k1} > p_{k2} \rightarrow E_{k1} > E_{k2}$; and from Equation 1.32 that $r_{s1} < r_{s2}$.

We are now in a position to complete Keynes's theory of monetary policy by building as follows upon Equations 1.27, 1.28, and 1.29:

$$NPV_1 = -Sp + E_{k1}/1 + r_{s1} = 0 > NPV_2 = -Sp + E_{K2}/1 + r_{s2} = 0 \tag{1.33}$$

$$Y_{k1} = I_{k1}/s > Y_{k2} = I_{k2}/s \tag{1.34}$$

$$n_{k1} = I_{k1}/s \ PN^s > n_{k2} = I_{k2}/s \ PN^s \tag{1.35}$$

In Equation 1.33, $NPV_1 > NPV_2$ because $E_{k1} > E_{k2}$ and $r_{s1} < r_{s2}$. Therefore, in Equations 1.34 and 1.35 respectively, $Y_{k1} > Y_{k2}$ and $n_{k1} > n_{k2}$. In short, the change from a discretionary monetary policy to one committed to maintaining a fixed-interest-rate structure by buying and selling at stated prices gilt-edged bonds of all maturities reduces the unemployment rate that characterizes the long-period equilibrium position of the economy from $1 - n_{k2}$ to $1 - n_{k1}$.

Section 1.3 Summary and Conclusions

Some orthodox economists argue the Federal Reserve should focus on keeping the inflation rate below 2 percent by maintaining a rate of growth of the stock of money that corresponds to the long-period rate of economic growth (i.e. the rate at which aggregate output tends toward its long-period equilibrium) and thus keep the money interest rate equal to the real interest rate. Other orthodox economists argue that it should also combat short-period unemployment by moving the money interest rate above the real interest rate during cyclical expansions, and below it during recessions.

These policy prescriptions are based on two assumptions and one causal claim. The two assumptions are that equilibrium aggregate output and the velocity of money are constant. The causal claim is that changes in the stock of money cause changes in the price level. In this chapter, I demonstrated that, once the difference between Keynes's concepts of probability and risk and the orthodox ones are taken into account, the assumption that equilibrium output is constant is invalid. Instead, it changes with the monetary policy pursued by the monetary authority.

I explained the difference between Keynes's concepts of probability and risk and the orthodox ones by analyzing their link to investment behavior, which can be summarized as follows (see, for example, Carabelli, 1988; O'Donnell, 1989; Gerrard, 1992). Looking backwards, we observe long-period trends shaping the growth and development of the economy. The confidence to undertake investment projects depends upon our ability to project these trends into the future. The problem is that we know these trends are not governed by natural laws but are instead the result of the series of investment projects undertaken by forward-looking investors in the past. In every given moment in which such investment projects were undertaken, the long-period trends of the economy would have taken off in a different direction, if those investment projects had not been undertaken.

For this reason, investors take a two-step approach to the evaluation of prospective investment projects. First, they project into the future long-period trends in technical innovations and the size and composition of both the labor force and the stock of capital by assigning probabilities to the likelihood of their continuance, and thereby calculate the expected profits (E_o).[19] Second, they contemplate the degree to which the principle of non-sufficient reason captures their uncertainty about the degree to which knowable but unknown or unknowable factors may cause future trends of the economy to differ from past ones, and thereby calculate the expected profit (E_k).

Monetary policy is a factor that has shaped the long-term trends in the economy. It is thus necessary for investors to assign a probability to the likelihood that the monetary authority will continue to act in the same way in the future that it has in the past, and incorporate it into the calculation of E_o. If the monetary authority has the discretion to act differently in the future than it has in the past, investors are compelled to contemplate monetary policy itself as a knowable but unknown or unknowable factor that may cause future trends in the economy to differ from past ones, and thus take it into account as a factor that makes $E_k < E_o$. If the monetary authority makes a credible commitment to maintaining a fixed-interest-rate structure by buying and selling at stated prices gilt-edged bonds of all maturities, this element of uncertainty would be alleviated, thereby reducing the difference between E_k and E_o. The purpose of this chapter has been to show that, as a result, the long-period equilibrium position of the economy would be characterized by less unemployment.

Notes

1   For example, if we specify C as (C/D) D, R as (R/D) D, and D as (D/D) D, then divide Equation 1.3 by Equation 1.2, we get:

$$M/H = [(C/D)D + (D/D)D]/[(C/D)D + (R/D)D]$$
$$= [(C/D + 1)D]/[(C/D + R/D)D$$
$$= (C/D + 1)/(C/D) + (R/D)$$

or:

$$M = \{[(C/D) + 1]/[(C/D) + (R + D)]\}H$$
$$= mH$$

2   The other factors supplying the monetary base are the size of the gold stock and Treasury deposits at the Federal Reserve, as well as Treasury currency and Treasury cash balances and the 'float.'

3   Nicholas Kaldor (1970, p. 15; 1982), combines as follows the notion of an unstable velocity of money with the claim that changes in the supply of bank reserves cause changes in the stock of money during periods of calm between financial crises, when the Federal Reserve need not intervene as lender of last resort:

> If one postulates that it is the fluctuations in the economy that causes the fluctuations in the money supply (and not the other way around), but that the elasticity in the supply of money (in response to changes in demand) is less than infinite, then, the greater the change in demand, the more *both* the supply of money and the 'velocity' will rise in consequence. If the supply of money responded less, the change in the velocity would have been greater; if the supply of money responded fully, no change in velocity would have occurred (under this hypothesis).

4   To reconstruct Keynes's theory of monetary policy I build upon the work of John Eatwell and Murray Milgate (1983a, 1983b; also see Eatwell, 1983; Milgate, 1982;

Bortis, 2013, 1997). In particular, I use the classical long-period method to model the relationships between the investment multiplier, the marginal efficiency of capital, and the interest rate—which constitute Keynes's theory—and I do so in such a way that the short-period fluctuations of the economy are around a long-period equilibrium position characterized by unemployment. See D'Orlando (2007) for a recent appraisal of the classical long-period method of analyzing the overall movements of the economy as tending toward a long-period equilibrium position characterized by a uniform rate of profit on the supply price of capital.

5 Keynes applies Equation 1.7 to capital assets rather than investment projects, and thereby obtains his concept of the marginal efficiency of capital. As Garegnani (1983) demonstrates, this application is incorrect because it implies that capital is a factor of production that yields a marginal product when plugged into a (aggregate) production function. However, as Pasinetti (1974, pp. 37–8) demonstrates, Equation 1.7 still applies to investment projects. To make clear that I am using Equation 1.7 in the valid sense of applying to investment projects, I drop the concept of the marginal efficiency of capital in favor of the concept of net present value.

6 Davidson (1996, p. 479; also see Solow, 1985, p. 330) emphasizes the role of the law of large numbers in orthodox probability theory. My analysis of the role of the principle of non-sufficient reason amplifies his analysis.

7 Fontana and Gerrard (2004, pp. 628–31) also make reference to the behavioral-finance literature to substantiate Keynes's theory of probability.

8 Thaler (1992, pp. 52–3) extends the oil-drilling example to the hypothetical case of a company which has won oil-drilling rights to a parcel of land. He asks us to assume that, if the company fails to find oil on the parcel of land, then under current management it will be worth nothing—$0 per share. However, if the company finds all the oil that it anticipated when bidding, then the company could be worth as much as $100 per share. Consider an investor who is contemplating a takeover of the company. The investor assumes that his/her superior management skills will make the company 50 percent more valuable under his/her direction than it is under current management. The investor also applies the principle of non-sufficient reason and assumes that, given the range of exploration outcomes, all share values between $0 and $100 are equally likely. Therefore, the investor estimates the expected value of the company as $50 under current management and $75 under his/her management.

The problem here is of course that the investor lacks a crucial piece of relevant information—namely, how much oil the company in question is finding. The company knows how much oil there is, and will only accept the takeover offer if it is in excess of its value based on this information. Therefore, the very fact of the offer being accepted will change the investor's calculations of expected value.

For example, assume that the investor offers $60 per share for the company and the offer is accepted. The range of equally likely values for each share of the company thus falls from $0-$100 to $0-$60. The expected value of the company, including the 50 percent mark-up for the investor's presumed superior management skill, thus falls to $45, meaning that there is now an expected loss of $15—and this would be true for any bid greater than $0: if it is accepted, the investor can expect to lose 25 percent of the amount bid.

9 See O'Donnell (1989), Gerrard (1992, 1994), and Dequech (1999) for alternative formulations of the concept of the weight of arguments. The fact of alternative formulations results in no small part from ambiguities in Keynes's analysis of the concept (see, for example, Runde, 1990; Dequech, 2000). But, as Ellsberg (1961; also see Camerer, 1994, p. 645) explains, ambiguity is often the consequence of situations in which a person does not know all the relevant facts. My formulation of the concept of the weight of arguments is motivated by the belief that facts unknown to Keynes have now emerged in the literature on behavioral finance.

10 See, for example, Hacking (1975; also see Dequech, 2000; O'Donnell, 2013), who analyzes these cases in terms of an "aleatory" dimension (that is, the knowable causal structure) and an "epistemic" dimension (that is, the investor's degree of belief in that causal structure).

11 See, for example, Davidson (1991; also see Keynes, 1937a, pp. 113–14; 1937b, 1937c) who analyzes these cases in terms of "non-ergodic uncertainty," as opposed to the "ergodic probability" of cases with an underlying causal structure which is knowable.

12 As Thaler and Tversky (1992) present it, the preference of the owners of wealth for Bet One is an unexplained anomaly from the perspective of orthodox probability theory. Behavioral economists attribute this anomaly to "loss aversion," which they define as an asymmetry of value whereby people tend to judge the disutility of giving up something they own to be greater than the utility of acquiring it anew (see, for example, Kahneman and Tversky, 1984). Or, dropping the language of utilitarianism, "loss aversion" denotes the fact that changes which make things worse loom larger in people's judgments of probability than changes which make them better. The results obtained in Equations 1.24 and 1.25 can thus be interpreted as a formulation of risk understood as loss aversion.

13 In particular, the Federal Reserve currently controls the federal funds rate, or the rate at which banks lend excess reserves to one another, by changing the supply of bank reserves. This fact preempts the analysis of the determination of the short-term interest rate by the schedule of liquidity preference and the supply of money, as Keynes does in chapter 13 of *The General Theory*. In this section, I derive Keynes's concept of liquidity preference from his analysis of it in chapter 17 of *The General Theory*.

14 "The short-term interest rate" denotes an index of all market yields on high-quality securities of short maturity (including federal funds) and "the long-term interest rate" denotes an index of all market yields on high-quality bonds of long maturity. Using such indexes is legitimate because all short-term market yields move in tandem, as do all long-term market yields. However, the short-term interest rate and the long-term interest rate do not move in tandem. Sometimes the yield curve is positively sloped, sometimes inverted, and sometimes flat.

15 Keynes (1936, p. 235) argues that "in the absence of money ... the rates of interest would only reach equilibrium when there is full employment." Following Harrod (1947) and Chick (1983), this passage, and others like it, is interpreted to mean that it is only an inflexibly high interest rate, when combined with net present value calculations, which causes long-period unemployment. My thesis is that this would be the case only if the expected profit is formulated in terms of Equation 1.10 and the long-term interest rate in the way proposed by orthodox economists.

16 Tobin's q proposes that the actual expected profits from investment projects, as determined in the stock market (E_a), influence long-term expectations (E_k) and thus the aggregate rate of investment undertaken in long-period equilibrium (I_k) (see, for example, Gordon, 2012, p. 528). In contrast, as formulated in Equation 1.27, E_a influences short-term expectations and thus the pace at which I_k is implemented in the short period.

17 For example, if the safe long-term interest rate (r_s) is 4 percent, then the actual long-term interest rate (r_a) is limited to a range of $0.04 - (0.04)^2 = 3.84$ percent to $0.04 + (0.04)^2 = 4.16$ percent. If r_s is 2 percent, then r_a is limited to range of $0.02 - (0.02)^2 = 1.96$ percent to $0.02 + (0.02)^2 = 2.04$ percent.

18 The short-period fluctuations of n_a around n_k have an upper bound, given by the supply of technologically augmented labor. However, this does not limit the short-period fluctuations of I_a and Y_a around I_k and Y_k: it simply defines the point at which those fluctuations cause what Keynes (1936, pp. 119, 303) calls "true inflation," or short-term inflationary pressures caused by excess aggregate demand during cyclical expansions. Keynes (1936, pp. 320–4; also see Robinson 1956, pp. 198–216) argues

that the appropriate government response in these circumstances is interventions to remove bottlenecks in the pipelines of production, leaving no role for the Federal Reserve.

19 D'Orlando (2005, 2007) also argues that probabilistic, as opposed to deterministic, dynamic models are compatible with the classical long-period method of analysis deployed by Keynes (1936).

Bibliography

Bazerman, M. H. and W. F. Samuelson. 1983. "I Won the Auction but Don't Want the Prize." *Journal of Conflict Resolution*, Vol. 27 (December), pp. 618–34.

Bernanke, Ben S. 1999. *Inflation Targeting: Lessons from the International Experience*. Princeton: Princeton University Press.

Blinder, Alan. 1999. *Central Banking in Theory and Practice*. Cambridge, MA: MIT Press.

Bortis, Heinrich. 2013. "Post-Keynesian Principles and Economic Policies." In *The Oxford Handbook of Post-Keynesian Economics: Volume Two: Critiques and Methodology*. Geoffrey C. Harcourt and Peter Kriesler (eds). New York: Oxford University Press, pp. 326–65.

Bortis, Heinrich. 1997. *Institutions, Behavior and Economic Theory: A Contribution to Classical-Keynesian Political Economy*. Cambridge: Cambridge University Press.

Burger, A. 1971. *The Money Supply Process*. Belmont, CA: Wadsworth.

Cagan, Phillip. 1965. *Determinants and Effects of Changes in the Stock of Money, 1867–1960*. New York: National Bureau of Economic Research.

Camerer, C. 1994. "Individual Decision Making." In J. Kagel and A. Roth (eds). *Handbook of Experimental Economics*. Princeton, NJ: Princeton University Press.

Capen, E. C., R. V. Clapp and W. M. Campbell. 1971. "Competitive Bidding in High-risk Situations." *Journal of Petroleum Technology*, Vol. 23 (June), pp. 641–53.

Carabelli, A. M. 1988. *On Keynes's Method*. New York: St. Martin's Press.

Carron, Andrew S. 1982. "Financial Crises: Recent Experiences in US and International Markets." *Brookings Papers on Economic Activity*, Vol. 2, pp. 395–422.

Chick, Victoria. 1983. *Macroeconomics after Keynes: A Reconsideration of the General Theory*. Cambridge, MA: MIT Press.

Davidson, Paul. 1991. "Is Probability Theory Relevant for Uncertainty? A Post Keynesian Perspective." *Journal of Economic Perspectives*, Vol. 5, pp. 129–43.

Davidson, Paul. 1996. "Reality and Economic Theory." *Journal of Post Keynesian Economics*. Vol. 18, pp. 479–508.

Dequech, D. 2000. "Fundamental Uncertainty and Ambiguity." *Eastern Economic Journal*, Vol. 26, pp. 41–60.

Dequech, D. 1999. "Expectations and Confidence under Uncertainty." *Journal of Post Keynesian Economics*, Vol. 21, pp. 415–30.

D'Orlando, R. 2007. "A Methodological Note on Long-Period Positions." *Contributions to Political Economy*, Vol. 29, pp. 633–54.

D'Orlando, R. 2005. "Will the Classical-type Approach Survive Sraffian Theory?" *Journal of Post Keynesian Economics*, Vol. 27, pp. 633–54.

Eatwell, John. 1983. "The Analytical Foundations of Monetarism." In *Keynes's Economics and the Theory of Value and Distribution*. John Eatwell and Murray Milgate (eds). New York: Oxford University Press, pp. 203–13.

Eatwell, John and Murray Milgate. 1983a. "Introduction." In *Keynes's Economics and the Theory of Value and Distribution*, John Eatwell and Murray Milgate (eds). New York: Oxford University Press.

Eatwell John and Murray Milgate. 1983b. "Unemployment and the Market Mechanism." In *Keynes's Economics and the Theory of Value and Distribution*. John Eatwell and Murray Milgate (eds). New York: Oxford University Press.

Ellsberg, D. 1961. "Risk, Ambiguity and the Savage Axioms." *Quarterly Journal of Economics*, Vol. 75, pp. 643–69.

Flaschel, Peter and Alfred Greiner. 2011. *A Future for Capitalism: Classical, Neoclassical and Keynesian Perspectives*. Northampton, MA: Edward Elgar.

Foley, Duncan K. and Thomas R. Michl. 1999. *Growth and Distribution*. Cambridge, MA: Harvard University Press.

Fontana, G. and B. Gerrard 2004. "A Post Keynesian Theory of Decision Making under Uncertainty." *Journal of Economic Psychology*, Vol. 25, pp. 619–37.

Friedman, Milton and Anna Jacobson Schwartz. 1963. *A Monetary History of the United States and Great Britain, 1867–1960*. Princeton, NJ: Princeton University Press.

Garegnani, Pierangelo. 1983. "Notes on Consumption, Investment and Effective Demand." In *Keynes's Economics and the Theory of Value and Distribution*. John Eatwell and Murrary Milgate (eds). New York: Oxford University Press.

Gerrard, B. 1994. "Beyond Rational Expectations: A Constructive Interpretation of Keynes's Analysis of Behavior under Uncertainty." *Economic Journal*, Vol. 104, pp. 327–37.

Gerrard, B. 1992. "From *A Treatise on Probability* to *The General Theory*: Continuity or Change in Keynes's Thought?" In B. Gerrard and J. V. Hillard (eds). *The Philosophy and Economics of John Marnard Keynes*. Aldershot, and Brookfield, WI: Edward Elgar, pp. 80–9.

Goldstein, Jonathan P. 2009. "An Introduction to a Unified Heterodox Macroeconomic Theory." In *Heterodox Macroeconomics: Keynes, Marx and Globalization*. Jonathan P. Goldstein and Michael G. Hillard (eds). New York: Routledge, pp. 36–53.

Goodhart, Charles A. E. 1991. *Money, Information and Uncertainty*. Second edition. Cambridge, MA: MIT Press.

Gordon, Robert. 2012. *Macroeconomics*. Twelfth edition. New York: Addison-Wesley.

Hacking, I. 1975. *The Emergence of Probability*. Cambridge: Cambridge University Press.

Harrod, Roy. 1947. "Keynes the Economist." In *The New Economics*. Seymour E. Harris (ed.). New York: Alfred A. Knopf, pp. 65–72.

Halevi, Joseph, Neil Hart and Peter Kriesler. 2013. "The Traverse, Equilibrium Analysis, and Post-Keynesian Economics." In *The Oxford Handbook of Post-Keynesian Economics: Volume Two; Critiques and Methodology*. Geoffrey S. Harcourt and Peter Kriesler (eds). New York: Oxford University Press, pp. 175–97.

Hershey, J. and P. J. H. Schomaker 1985. "Probability versus Certainty Equivalence Methods in Utility Measurement: Are They Equivalent?" *Management Science*, Vol. 31 (October), pp. 1213–31.

Hester, D. D. 1981. "Innovations and Monetary Control." *Brookings Papers on Economic Activity*. Vol. 1, pp. 141–99.

Holmes, A. 1969. "Operational Constraints on the Stabilization of Money Supply Growth." In *Controlling Monetary Aggregates*. Boston: Federal Reserve Bank of Boston.

Ingersoll, J. E. 1989. "Interest Rates." In *The New Palgrave: Finance*. John Eatwell, Murray Milgate and Peter Newman (eds). New York: W. W. Norton.

Johannes, J. M. and Rasche, R. H. 1981. "Can the Reserves Approach to Monetary Control Really Work?" *Journal of Money, Credit and Banking*. Vol. 13, No. 3 (August), pp. 298–313.

Kagel, J. H. and D. Levin. 1986. "The Winner's Curse and Public Information in Common Value Auctions." *American Economic Review*, Vol. 76 (December), pp. 894–920.

Kahneman, Daniel and Amos Tversky. 1984. "Choices, Values and Frames." *American Psychologist*, Vol. 39 (April), pp. 341–50.

Kaldor, Nicholas. 1982. *The Scourge of Monetarism*, New York: Oxford University Press.

Kaldor, Nicholas. 1970. "The New Monetarism." *Lloyds Bank Review* (July).

Keynes, John Maynard. 1937a [1973]. The Theory of the Rate of Interest. In *The General Theory and After: Part II: Defense and Development*. London: Macmillan, pp. 101–8.

Keynes, John Maynard. 1937b [1973]. "The General Theory of Employment." In *The General Theory and After: Part II: Defense and Development*. London: Macmillan, pp. 109–23.

Keynes, John Maynard. 1937c [1979]. "Letter to H. Townsend: April 11, 1937." In *The General Theory and After: A Supplement*. London: Macmillan, pp. 258–9.

Keynes, John Maynard. 1936 [1964]. *The General Theory of Employment, Interest, and Money*, New York: Harcourt, Brace Jovanovich.

Keynes, John Maynard. 1921 [1973]. *A Treatise on Probability*. New York: St. Martin's Press.

Kindleberger, Charles P. 1978 [2005]. *Manias, Panics, and Crashes: A History of Financial Crises*. New York: Wiley.

Markowitz, Harry M. 1959 [1991]. *Portfolio Selection: Efficient Diversification of Investments*. Malden, MA: Blackwell.

Marx, Karl. 1894 [1967]. *Capital: The Process of Capitalist Production as a Whole*. Volume Three. New York: International Publishers.

Meltzer, Allan. 2009. *A History of the Federal Reserve*. Volume Two. Chicago: University of Chicago Press.

Meltzer, Allan. 2003. *A History of the Federal Reserve*. Volume One. Chicago: University of Chicago Press.

Meltzer, Allan. 1982. "Comment on Federal Reserve Control of the Money Stock." *Journal of Money, Credit, and Banking*, Vol. 14 (November), pp. 632–40.

Meltzer, Allan. 1969. "Controlling Money." *Federal Reserve Bank of St. Louis Review*. Vol. 51, No. 5 (May).

Michl, Thomas R. and Duncan K. Foley. 2004. "A Classical Alternative to the Neoclassical Growth Model." In *Growth, Distribution, and Effective Demand: Alternatives to Economic Orthodoxy*. George Argyrous, Mathew Forstater and Gary Mongiovi (eds). New York: M.E. Sharpe, pp. 35–60.

Milgate, Murray. 1982. *Capital and Employment: A Study of Keynes's Economics*. New York: Academic Press.

Moore, Basil. 1989. "On the Endogeneity of Money Once More." *Journal of Post Keynesian Economics*, Vol. 11, No. 3 (Spring), pp. 479–87.

Moore, Basil J. 1988. *Horizontalists and Verticalists: The Macroeconomics of Credit Money*. New York: Cambridge University Press.

Moore, Basil J. 1979. The Endogenous Money Stock. *Journal of Post Keynesian Economics*, Vol. 1, No. 2 (Fall), pp. 49–71.

O'Donnell, Rod. 2013. "Two Post-Keynesian Approaches to Uncertainty and Irreducible Uncertainty." In *The Oxford Handbook of Post-Keynesian Economics: Volume Two: Critiques and Methodology*. Geoffrey C. Harcourt and Peter Kriesler (eds). New York: Oxford University Press, pp. 124–42.

O'Donnell, Rod. 1989. *Keynes: Philosophy, Economics and Politics*. London: Macmillan.

Palley, Thomas I. 1987–8. "Bank Lending, Discount Window Borrowing, and the Endogenous Money Supply: A Theoretical Framework." *Journal of Post Keynesian Economics*, Vol. 10, No. 2 (Winter), pp. 282–304.

Pasinetti, Luigi L. 1974. "The Economics of Effective Demand." In *Growth and Income Distribution*. Cambridge: Cambridge University Press.

Rasche, R. 1972. "A Review of Empirical Studies of the Money Supply Mechanism." *Federal Reserve Bank of St. Louis Review*. Vol. 54 (July).

Ricardo, David. 1817 [1951]. *On the Principles of Political Economy and Taxation*. Piero Sraffa (ed.). Cambridge: Cambridge University Press.

Robinson, Joan. 1956. *The Accumulation of Capital*. Philadelphia: Porcupine Press.

Rousseas, Stephen W. 1989. "On the Endogeneity of Money Once More." *Journal of Post Keynesian Economics*, Vol. 1, No. 3 (Spring), pp. 474–8.

Rottenstreich, Y. and A. Tversky. 1997. "Unpacking, Repacking and Anchoring: Advances in Support Theory." *Psychology Review*, Vol. 104, pp. 406–15.

Runde, J. 1990. "Keynesian Uncertainty and the Weight of Arguments." *Economics and Philosophy*, Vol. 6, pp. 275–92.

Sardoni, Claudio. 2013. "Marx and the Post-Keynesians." In *The Oxford Handbook of Post-Keynesian Economics: Volume Two: Critiques and Methodlogy*. Geoffrey S. Harcourt and Peter Kriesler (eds). New York: Oxford University Press, pp. 231–44.

Shaikh, Anwar. 2004. "Labor Market Dynamics within Rival Macroeconomic Frameworks." In *Growth, Distribution, and Effective Demand: Alternatives to Economic Orthodoxy*. Argyrous, G., Matthew Forstater and Gary Mongiovi, G. (eds). Armonk, NY: M.E. Sharpe.

Solow, Robert. 1985. "Economic History and Economics." *American Economic Review, Papers and Proceedings*, Vol. 75, pp. 328–31.

Thaler, Richard H. 1992. "The Winner's Curse." In *The Winner's Curse: Paradoxes and Anomalies of Economic Life*. R. H. Thaler (ed.). Princeton, NJ: Princeton University Press, pp. 50–62.

Thaler, Richard H. and Amos Tversky. 1992. "Preference Reversals." In *The Winner's Curse: Paradoxes and Anomalies of Economic Life*. R. H. Thaler (ed.). Princeton, NJ: Princeton University Press, pp. 79–91.

Wojnilower, Albert M. 1980. "The Central Role of Credit Crunches in Recent Financial History." *Brookings Papers on Economic Activity*, Vol. 2, pp. 277–325.

Wray, L. Randall. 1999. "The 1966 Financial Crisis: Financial Instability of Political Economy?" *Review of Political Economy*. Vol. 11, No. 4, pp. 415–26.

Wray, L. Randall. 1998. *Understanding Modern Money: The Key to Full Employment and Price Stability*. Northampton, MA: Edward Elgar.

2 The Origin of the Federal Reserve System

The Institutionalization of the Alliance between the Large New York Banks and the Large Regional Banks

Central banks exist to perform two contradictory functions—namely, acting as lender of last resort for private banks and exercising monetary control over the money supply. In Chapter 1, I defined the art of central banking as exercising monetary control during periods of calm between financial crises despite the fact that central banks must intervene, and financial-market participants know they must intervene, as lenders of last resort when financial crises occur. Henceforward, I will refer to this art as attempting to stabilize the economy on a non-inflationary growth path, or at full employment with price stability.

In this chapter, I explain how the Federal Reserve System evolved out of failed attempts of bank clearinghouses to stabilize the economy on a non-inflationary growth path. My thesis is that private, profit-maximizing banks need a public, non-profit-maximizing central bank to accomplish this goal.

In Section 2.1, I explain why private banks needed a central bank to act as lender of last resort and in Section 2.2 I explain why they needed one to exercise monetary control. In both cases, at the center of analysis is the struggle of individual banks to increase their profits at the expense of other banks. In the case of the evolution of the monetary-control function, I also show the fundamental role played by the struggle of the banks, taken as a whole, to increase their profits at the expense of other social classes. In Section 2.3, I then explain why, until the New Deal, other social classes acquiesced to the establishment and operation of an institution opposed to their interests. In this way, my analysis goes beyond strictly economic terms. As Charles Goodhart (1989, p. xiv) puts it:

> Our subject has been rightly called 'political economy', and those who choose to leave out politics in pursuit of rigor, or the avoidance of value judgments, or whatever, are to my mind losing too much that is important for the relevance and immediacy of the subject.

In Section 2.4, I provide a summary and conclusions.

Section 2.1 The Origin of the Federal Reserve System as Lender of Last Resort

The Federal Reserve System was established in the context of the gold exchange standard under which the dollar had a fixed value in terms of gold but bank notes were the primary form of dollars used in transactions.[1] In the first instance, bank notes were receipts acknowledging gold deposits at banks. However, since the bank notes could be used to purchase goods and services, they were the instrument used by banks to make loans.

For example, assume one-hundred people deposit one ounce of gold with a bank, each one receiving a bank note representing one ounce of gold in exchange. Also assume, on average, ten people redeem their bank notes for gold each day. Therefore, the bank must hold ten ounces of gold as a reserve and can lend out the other ninety ounces of gold. Or, to speak more precisely, for every ten ounces of gold a bank has on deposit, it can print additional bank notes representing ninety ounces of gold in order to make loans. With the one hundred ounces of gold on deposit, it can thus have bank notes in circulation representing one thousand ounces of gold.

Bank loans typically took the form of discounting bills of exchange. For example, assume a U.S. exporter contracts for delivery of $100 of goods in a foreign port in three months. The contract is a bill of exchange, or the importer's promise to pay upon delivery. The exporter then takes the bill of exchange to a bank and receives a loan of $99 of the bank's notes in exchange for a promise to turn over the $100 of bank notes it will receive upon delivery of the goods. The difference between the $99 of bank notes received by the exporter now and the $100 of bank notes it repays in three months constitutes an annualized discount rate of approximately 4 percent, the source of the bank's profit.

The bank notes the bank received in repayment of the loan were unlikely to be its own. Consequently, the bank needed to join a clearinghouse. All banks which joined a clearinghouse placed their gold reserves with other member banks, then deposited all the bank notes they received that were not their own at the clearinghouse. Banks which placed more such notes on deposit than the clearinghouse received of the banks' own notes were creditors, while banks that deposited fewer notes than the clearinghouse received of their notes were debtors.

In the nineteenth century, large banks in Boston and Philadelphia established clearinghouses, but the New York Clearinghouse was unique in issuing "specie certificates" to its creditors, representing the amount of their credit. Creditor banks either held the specie certificates or exchanged them for the gold reserves of the banks that were debtors of the clearinghouse. If the creditor banks converted their specie certificates into gold, then the debtor banks turned to the New York Clearinghouse for "loan certificates."

The New York Clearinghouse issued loan certificates to member banks in exchange for bonds as collateral and a promise to pay 6 percent interest on the face value of the loan certificates. In this way, the New York Clearinghouse performed the principal function of a central bank as explained by Walter Bagehot (1893) in *Lombard Street*—namely, lending freely at a penalty rate of interest.[2] Also in this way, bonds held by the New York Clearinghouse gradually supplanted gold as the principal reserve banks held against their outstanding bank notes.

During the 1893 financial crisis, when the public as well as other banks demanded gold in exchange for bank notes, the debtor banks of the New York Clearinghouse exchanged their loan certificates for "clearinghouse currency." Clearinghouse currency was nothing more than the loan certificates denominated in a manner convenient for the public—as low as 25 cents. The debtor banks then gave the clearinghouse currency to the public in exchange for their bank notes, instead of gold, thereby transforming the New York Clearinghouse into a lender of last resort to the large New York banks (Gorton, 1984, pp. 5–6, 8; White, 1983, pp. 281*ff.*).

However, the 1907 financial crisis was caused by the fact that the New York Clearinghouse could not perform the lender-of-last-resort function efficiently. It began on October 21, when the National Bank of Commerce refused to accept specie certificates representing bank notes issued by the Knickerbocker Trust Company, a persistent debtor of the New York Clearinghouse. Knickerbocker met all its interest obligations on the loan certificates it received, and paid them back in full upon maturity. Nonetheless, the National Bank could not resist an opportunity to try to "eliminate a rival, or rather a set of rivals; for the run on Knickerbocker immediately turned into a stampede of depositors onto all the trust companies and eventually back onto the national banks themselves." In short, the large New York banks needed a public, non-profit-maximizing institution (i.e. the Federal Reserve) to act as lender of last resort, because the temptation of forcing competitors into bankruptcy then purchasing their assets (i.e. loans) at fire-sale prices was a far more attractive alternative for private, profit-maximizing banks, like the National Bank of Commerce (Goodhart, 1969, pp. 118–9; 1988).[3]

Section 2.2 The Origin of the Federal Reserve System as Controller of the Money Supply

In Chapter 1, I explained why the money-supply process is not properly understood in terms of orthodox monetary theory (i.e. the quantity theory of money), but I did not propose an alternative explanation of it. Short-term and long-term interest rates are the only monetary variables in my reconstruction of Keynes's theory of monetary policy (Keynes, 1936).

In this section, I rectify this lacuna by incorporating into my reconstruction of Keynes's theory of monetary policy the equation for bank profit margins (PM), which distinguishes between two short-term interest rates—namely, the ask price (AP) and the bid price (BP) banks receive on loans and pay for deposits respectively:

$$PM = AP - BP \qquad (2.1)$$

So long as $AP > BP$, banks have an incentive to make loans, creating deposits in the process (see, for example, Goodhart, 1989, pp. 24, 109, 125–6). In the process of expanding the money supply (defined as bank deposits plus currency in circulation), banks must bid for the reserves required to back the deposits (or bank notes), thereby putting upward pressure on *BP*.

In other words, during cyclical expansions, when the demand for loans is increasing, there is a tendency for bank profit margins (*PM*) to be squeezed, and ultimately reduced to zero.[4] At that point, if there is any net benefit to liquidity, or obtaining bank services, then the stock of money will expand without limit. As Charles Goodhart (1989, p. 102) puts it, when *PM* = *0* because banks have bid the interest rate on deposits (*BP*) to equality with the interest rate on loans (*AP*):

> it would be sensible for all agents to sell assets to, and borrow assets from, the banks up to an infinite amount, increasing their bank deposits without limit at the same time. In other words, the demand for intermediary services is a function of the price-cost of intermediation itself—i.e., the spread.
>
> (See, too, Miller and Sprenkle, 1980).

Bank clearinghouses, and the Federal Reserve System that evolved out of them, were established to prevent the money supply from expanding without limit during economic expansions. For this reason, they are essentially "managers of a club of banks," or of "bank cartels," which exist to maintain positive bank profit margins by restricting the money supply (Goodhart, 1989, p. 176, also see pp. 136–7, 178–80; Epstein, 1982, p. 220).

Cartels are common, not just in banking, but in all professional services—such as law, insurance, medicine, etc.—where the quality of the services provided is not guaranteed by the incentive to obtain repeat business. An individual's demand for professional services is infrequent and largely non-repetitive. Consequently, there is a "free-rider" problem in the sense that less reputable suppliers have an incentive to use the cover of their association with reputable lawyers, bankers, etc. to increase profit margins by providing shoddy services, thereby squeezing the profit margins of the purveyors of quality services. Cartels are formed to combat this free-rider problem.

In the case of banking, clearinghouses and the Federal Reserve System exist to impose quality control standards on free riders, or to exercise monetary control over them, in order to preserve and enhance the profit margins of their members. For example, prior to their replacement by Federal Reserve notes with the establishment of the Federal Reserve System in 1913, the free-rider problem took the form of an incentive for banks to increase their profit margins by placing "themselves at long distances from the most important centers of business" then flood those centers with their bank notes. It was impossible for the public to assess the relative quality of all the bank notes in circulation. All bank notes were convertible into gold in principle. Therefore, once they were discounted to take into account "the transportation costs of shipping the notes from the point of quotation to the redemption point and the costs of shipping the gold back," all bank notes were equally acceptable in practice (Klein, 1974, p. 440; Smith, 1936, p. 42).

The issue here is banks' bid prices (*BP*), particularly the cost of reserves included in them. In the example in Section 2.1, I explained the amount of money in circulation on the assumption that banks needed to hold 10 percent of the gold they received as a reserve against deposit withdrawals. In fact, it was a function of the probability of redemption, or how far a bank's offices were from where its bank notes circulated. The greater the distance between where a bank's notes circulated and where they could be redeemed, the less likely it was that people would incur the transportation costs of redeeming bank notes. And the smaller the chance that the bank notes would be presented for conversion into gold, the greater the amount of them that could be issued on the basis of a given gold reserve.

The large banks in Boston, Philadelphia, and New York established clearing-houses not to act as lenders of last resort, but to combat this way of minimizing required gold reserves, and thus the ability of free riders to hold down their bid prices. Banks that were members of the clearinghouses became their creditors or debtors. But banks that placed themselves at long distances from Boston, Philadelphia, and New York to reduce the likelihood that their bank notes would be redeemed for gold were not members of the clearinghouses. The primary purpose of the clearinghouses was to accumulate the banks notes of the non-member regional banks then incur the transportation costs to redeem them. This solved the free-rider problem, since the only way the large regional banks could protect themselves from having their notes systematically collected by the clearinghouses for redemption was to join the clearinghouses and thus submit to the rigorous quality-control standards the clearinghouses enforced at the daily clearing of balances (see, for example, Trivoli, 1979, especially pp. 18–19). In effect, the bank clearinghouses were bank cartels that raised the price of money (i.e. interest rates) by restricting its supply (Goodhart, 1989, p. 180; Epstein, 1982, p. 220).

However, by solving the free-rider problem in this way, the bank clearinghouses also defeated the whole point of banks setting up their offices at long distances from the most important centers of business in Boston, Philadelphia, and New York. Not surprisingly, the large regional banks mobilized against this threat to their reason for being, giving rise to the Bank Wars of the Jackson Era and the sustained campaign for Bimetallism (i.e. giving silver equal status to gold in bank reserves) in the post-Civil War period (Trivoli, 1979, pp. 18–19*ff*; Schlesinger, 1953, pp. 74–87; Friedman and Schwartz, 1963, pp. 113–19; Timberlake, 1993, pp. 152–65).

The rise of the populist movement prompted the large regional banks to shift their allegiance back to the gold exchange standard and, for this reason, explains why the Federal Reserve was established, not just to act as lender of last resort, but also to exercise monetary control over the amount of money in circulation. The original target of the populist movement was the crop lien system in the South. The crop lien system, established during Reconstruction, was characterized by "furnishing merchants" who lent farmers all the necessities of life between harvests in exchange for, first, a commitment to plant only cotton, and, second, first claim on the proceeds from the sale of the cotton. Each year, the farmers discovered that the proceeds from the sale of the cotton fell short of what they owed the furnishing merchants. It could not have been otherwise. For the furnishing merchants charged exorbitant interest rates, usually over 100 percent and sometimes over 200 percent; high enough, at any rate, to ensure that the value of the farmers' crops was less than their bills to the furnishing merchants (Goodwyn, 1978, p. 22).

In an effort to break out of the crop lien system, Southern farmers set up purchasing and marketing cooperatives which eventually spread to the Midwest and West. However, the cooperative movement floundered on the fact that the large regional banks would not finance their purchases. The cooperatives produced tokens and script for exchanges among members, but they were of no use in obtaining the farm implements and other commodities the farmers did not produce themselves. The large regional banks would lend only to the furnishing merchants to finance such purchases (Goodwyn, 1978, p. 68).

What began as a cooperative movement to break out of the crop lien system was thus transformed into a political movement, organized around a "sub-treasuries" plan for a central bank, the purpose of which was to break the stranglehold of the large regional banks on the money supply in the South, Midwest, and West. The sub-treasuries were to be government-run warehouses and grain elevators in every county with significant agricultural production. But they were also to be a central bank since, in exchange for crops put in storage, the sub-treasuries would be empowered to issue bank notes, only now the bank notes would be receipts for cotton and grain put on deposit at the sub-treasuries, rather than for gold put on deposit at a bank. Farmers would return the bank notes when their crops were sold and thus removed from storage at the sub-treasuries. Consequently, the money supply would automatically expand and contract to meet the seasonal needs of trade in a predominantly agricultural economy. By the turn of the twentieth century, the populist movement, based on this campaign for a money supply based on cotton and grain, had gained control of the congressional delegations, State legislatures, and governorships in most of the States in the South, Midwest and West (Kolko, 1963, chapter 9; Greider, 1987, pp. 261–73).

In the face of the populist threat to their control of a money supply based on gold, the large regional banks in the South, Midwest, and West aligned themselves with the demand of the large New York banks for a central bank that would both maintain the gold exchange standard and act as lender of last resort. However, to gain this support from the large regional banks, the large New York banks had to agree to a decentralized central bank, with twelve equally powerful Regional Reserve banks created to give equal power to the bankers in each region of the country: three in the East (Boston, Philadelphia, and New York), three in the South (Atlanta, Dallas, and Richmond), three in the Midwest (Chicago, Cleveland, and Minneapolis), and three in the West (Kansas City, San Francisco, and St. Louis). The banks in each of the twelve Federal Reserve Districts elect six of the nine members of the Board of Directors of the Regional Reserve Bank in their District, thereby ensuring their control of them. The large regional banks and the large New York banks thus assured themselves of both a lender of last resort and a means to exercise monetary control over those who are too weak politically to keep themselves from being rationed out of credit markets—in the first instance, the farmers who supported the populist movement.

Section 2.3 Stabilizing the Economy at Full Employment with Price Stability

Why do borrowers—in the first instance, the populist farmers—acquiesce to a Federal Reserve System which exists to preserve and enhance bank profit margins by restricting the supply of money available to them? Because borrowers know that banks know more about credit-market conditions than borrowers do. Banks have an incentive to take advantage of the information asymmetry, exaggerate the tightness of credit markets, and thereby justify higher interest rates. To the degree that the Federal Reserve must justify higher interest rates as necessary to stabilize the economy at full employment with price stability, borrowers can ameliorate the disadvantage this information asymmetry places them in by insisting that the banks link increases in their ask prices for loans to a tightening of monetary policy (see, for example, Goodhart, 1989, pp. 17–18).

In effect, the Federal Reserve can act as a cartel manager for the banks and use tight monetary policy to preserve and enhance bank profit margins only to the degree that it is plausible to argue that the Federal Reserve is *not* using tight monetary policy to preserve and enhance bank profit margins but rather to stabilize the economy on a non-inflationary growth path. In the Federal Reserve Act of 1913, this fact was enshrined in the imperative for the newly established Federal Reserve System to implement the real-bills doctrine, according to which banks could bring bills of exchange they received as collateral for loans to the Federal Reserve for re-discounting. This imperative appeared to make monetary policy about more than merely preserving and enhancing bank profit margins. In particular, the real-bills doctrine pleased the populists because, as with the sub-treasuries plan, the money supply would ostensibly expand and contract auto-matically to meet the seasonal needs of trade, as represented by the amount of bills of exchange in need of discounting and re-discounting. Unfortunately, the populists failed to notice that, whereas the sub-treasuries plan would have made the money supply endogenous for the majority of U.S. citizens who were still farmers in 1913, under the real-bills doctrine the money supply remained under the control of the large banks, and thus exogenous for those farmers "in most need of it" (Rousseas, 1986, p. 476). Nonetheless, the Federal Reserve's efforts to implement the real-bills doctrine introduced enough randomness into the relationship between bank profit margins and its monetary control of gold reserves to make it plausible to argue that the Federal Reserve was not using tight monetary policy to preserve and enhance bank profit margins but rather was acting to stabilize the economy on a non-inflationary growth path.

Moreover, the fact that the Federal Reserve is essentially a bank-cartel manager is obfuscated by a second concession to the populists—namely, the creation of a Board of Governors, or Federal Reserve Board, in Washington. With seven members appointed by the President and confirmed by the Senate, the Board of Governors created a simulacrum of democratic control, as opposed to banker control, of the newly established central bank. However, as Jane D'Arista (1994, pp. 15–20*ff.*) demonstrates for the 1920s, and, as we will see in Chapter 3, for the post-Second World War period, the Federal Reserve Board has never challenged banker control of U.S. monetary policy. In sum, as Lawrence Goodwyn (1978, p. 267) puts it, the establishment of the Federal Reserve not only centralized and rationalized the financial system

> in ways harmonious with the preferences of the New York banking community, its method of functioning also removed the bankers from the harsh glare of public view. Popular attention thenceforth was to focus upon "the Fed" and not upon the actions of the New York commercial bankers.

The only break in banker control was between the New Deal financial reforms of 1933–5 and the Treasury-Federal Reserve Accord of 1951, when the government forced the Federal Reserve to abide by a fixed-interest-rate rule. For example, whereas the interest rate on the government's three-month Treasury bills stayed well above one percent prior to the New Deal, the fixed-interest-rate rule kept it at three eighths of one percent. Indeed, Epstein and Ferguson (1984, p. 970) show that the bank cartel kept the Federal Reserve from pushing the Treasury-bill rate below one percent in the depths of the Great Depression in 1932 and, in Chapter 3, I show that it did the same thing again in 1953–4, the first recession after the bank cartel regained control of the Federal Reserve. No wonder, then, the extraordinary lengths to which the bank cartel went to end the fixed-interest-rate rule in 1951, as documented in Epstein and Schor (1995).

Section 2.4 Summary and Conclusions

In this chapter, I have argued that the Federal Reserve is essentially the manager of a cartel composed of the large New York banks and the large regional banks. Its primary function is to preserve and enhance the profit margins of cartel members by exercising monetary control over the supply of reserves available to banks and other financial institutions that are not members of the bank cartel, and thus the amount of money and credit available to their customers. In the early twentieth century, farmers were the victims. As I show in Chapter 6, workers trying to get mortgages to buy homes were the primary victims in the late twentieth century.

The Federal Reserve also acts as lender of last resort. I showed how the competitive struggle for market share among private, profit-maximizing banks prevents them from acting as lenders of last resort for each other, in much the same way that the need to justify to borrowers exercising monetary control as serving a larger purpose than bankers' greed prevents banks from restricting the money supply on their own.

Notes

1 If the persistent and systematic forces at work in the economy cause it to tend toward an equilibrium characterized by full employment, then the gold-exchange standard

reinforces this tendency. Trade deficits mean money outflows, falling prices, and thus relatively cheaper exports and more expensive imports. Similarly, trade surpluses mean money inflows, rising prices, and thus relatively more expensive exports and cheaper imports (see, for example, Eichengreen, 1985). Unfortunately, if the underlying tendency of the economy is toward an equilibrium characterized by unemployment, then the gold-exchange standard also reinforces that tendency. The money outflows caused by trade deficits reduce expected profits and increase the safe interest rate. Meanwhile, the money inflows caused by trade surpluses can be sterilized by central-bank sales of securities.

2 In Chapter 4, we will see that the Federal Reserve also attempted to implement a penalty-rate policy in the late 1950s.

3 Establishing this point is the reason why Charles Goodhart wrote *The Evolution of Central Banks* (1988).

4 As Charles Goodhart (1989, p. 109) puts it:

> The gap between the zero nominal yield on legal tender ... and the positive yield on longer-dated assets thus makes it profitable for intermediaries to bid for cash until the marginal cost of attracting another unit equals the marginal return obtained from buying some other longer-dated asset.

See, too, Goodhart, 1989, pp. 24, 125–6). In Chapter 5, I explain how this process has played out in practice.

Bibliography

Bagehot, Walter. 1893. *Lombard Street*. London: Henry S. King.

D'Arista, Jane W. 1994. *The Evolution of U.S. Finance, Vol. 1, Federal Reserve Monetary Policy: 1915–1935*. Armonk, NY: M. E. Sharpe.

Eichengreen, Barry. 1985. *The Gold Standard in Theory and History*. New York: Methuen.

Epstein, Gerald. 1982. "Federal Reserve Politics and Monetary Instability." In *The Political Economy of Public Policy*. A. Stone and E. J. Harphan (eds). Beverly Hills, CA: Sage Publications.

Epstein, Gerald and Juliet Schor. 1995. "The Federal Reserve Treasury Accord and the Construction of the Postwar Monetary Regime in the United States." *Social Concept*, Vol. 7, No. 1, (July), pp. 7–48.

Epstein Gerald and Thomas Ferguson. 1984. "Monetary Policy, Loan Liquidation and Industrial Conflict: The Federal Reserve and Open Market Operations in 1932." *Journal of Economic History*, Vol. 64, No. 4, pp. 957–83.

Friedman, Milton and Anna Jacobson Schwartz. 1963. *A Monetary History of the United States and Great Britain, 1867–1960*. Princeton, NJ: Princeton University Press.

Goodhart, Charles. 1989. *Money, Information and Uncertainty*. Second edition. Cambridge, MA: MIT Press.

Goodhart, Charles. 1988. *The Evolution of Central Banks*. Cambridge, MA: MIT Press.

Goodhart, Charles. 1969. *The New York Money Market and the Finance of Trade, 1900–1913*. Cambridge, MA: Harvard University Press.

Goodwyn, Lawrence. 1978. *The Populist Movement: A Short History of the Agrarian Revolt in America*. New York: Oxford University Press.

Gorton, Gary. 1984. "Private Clearinghouses and the Origins of Central Banking." *Federal Reserve Bank of Philadelphia Business Review*, January–February.

Greider, William. 1987. *Secrets of the Temple: How the Federal Reserve Runs the Country*. New York: Simon and Schuster.

Keynes, John Maynard. 1936 [1964]. *The General Theory of Employment, Interest, and Money*, New York: Harcourt, Brace Jovanovich.

Klein, Benjamin. 1974. "The Competitive Supply of Money." *Journal of Money, Credit and Banking*, Vol. 6, No. 4, pp. 423–53.

Kolko, Gabriel. 1963. *The Triumph of Conservatism: A Reinterpretation of American History, 1900–1916*. New York: Macmillan.

Miller, M. and C. M. Sprenkle. 1980. "The Precautionary Demand for Narrow and Broad Money." *Economica*, Vol. 47, No. 188, pp. 407–21.

Rousseas, Stephen W. 1986. *Post Keynesian Monetary Economics*. Armonk, NY: M. E. Sharpe.

Schlesinger, Arthur, Jr. 1953. *The Age of Jackson*. Boston, MA: Little Brown and Co.

Smith, Vera C. 1936. *The Rationale of Central Banking*. London: P. S. King & Sons.

Timberlake, Richard H. 1993. *Monetary Policy in the United States: An Intellectual and Institutional History*. Chicago: The University of Chicago Press.

Trivoli, George. 1979. *The Suffolk Bank: A Study of a Free-enterprise Clearing System*. London: The Adam Smith Institute.

White, Lawrence H. 1983. "Competitive Money, Inside and Out." *Cato Journal*, Vol. 3, No. 1, pp. 281–99.

3 Democratic Control versus Banker Control of the Federal Reserve System

In March 1951, the Federal Reserve was given independence from democratic control in order to stabilize the economy at full employment with price stability. In this chapter, I present both archival and econometric evidence to show that to the degree the Federal Reserve became independent of democratic control it became dependent on the U.S. bank cartel, which compromises its ability to stabilize the economy. The statistical evidence covers the period from 1951 to 1988. However, the archival evidence focuses on the 1953–4 recession, the first opportunity the newly independent Federal Reserve had to stabilize the economy at full employment. Taken together, the statistical and archival evidence suggest that an independent Federal Reserve System, dependent on the U.S. bank cartel, will not stabilize the economy, unless it is in the interests of the bank cartel for it to do so. During the 1953–4 recession, it was not in the cartel's interests, so the Federal Reserve did not stabilize the economy.[1]

Banker influence on U.S. monetary policy was not new in the period since 1951. From its establishment in 1913 to the New Deal banking reforms of 1933–5, the Federal Reserve was also largely controlled by the U.S. bank cartel (Kolko, 1963, chapter 9; D'Arista, 1994). Epstein and Ferguson (1984) show that, because of the excessive banker influence, the Federal Reserve failed to stabilize the economy during the Great Depression of the early 1930s. This failure, which was widely perceived as an egregious mistake, prompted the banking reforms of 1933–5 that increased democratic control, and thus reduced banker influence, on monetary policy.

The level of interest rates on short-term government securities, especially on Treasury bills, illustrates the trade-off between democratic and banker control of monetary policy. During the 1935–51 period of democratic control, the Treasury-bill rate was typically kept well below 1 percent (Table 3.1).

In contrast, from when data are first available in 1920 until 1932, the yields on short-term government securities were well above 1 percent. Indeed, Epstein and Ferguson (1984, p. 970) show that the bank cartel successfully lobbied the Federal Reserve to abandon an expansionary monetary policy in 1932 because it pushed the Treasury-bill rate below 1 percent.

In Section 3.3, I provide econometric evidence that the bank cartel did the same thing during the 1953–4 recession that they did in 1932. At the same time,

Table 3.1 Yields on short-term U.S. government securities, 1920–54 (percent per annum)

Three-to six-month Treasury notes and certificates, 1920–31 (average of daily rates)		Three-month Treasury-bill rate, 1934–54 (secondary market yields)	
1920	5.42	1934	0.28
1921	4.83	1935	0.17
1922	3.47	1936	0.14
1923	3.93	1937	0.45
1924	2.77	1938	0.05
1925	3.03	1939	0.02
1926	3.23	1940	0.01
1927	3.10	1941	0.13
1928	3.97	1942	0.34
1929	4.42	1943	0.38
1930	2.23	1944	0.38
1931	1.15	1945	0.38
		1946	0.38
Three-month Treasury-bill		1947	0.61
rate, 1931–4 (average rate		1948	1.05
on new issues)		1949	1.11
		1950	1.20
1931	1.40	1951	1.52
1932	0.88	1952	1.72
1933	0.52	1953	1.90
1934	0.26	1954	0.94

Source: Board of Governors of the Federal Reserve System (1976, pp. 693–94; 1943, p. 460).

I provide evidence that banker influence was a highly statistically significant influence on U.S. monetary policy for the entire period from 1951 to 1988, thereby providing essential background for the material I present in Chapters 5 and 6.

Section 3.1, while focused on explaining the Federal Reserve's behavior in the early 1950s, is also designed to provide essential background to the material presented in subsequent chapters. In Section 3.1, I review the literature on the Federal Reserve's behavior in the early 1950s, in which there is no dispute that the Federal Reserve failed to achieve its goal of stabilizing the economy at full employment with price stability. However, these were the first years of William McChesney Martin's tenure as Chair of the Board of Governors of the Federal Reserve System, a position he held from 1951 to 1970. During Martin's tenure, the consensus in the literature is that the Federal Reserve tried to stabilize the economy—to "lean against the wind," as Martin often put it—by moving free reserves countercyclically. Consequently, the arguments presented in Section 3.1 explaining the Federal Reserve's behavior in the early 1950s are also applied by their advocates to the entire 1951–70 period. In Chapter 4, I supplement the material in Section 3.1 with a review of the literature interpreting the Federal

Reserve's behavior in the 1970–5 period, after Martin was replaced as Chair of the Board of Governors by Arthur F. Burns.

In Section 3.2, I use archival evidence to substantiate three hypotheses about the 1951–6 period. First, I show how the "art of central banking" worked in practice. That is to say, the Federal Reserve exercised monetary control by restricting the supply of bank reserves during periods of calm between financial crises, only to reverse course and flood the financial markets with reserves during financial crises. Second, I show that the bank cartel lobbied the Federal Reserve to keep the Treasury-bill rate above 1 percent during the 1953–4 recession. Last, I show that the Federal Reserve did in fact try to stabilize the economy at full employment with price stability during the period from May 1954 to March 1956.

In Section 3.4, I provide a summary and conclusions.

Section 3.1 The Mainstream Literature

Economists working in the Keynesian and Monetarist traditions agree that, after the Federal Reserve was given independence to stabilize the economy at full employment with price stability in March 1951, it tried, but failed, to do so by moving free reserves countercyclically. Free reserves (FR) are defined as follows:

$$FR = NBR - RR \tag{3.1}$$

where NBR is nonborrowed reserves and RR is required reserves.[2]

As defined in Equation 3.1, free reserves provide an excellent gauge of the amount of pressure the Federal Reserve is putting on the supply of bank reserves. In particular, if free reserves are negative, so that banks are forced to hold net borrowed reserves, or borrow from the Federal Reserve to meet their reserve requirements, then banks are in effect insolvent and can avoid bankruptcy only at the sufferance of the Federal Reserve's willingness to lend to them at the discount rate. Under such circumstances, the Federal Reserve has enormous power to determine both the interest rate (the discount rate) at which it will lend to banks and other terms on which it is willing to lend, such as the collateral (the types of loan) it is willing to lend against. Contrariwise, to the degree that banks have free reserves at their disposal, they are free to act without regard for the wishes of the Federal Reserve.

In Table 3.2, we can see that the Federal Reserve did in fact move free reserves countercyclically in the 1950s.[3]

Free reserves (FR) increased by 53 percent during the 1953–4 recession, decreased by 183 percent during the 1954–7 expansion, increased again by 204 percent during the 1957–8 recession, and fell by 136 percent during the 1958–60 expansion.

Monetarists (and their progeny, New Classical economists) point to the last column of Table 3.2 as proof that the Federal Reserve's countercyclical monetary policy failed, for the countercyclical movement of free reserves did not result in a countercyclical movement of the stock of money, defined as demand deposits, traveler's checks, and currency in circulation (M_1). Instead, M_1 increased by

Table 3.2 The cyclical movement of free reserves (FR) and the stock of money (M_1), 1953–60

	FR (millions of $)	% change in FR	M_1 (billions of $)	% change in M_1
July 1953 (peak)	366		128.6	
May 1954 (trough)	561	53	129.7	0.8
August 1957 (peak)	−471	−183	137.1	5.7
April 1958 (trough)	492	204	137	−0.07
April 1960 (peak)	−180	−136	143	4.4

Source: CITIBASE, Chapter 1, sections 1 and 4.

eight-tenths of a percentage point during the 1953–4 recession, increased by 5.7 percent during the 1954–7 expansion, stagnated during the 1957–8 recession, and increased by 4.4 percent during the 1958–60 expansion.

Monetarists attribute this failure of the countercyclical movement of free reserves to translate into a countercyclical movement of M_1 to the Federal Reserve's failure to distinguish between the supply and the demand for free reserves. For example, during the recessions, the Federal Reserve increased free reserves in $50–$100 million increments. But if banks were simultaneously increasing their demand for free reserves because of growing uncertainty concerning the quality of their loans outstanding, then the increase in free reserves would not increase the stock of money (M_1). Similarly, if exuberant expectations during the economic expansions caused banks to reduce their assessments of liquidity needs, then reducing free reserves in $50–$100 million increments would not have caused them to reduce their lending, and thus deposit expansion (see, for example, Meigs, 1962; Dewald and Johnson, 1963; Brunner and Meltzer, 1964; Guttentag, 1966; Lombra and Torta, 1973; Lombra, 1980; Meltzer, 1982; Gordon, 1983; Wicker, 1990; Meltzer, 2003).

Economists working in the Keynesian tradition take issue with this interpretation of U.S. monetary policy on the grounds that it is changes in interest rates, not changes in the stock of money, that represent changes in monetary policy. In Chapter 1, I explain the theoretical foundations of this difference of opinion.[4] At a more practical level, Ahearn (1963) takes issue with the fact that (except for a brief period in the early 1960s, explained in Chapter 4) the Federal Reserve only bought and sold Treasury bills in order to move free reserves countercyclically. Ahearn argues that the Federal Reserve should have bought and sold long-term government bonds instead because changes in long-term interest rates have a greater effect than changes in short-term interest rates on output and employment. Fazzari (1994–5) argues that even changing long-term interest rates to affect output and employment would be self-defeating because the ensuing loss of investments and output will cause the rate of growth of labor productivity to fall as rapidly as, if not more rapidly than, wages. And Weintraub (1978) argues that it was because of a genuine belief in Monetarism that the Federal Reserve engaged in such self-defeating behavior. In short, economists working in the Keynesian tradition have generally accepted the notion that the Federal Reserve was trying to stabilize the economy at full employment with price stability. They just disagree with the Monetarists and New Classical economists about why the Federal Reserve failed to do so.

Reaction functions are usually used to resolve questions concerning the motives of central banks (see, for example, Epstein, 1990; Epstein and Schor, 1990; Khoury, 1990). Reaction functions are multiple regression analyses that use a monetary aggregate (e.g., M_1), an interest rate, or on rare occasions a measure of bank reserves (e.g. free reserves) as a proxy for the motives of the monetary authorities. The proxy is regressed on an array of independent variables, testing to see if the monetary authorities were sensitive to them.

Unfortunately, reaction functions cannot distinguish between what central banks intend to do and what they are compelled to do. In other words, the proxies used in reaction functions to represent the motives of the monetary authorities are only partly determined by the monetary authorities. This is obvious in the case of monetary aggregates, which are at least partly determined by demand-side factors (see, for example, Goodhart, 1989). But it is also true in the case of short-term interest rates. For example, I show in Chapter 4 that market forces pushed the Treasury-bill rate above the level desired by the Federal Reserve for long periods of time in the late 1950s, and the same thing happened with the federal funds rate, or the interbank lending rate, when the Federal Reserve was using it as a control variable in the early 1970s. I also show that, during the 1957–8 recession and again in the summer of 1959, external political pressures compelled the Federal Reserve to keep short-term interest rates below the level it desired. As a result, conclusions drawn from reactions functions concerning what the Federal Reserve was trying to do during these periods are in error.

It follows that archival research is necessary to determine what the monetary authorities intended to do, regardless of whether they were able to do it or not (Friedman and Schwartz, 1963; Epstein and Ferguson, 1984; Romer and Romer, 1990; Romer and Romer, 1993; Epstein and Schor, 1995; Meltzer, 2009; Meltzer, 2003). In Section 3.2, I show that, from May 1954 to March 1956, the Federal Reserve did in fact try to stabilize the economy at full employment with price stability. But we will see in Chapter 4 that this was only because the political-economic conjuncture at that time left the Federal Reserve with no role to play in using monetary policy in the conflict between capital and labor over the terms of the employment relation. The archival research I report in Chapter 4 shows that it was not a mistaken effort to stabilize the economy at full employment with price stability but a desire to strengthen capital against labor that explains the Federal Reserve's behavior, and there are numerous reasons to believe that tight monetary policy strengthens capital against labor (Kalecki, 1971, pp. 138–45; Boddy and Crotty, 1975; Pivetti, 1985; Schor, 1985; Epstein, 1987; Schor, 1987; Panico, 1988; Epstein and Schor, 1990; Epstein, 1992).

In Section 3.3, I also use archival research to demonstrate that, in contrast to the consensus of economists working in both the Keynesian and Monetarist traditions, which assumes that the Federal Reserve could have stabilized the economy but failed to do so because of incorrect operating procedures, the Federal Reserve was not trying to stabilize the economy during the 1953–4 recession because there were no democratic controls in place to compel it to do so.

Section 3.2 Banker Influence and the Use of Monetary Policy to Stabilize the Economy at Full Employment with Price Stability

In this section, I use archival materials[5] to show that the widespread belief that the Federal Reserve tried to stabilize the economy at full employment with price stability is only true for the period from May 1954 to March 1956. First, I explain the operating procedure—free-reserve targeting—used to stabilize the economy. Second, I explain why, even though it was given authority to stabilize the economy at full employment with price stability in March 1951, it was not until May 1954 that the Federal Reserve actually tried to do so. Last, I explain the operating procedure that took the place of free-reserve targeting in March 1956—namely, a penalty-rate policy. I do not examine the reasons why the Federal Reserve shifted from free-reserve targeting to a penalty-rate policy until Chapter 4.

The Federal Reserve was given authority to stabilize the economy at full employment with price stability in March 1951. Prior to March 1951,[6] the Treasury Department, after consulting with the Federal Reserve, had set the prices of government securities. The Federal Reserve then conducted open market purchases of government securities as necessary to keep their prices at the level set by the Treasury Department. Consequently, even though the Federal Reserve received authority to stabilize the economy in March 1951, before it could do so the Federal Reserve had to habituate the government-securities market to the idea that the prices of government securities set by the Treasury Department would not be sustained regardless of circumstances, such as how rapidly the economy was growing.

The first step in habituating the government-securities market to flexible prices was taken on 8 March 1951, which was "the first day in more than ten years on which the market for Government securities had been entirely without support from [Federal Reserve] System open market operations" (Federal Open Market Committee (FOMC) *Minutes*, 8 March 1951, p. 2). The next step was taken in December 1952 when the Treasury Department carried out its first refunding of maturing government securities with no open market purchases by the Federal Reserve (FOMC *Minutes*, 3 March 1954, p. 19). Then, in March 1953, when the Treasury Department stopped consulting with it prior to setting the prices of government securities,[7] the Federal Reserve was finally free to stabilize the economy at full employment with price stability (FOMC *Minutes*, 4–5 March 1953, pp. 27–8). Nonetheless, as I will now show, it was not until the 1953–4 recession ended, in May 1954, that the Federal Reserve actually tried to stabilize the economy.

The problem facing the Federal Reserve was twofold. First, even though the Federal Reserve was free after March 1953 to stabilize the economy, fear of precipitating financial crises made it reluctant to do so. In May 1953, the Treasury Department underpriced its first new issue of securities without the Federal Reserve's recommendations to follow. The Federal Reserve thus felt compelled to flood the market with reserves (Wojnilower, 1980, p. 281–2). Second, when the 1953–4 recession began, in July 1953, the Federal Reserve decided against a stabilization policy because it did not want to create sloppy financial markets, where "sloppy" financial markets meant a Treasury-bill rate below 1 percent (Wicker 1990; Federal Advisory Council (FAC) *Minutes*, 14 February 1951, pp. 6–7; FAC *Minutes*, 16 May 1954, p. 7; FAC *Minutes*, 14 November 1964, pp. 3–4).

"Sloppy" financial markets, defined as a Treasury-bill rate below 1 percent, were a primary concern of the bankers on the Federal Advisory Council. The Federal Open Market Committee—the policymaking council within the Federal Reserve System—is dominated by the Federal Reserve's Board of Governors. The Board of Governors, in turn, meets with the Federal Advisory Council four times a year. The Federal Advisory Council is composed of twelve bankers, one appointed by the boards of directors of each of the twelve regional banks.[8] During the 1953–4 recession, the banks became increasingly dependent on earnings from their holdings of government securities. As a result, the Federal Advisory Council became increasingly emphatic that the Federal Reserve should keep the Treasury-bill rate above 1 percent.

As noted above, the first postwar financial crisis occurred in May 1953. In Table 3.3, we see that, at that time, the loans outstanding at all commercial banks had reached a postwar peak of 112 percent of bank holdings of government securities.

The banks' relatively small reliance on interest income from government securities prompted the Federal Advisory Council (FAC) to recommend to the Board of Governors that "some relief should now be given to the money market" (FAC *Minutes*, 19 May 1953, pp. 3–4).

In contrast, when the onset of recession in July 1953 caused non-financial firms to reduce their demand for loans, the FAC began to reconsider its support for easy monetary policy. In November 1953, with bank loans outstanding down to 106 percent of the banks' holdings of government securities, the FAC reversed its position and argued that

> the Board [of Governors] in its Open Market operations should be as ready to sell short term securities if bank loans are repaid in volume and money rates are disorderly on the downward side, as to purchase securities if the level of interest rates and any difficulty in obtaining credit should threaten to accelerate a business decline.
>
> (FAC *Minutes*, 17 November 1953, p. 2)

At the next meeting of the FAC with the Board of Governors, the FAC was emphatic about what it considered the implications for monetary policy of the falling demand for loans. In February 1954, with the demand for loans by

Table 3.3 The ratio of bank loans outstanding to banks' holdings of government securities (percent)

Date	All commercial banks	Weekly reporting banks	Date	All commercial banks	Weekly reporting banks
1948			1951 (contd)		
Feb.	57	40	July	93	62
Mar.	59	41	Aug.	93	62
Apr.	59	40	Sept.	94	64
May	60	40	Oct.	93	65*
June	62	41	Nov.	93	66
July	62	42	Dec.	94	66
Aug.	62	42	1952		
Sept.	67	44	Jan.	93	66
Oct.	66	46	Feb.	94	65
Nov.	67	47	Mar.	95	66
Dec.	68	47	Apr.	96	67
1949			May	96	65
Jan.	67	46	June	97	64
Feb.	68	46	July	95	61
Mar.	70	46	Aug.	97	63
Apr.	67	44	Sept.	99	67
May	65	41	Oct.	99	67
June	65	39	Nov.	99	70
July	63	37	Dec.	101	70
Aug.	62	35	1953		
Sept.	62	35	Jan.	102	71
Oct.	62	36	Feb.	104	72
Nov.	64	37	Mar.	108	75
Dec.	64	37	Apr.	111	79
1950			May	112	79
Jan.	63	37	June	111	78
Feb.	64	37	July	104	72
Mar.	66	38	Aug.	106	71
Apr.	67	38	Sept.	106	73
May	67	37	Oct.	108	73
June	68	37	Nov.	106	72
July	71	38	Dec.	107	71
Aug.	74	41	1954		
Sept.	78	44	Jan.	104	69
Oct.	80	48	Feb.	106	69
Nov.	83	50	Mar.	111	71
Dec.	84	51	Apr.	107	71
1951			May	106	68
Jan.	88	55	June	106	65
Feb.	91	60	July	105	64
Mar.	93	62	Aug.	99	57
Apr.	93	62	Sept.	100	58
May	94	63	Oct.	97	56
June	94	62			

Date	All commercial banks	Weekly reporting banks	Date	All commercial banks	Weekly reporting banks
1954 (contd)			1958		
Nov.	99	58	Jan.	160	118
Dec.	102	60	Feb.	158	113
1955			Mar.	156	108
Jan.	102	61	Apr.	149	102
Feb.	107	62	May	147	96
Mar.	113	66	June	149	92
Apr.	111	66	July	146	87
May	114	68	Aug.	142	83
June	119	71	Sept.	146	87
July	120	73	Oct.	144	89
Aug.	124	76	Nov.	142	90
Sept.	126	80	Dec.	148	90
Oct.	126	81	1959		
Nov.	133	85	Jan.	145	90
Dec.	134	88	Feb.	149	90
1956			Mar.	157	95
Jan.	135	87	Apr.	159	97
Feb.	140	90	May	164	101
Mar.	144	94	June	172	105
Apr.	147	98	July	173	92
May	150	102	Aug.	178	98
June	153	105	Sept.	182	101
July	155	107	Oct.	181	105
Aug.	153	108	Nov.	187	107
Sept.	155	110	Dec.	188	108
Oct.	154	113	1960		
Nov.	154	115	Jan.	189	110
Dec.	154	116	Feb.	196	115
1957			Mar.	206	122
Jan.	154	114	Apr.	202	122
Feb.	157	116	May	206	120
Mar.	163	120	June	212	122
Apr.	158	120	July	201	116
May	160	121	Aug.	203	114
June	168	124	Sept.	200	112
July	164	123	Oct.	190	111
Aug.	165	127	Nov.	191	108
Sept.	167	129	Dec.	193	106
Oct.	162	124	1961		
Nov.	163	126	Jan.	185	103
Dec.	161	122	Feb.	190	102

Source: Board of Governors of the Federal Reserve System (1976, pp. 27–8, and pp. 188–213).
*Calculated without one week due to misprint in text.

non-financial corporations still languishing (Table 3.3), the FAC criticized the Board of Governors for

> buying on balance rather than selling in connection with its Open Market operations. ... the Open Market Committee should have sold securities. ... At a time when loans were still decreasing, the [Federal Advisory] Council feels the Board's policy should have been to continue to sell [Treasury] bills to an amount approximately offsetting the decline in loans.
>
> (FAC *Minutes*, 14 February 1954, pp. 6–7)

The FAC thus insisted on a tightening of monetary policy despite the 1953–4 recession. The FAC did not care about stabilizing the economy at full employment with price stability. Its only concern was that the prices of government securities were increasing at a time when the reduced demand for loans meant the banks were making heavy purchases of them.

The FAC continued to lobby the Board of Governors to increase the yields on government securities until the loans outstanding at all commercial banks bottomed out at 97 percent of the banks' holdings of government securities in October 1954 (Table 3.3).

The effects of the 1953–4 recession on the portfolios of the weekly reporting banks were even more pronounced than they were on all commercial banks.[9] At the onset of the May 1953 financial crisis, the weekly reporting banks' business loans outstanding were 79 percent of their holdings of government securities[10] (Table 3.3). By October 1954, the business loans outstanding at weekly reporting banks were down to 56 percent of their holdings of government securities.

There was also a shortening of the maturities of the weekly reporting banks' holdings of government securities. As shown in Table 3.4, the ratio of the weekly reporting banks' holdings of Treasury bills to their holdings of government securities increased from 5.1 percent to 8.7 percent in the wake of the May 1953 financial crisis, and remained at 7.8 percent at the end of the recession in May 1954.

Consequently, the FAC told the Board of Governors that

> a [Treasury] bill rate below one per cent is too low ... open market operations could have been conducted so that the bill rate would not have fallen as low as it has recently.
>
> (FAC *Minutes*, 16 May 1954, p. 7)

> the bill rate has been sloppy ... a bill rate of 1.05 per cent to 1.25 per cent would be better than .85 per cent to .88 per cent ... Open market operations should be conducted to bring the bill rate up to a figure of 1.10 per cent to 1.25 per cent.
>
> (FAC *Minutes*, 14 November 1954, p. 7)

In the next section, I present econometric evidence which suggests that the Federal Reserve ignored the fact that the economy was in a recession in order to

Table 3.4 The ratio of the weekly reporting banks' holdings of treasury bills to their holdings of government securities (percent)

Date	Weekly reporting banks	Date	Weekly reporting banks	Date	Weekly reporting banks
1948		1951 (Contd.)		1954 (Contd.)	
Feb.	6.2	June	7.7	Oct.	7.1
Mar.	5.6	July	7.8	Nov.	7.0
Apr.	5.9	Aug.	8.5	Dec.	6.7
May	6.5	Sept.	8.6	1955	
June	5.6	Oct.	10.0	Jan.	6.5
July	5.3	Nov.	11.1	Feb.	5.3
Aug.	6.4	Dec.	13.1	Mar.	5.0
Sept.	5.8	1952		Apr.	5.0
Oct.	6.2	Jan.	13.0	May	4.0
Nov.	7.1	Feb.	12.5	June	3.4
Dec.	6.4	Mar.	12.5	July	3.4
1949		Apr.	11.1	Aug.	3.3
Jan.	6.6	May	11.0	Sept.	3.3
Feb.	5.6	June	12.1	Oct.	3.4
Mar.	5.4	July	10.4	Nov.	2.6
Apr.	5.0	Aug.	8.5	Dec.	3.8
May	6.3	Sept.	8.2	1956	
June	6.3	Oct.	11.0	Jan.	4.7
July	7.0	Nov.	11.4	Feb.	3.4
Aug.	7.8	Dec.	13.3	Mar.	3.3
Sept.	8.3	1953		Apr.	2.8
Oct.	7.5	Jan.	12.2	May	2.5
Nov.	6.6	Feb.	10.4	June	2.6
Dec.	6.8	Mar.	9.3	July	2.2
1950		Apr.	5.8	Aug.	2.1
Jan.	7.9	**May**	**5.1**	Sept.	2.3
Feb.	6.7	June	7.9	Oct.	2.8
Mar.	5.8	**July**	**8.7**	Nov.	3.6
Apr.	4.8	Aug.	8.1	Dec.	6.0
May	5.3	Sept.	7.0	1957	
June	6.4	Oct.	6.9	Jan.	7.3
July	6.5	Nov.	7.0	Feb.	5.4
Aug.	5.1	Dec.	7.6	Mar.	5.6
Sept.	7.7	1954		Apr.	4.3
Oct.	7.1	Jan.	8.3	May	4.2
Nov.	6.8	Feb.	6.8	June	5.6
Dec.	7.5	Mar.	7.2	July	7.0
1951		Apr.	8.0	Aug.	6.0
Jan.	6.6	**May**	**7.8**	Sept.	5.8
Feb.	4.8	June	7.5	Oct.	4.5
Mar.	5.9	July	8.1	Nov.	3.9
Apr.	6.0	Aug.	9.7	Dec.	5.4
May	5.8	Sept.	8.4		

(Continued)

Table 3.4 Continued

Date	Weekly reporting banks	Date	Weekly reporting banks	Date	Weekly reporting banks
1958		1959		1960	
Jan.	5.7	Jan.	6.5	Jan.	8.7
Feb.	5.3	Feb.	6.7	Feb.	6.7
Mar.	7.5	Mar.	7.1	Mar.	5.7
Apr.	6.9	Apr.	7.5	Apr.	5.0
May	6.2	May	7.9	May	5.0
June	6.6	June	7.0	June	4.8
July	6.1	July	9.0	July	9.3
Aug.	5.1	Aug.	7.8	Aug.	9.4
Sept.	4.5	Sept.	7.5	Sept.	10.0
Oct.	5.5	Oct.	6.7	Oct.	10.9
Nov.	5.8	Nov.	5.9	Nov.	12.2
Dec.	6.9	Dec.	8.3	Dec.	12.4

Source: Board of Governors of the Federal Reserve System (1976, pp. 188–239).

respond to these statements by the FAC expressing their preference for using open market sales of Treasury bills to prop up the Treasury-bill rate. Therefore, the Federal Reserve failed to carry out the mandate it was given in March 1951 to stabilize the economy at full employment with price stability by lowering interest rates during recessions.

When an economic recovery began in May 1954, the Federal Reserve was finally ready to stabilize the economy at full employment with price stability by restricting the supply of bank reserves. In particular, it set out to reduce the supply of free reserves to the point where banks would have insufficient nonborrowed reserves to meet the rapidly expanding demand for required reserves as bank lending grew in tandem with the economic recovery. That is to say, the Federal Reserve's aim was to make free reserves negative. So long as the Treasury-bill rate was less than the discount rate, the banks would then sell Treasury bills to make up the reserve deficiency. If the Treasury-bill rate rose above the discount rate, then banks would borrow from the Federal Reserve to make up the reserve deficiency.[11] However, the Federal Reserve also hoped that the banks would feel compelled to ration credit.

The Federal Reserve began its stabilization policy in May 1954 by aiming for free reserves between $400 million and $700 million (Executive Committee (EC) *Minutes*, 8 June 1954, p. 5; EC *Minutes*, 23 June 1954, pp. 7, 9). In early September 1954, it used open market sales of securities to the banks to move their free reserves to the lower end of the $400–$700 million range (EC *Minutes*, 8 September 1954, p. 5). By late December, the Federal Reserve succeeded in moving free reserves to the lower end of a $300–$500 million target range (EC *Minutes*, 28 December 1954, p. 12). Finally, in mid January 1955, the banks felt the first monetary restraint of the postwar period, when the Federal Reserve successfully targeted zero free reserves (EC *Minutes*, 11 January 1955, p. 2; EC *Minutes*, 8 February 1955, p. 13).

Since the Treasury-bill rate was less than the discount rate, the banks responded to the insufficient supply of nonborrowed reserves by selling Treasury bills, thereby putting upward pressure on their yield. In April 1955, the Treasury-bill rate was thus pushed to equality with the discount rate, and the Federal Reserve increased the discount rate out of a perceived need to prevent the banks from borrowing from it in order to purchase Treasury bills (EC *Minutes*, 26 April 1955, pp. 13–14). Discount-rate increases were sufficiently novel at the time to cause a minor panic among government-securities dealers, the second financial crisis of the postwar period. As a result, the Federal Reserve felt compelled to abandon free-reserve targeting in favor of stabilizing the government-securities market (EC *Minutes*, 26 April 1955, p. 14; EC *Minutes*, 10 May 1955, pp. 7–8; EC *Minutes*, 24 May 1955, pp. 7–9; FOMC *Minutes*, 12 July 1955, p. 29).

In mid July 1955, the government-securities market stabilized, and the Federal Reserve returned to its policy of refusing to supply sufficient nonborrowed reserves for the banks to meet reserve requirements. Its first target was free reserves below $100 million (FOMC *Minutes*, 12 July 1955, p. 25). By August, the Federal Reserve was aiming for negative free reserves, or net borrowed reserves, between $400 million and $500 million and the banks' efforts to overcome their reserve deficiency by means of sales of Treasury bills triggered a second discount-rate increase (FOMC *Minutes*, 23 August 1955, pp. 9–10). The same thing happened for a third time in September, but a fourth discount-rate increase in November once again destabilized the government-securities market, forcing the Federal Reserve to abandon free-reserve targeting in favor of a return to pegging the Treasury-bill rate for the first time since it had finally freed itself of this imperative in March 1953 (FOMC *Minutes*, 14 September 1955, p. 16; FOMC *Minutes*, 4 October 1955, p. 25; FOMC *Minutes*, 25 October 1955, p. 11; FOMC *Minutes*, 16 November 1955, pp. 9–10, 13–16, 21, 25; FOMC *Minutes*, 8 December 1955, p. 2).

In March 1956, the government-securities market stabilized sufficiently for the Federal Reserve to reestablish a target for negative free reserves, or net borrowed reserves, between $400 million and $500 million (FOMC *Minutes*, 6 March 1956, p. 38). But before another discount-rate increase could be triggered by the Treasury-bill rate moving above it, the Federal Reserve had changed to a new operating procedure whereby discount-rate increases would lead, rather than follow, increases in the Treasury-bill rate.

From May 1954 to March 1956, discount-rate increases were semiautomatic technical adjustments to a rising Treasury-bill rate, designed to keep the banks from having a profit opportunity to borrow from the Federal Reserve in order to purchase Treasury bills. In August 1955, to obtain the flexibility to increase the discount rate regardless of the level of the Treasury-bill rate, William McChesney Martin Jr., Chair of the Board of Governors, began advocating for a new operating procedure. At that time, Martin had the Secretary of the Board of Governors (Winfield Riefler) present the following statement:

> the procedure has been to initiate restraint through open market operations by reducing available reserves. When the market rate [i.e., the Treasury bill rate] finally went above the discount rate as a result of this action, it constituted an almost automatic signal for an increase in the discount rate. ... There is another approach to restraint that has never been taken. Under this approach the [Federal Reserve] System could avoid exerting so much pressure through open market operations as to raise market rates actually above the discount rate. Rather open market operations would be used to maintain a volume of negative free reserves sufficient to make market rates of interest highly responsive to the discount rate, but not in such large volume as to raise, say, the [Treasury] bill rate above the discount rate. That procedure would always keep the discount rate in the position of being a penalty rate. ... Under this approach, the discount rate would be used to lead in applying a policy of restraint. [Treasury] bill rates would move up with the discount rate because it would be less costly for banks to adjust to temporary shortages by selling bills than by discounting.
>
> (Riefler, FOMC *Minutes*, 23 August 1955, pp. 10–11)

The new operating procedure advocated by Martin had a fundamental technical flaw. It assumed that open market operations would be used to keep free reserves negative. Otherwise, the banks would not be under pressure to reduce, or at least restrain the rate of growth of, their lending, sell Treasury bills, or borrow from the Federal Reserve, and the discount rate would be of little consequence. But with free reserves negative and the discount rate greater than the Treasury-bill rate, the banks would sell Treasury bills relentlessly. The bank sales of Treasury bills would be especially large between Thanksgiving and Christmas and Jewish holidays, as well as at other times of sharp seasonal increases in the demand for credit. Consequently, the only way the Federal Reserve would be able to keep the discount rate greater than the Treasury-bill rate during these periods would be either to allow free reserves to become positive or to increase the discount rate over and over again.

In September 1955, Allan Sproul, President of the Federal Reserve Bank of New York, pointed out this technical problem with the operating procedure advocated by Martin. Long before the Federal Reserve adopted the new operating procedure in March 1956, Sproul argued that both of the Federal Reserve's possible responses to seasonal increases in the demand for credit—allowing free reserves to become positive or increasing the discount rate over and over again—were unpalatable. On the one hand, he contended that, if free reserves were allowed to become positive, the Federal Reserve would "lose rather than gain control of the credit situation" (FOMC *Minutes*, 14 September 1955, p. 22). On the other hand, Sproul argued that, if negative free reserves, or net borrowed reserves, were maintained, "we would seem to have acquired a built in device for shoving the discount rate up, during periods of credit restraint, with real risk of creating disorderly conditions in the capital markets" (FOMC *Minutes*, 14 September 1955, pp. 22–4).

Sproul was right, but the new operating procedure was adopted in spite of this fundamental technical flaw because, after a five-year hiatus, leading sections of the industrial proletariat were using the strike weapon to obtain greater wages and benefits. In Chapter 4, I show that the Federal Reserve hoped the greater flexibility the new operating procedure offered for increasing the discount rate, regardless of the level of the Treasury-bill rate, would permit it to intervene more effectively in the renewed capital–labor conflict over the terms of the employment relation.

Section 3.3 Banker Influence and U.S. Monetary Policy during the 1953–4 Recession

In this section, I test the hypothesis that the Federal Advisory Council's (FAC) monetary-policy preferences were a determinant of monetary policy. Since the FAC's statements I reported in Section 3.2 make clear that the Federal Reserve would have responded, if at all, to the FAC's preferences for a tighter monetary policy during the 1953–4 recession by increasing the Treasury-bill rate, the Treasury-bill rate (Tbill) is used as a proxy for monetary policy.[12]

To quantify the FAC's preferences, I constructed an FAC index by assigning values between -1 and $+1$ to each meeting of the FAC with the Board of Governors. The period analyzed is from the second quarter of 1951, when the Federal Reserve obtained sufficient independence from democratic control to change the Treasury-bill rate, to the second quarter of 1988, the last quarter for which the *Minutes* of FAC meetings with the Board of Governors are available.

Thomas Havrilesky (1990) made the first use of the FAC index – and he (1993, chapter 8) extended the analysis of banker influence on monetary policy from the 1973–85 period examined in his original paper to the 1969–88 period. This section extends the analysis back to the March 1951 Federal Reserve-Treasury Accord. Using Havrilesky's method, I show that there was highly statistically significant banker influence on monetary policy during the entire 1951–88 period. In this chapter, the economic significance of the empirical results is that, despite the 1953–4 recession, the banks' lobbying efforts for a higher Treasury-bill rate, as reported in Section 3.2, were successful.

Following Havrilesky (1990; 1993, chapter 8), I assigned a $+1$ to each meeting where the FAC lobbied the Board of Governors for an easier monetary policy, a -1 to each meeting where the FAC lobbied the Board of Governors for a tighter monetary policy, a 0 to each meeting where the FAC expressed support for monetary policy, a $+\frac{1}{2}$ to each meeting where the FAC expressed support for monetary policy but also suggested that monetary policy could be easier, and a $-\frac{1}{2}$ to each meeting where the FAC expressed support for monetary policy but also suggested that it could be tighter. The most revealing statements by the FAC, and the values assigned to them, are in the Appendix.

If the Federal Reserve responded to the monetary policy preferences of the FAC, then the Treasury-bill rate and the FAC index will move inversely. When the

FAC lobbied the Board of Governors for an easier monetary policy, reflected in positive values in the FAC index, the Treasury-bill rate should fall. When the FAC lobbied for a tighter monetary policy, reflected in negative values in the FAC index, the Treasury-bill rate should rise. Equations 3.2–3.4 show that this is in fact the case.

$$\text{Tbill}_t = 0.168 + 0.956 \quad \text{Tbill}_{t-1} \quad -0.590 \quad \text{FACindex}_t$$
$$(1.307) \quad (46.301) \qquad (-3.734)$$
$$R^2 = 0.94 \quad \text{Durbin } h = 1.23 \quad n = 146 \tag{3.2}$$

Comparing this result to the same regression without the FAC index,

$$\text{Tbill}_t = 0.244 + 0.060 \quad \text{Tbill}_{t-1}$$
$$(1.820) \quad (44.304)$$
$$R^2 = 0.93 \quad \text{Durbin } h = 2.33 \quad n = 148 \tag{3.3}$$

Specifying the dependent variable as a first difference, the result is

$$\Delta\text{Tbill}_t = -0.063 \quad -0.584 \quad \text{FACindex}_t$$
$$(-0.937) \quad (-4.085)$$
$$R^2 = 0.08 \quad \text{DW} = 1.82 \quad n = 146 \tag{3.4}$$

In Equation 3.2, the Durbin h statistic indicates that we cannot reject the null hypothesis of no serial correlation at the 0.05 level and, in Equation 3.4, the Durbin–Watson statistic indicates the same thing. The fit improves from Equation 3.3 to Equation 3.2.[13]

The t-statistics are in parentheses. They indicate that the estimated coefficients for the FAC index are highly statistically significant in Equations 3.2 and 3.4. That is to say, during the 1951–88 period, there is reason to believe that the Federal Reserve changed the Treasury-bill rate in accordance with the monetary policy preferences expressed by the FAC to the Board of Governors. In particular, the statistical significance of the FAC index in Equations 3.2 and 3.4 suggests that the Federal Reserve responded to the banks' lobbying for a higher Treasury-bill rate during the 1953–4 recession.

To focus the analysis more on the banks' lobbying of the Board of Governors for a higher Treasury-bill rate during the 1953–4 recession, in Equations 3.5 and 3.6, the FAC index is divided into a FACE index and a FACT index. The FACE index is composed of all the FAC's expressions of a preference for an easier monetary policy and the FACT index is composed of all its expressions of a preference for a tighter monetary policy (Havrilesky, 1990, p. 43). If the Federal Reserve was responsive to the FAC's lobbying for a higher Treasury-bill rate during the 1953–4 recession, then the FACT index should have a negative and statistically significant coefficient. This is in fact the case.

$$\text{Tbill}_t = 0.132 + 0.950 \ \text{Tbill}_{t-1} - 0.135 \ \text{FACEindex}_t - 0.791 \ \text{FACTindex}_t$$
$$(1.011) \quad (45.238) \quad (-0.393) \quad (-3.826)$$
$$R^2 = 0.94 \ \text{Durbin} \ h = 1.21 \ n = 146 \tag{3.5}$$

$$\Delta\text{Tbill}_t = 0.110 - 0.275 \ \text{FACEindex}_t - 0.720 \ \text{FACTindex}_t$$
$$(1.322) \quad (-0.803) \quad (-3.463)$$
$$R^2 = 0.08 \ \text{Durbin} \ W = 1.82 \ n = 146 \tag{3.6}$$

In Equation 3.5, the Durbin h statistic indicates that we cannot reject the null hypothesis of no serial correlation at the 0.05 level and, in Equation 3.6, the Durbin–Watson statistic indicates the same thing. The fit improves from Equation 3.3 to Equation 3.5.

The t-statistics indicate that the estimated coefficients for the FACT index, but not the FACE index, are highly statistically significant in Equations 3.5 and 3.6. This suggests that the Federal Reserve responded to the FAC's expressions of a preference for a higher Treasury-bill rate, but ignored the FAC's expressions of a preference for a lower Treasury-bill rate.

To placate the FAC's demands for a tighter monetary policy, the Federal Reserve had no alternative to raising interest rates. The Federal Reserve had more flexibility, however, when the FAC lobbied for an easier monetary policy. In fact, as we will see in Chapter 4, the FAC often lobbied for an easier monetary policy in the hope of convincing the Federal Reserve to lower reserve requirements.

In addition, the Federal Reserve administered interest-rate ceilings on how much the banks could pay for time deposits. When the Federal Reserve increased the Treasury-bill rate above the interest-rate ceilings on time deposits, it caused households and non-financial corporations to shift funds from time deposits to Treasury bills (i.e. a Treasury-bill rate above the interest-rate ceilings on time deposits caused bank disintermediation). Under such circumstances, as we will see in Chapter 5, the Federal Reserve could placate the FAC's demands for an easier monetary policy by raising the interest-rate ceiling on time deposits.

In short, the Federal Reserve could often respond to the FAC's lobbying for an easier monetary policy by either reducing reserve requirements or raising the interest-rate ceilings on time deposits, rather than decreasing the Treasury-bill rate. Therefore, it is not surprising that the FACE index is not statistically significant in Equations 3.5 and 3.6.

On the other hand, the fact that the FACT index is highly statistically significant in Equations 3.5 and 3.6 reinforces our suspicion that the Federal Reserve responded to the FAC's lobbying efforts, reported in Section 3.2, by increasing the Treasury-bill rate during the 1953–4 recession.

It is possible, however, that Equations 3.2–3.6 do not indicate that banker preferences were causing changes in monetary policy. They may indicate, instead, that changes in other factors, like state-of-the-economy variables, were causing simultaneous changes in both banker preferences and monetary policy. Following Havrilesky (1990, p. 43), this possibility is alleviated by regressing the FAC index

Table 3.5 *F*-Test on four geometrical distributed lags

Regression	F-ratio
Treasury bill rate on FAC index	8.53*
FAC index on treasury bill rate	1.19
5% significance level	2.27
1% significance level	3.17

*The *F*-ratio is highly statistically significant.

on the Treasury-bill rate. For the 1951–88 period, the Treasury-bill rate was not a statistically significant determinant of the FAC index.

Granger causality tests can further alleviate the possibility that changes in other factors were causing simultaneous changes in both banker preferences and monetary policy. Following Havrilesky (1993, pp. 265–6), I ran two regressions using current values of the Treasury-bill rate and lagged values of the Treasury-bill rate as arguments. I then ran the two basic regressions with the dependent and explanatory variables reversed. Following Robert Pollin (1991, p 387), the Treasury-bill rate was given the following geometric distributed lag structure.[14]

$$\text{Tbill}_t = \text{Tbill}_{t-1} + w\ \text{Tbill}_{t-2} + w^2 \text{Tbill}_{t-3} + w^3 \text{Tbill}_{t-4} \tag{3.7}$$

I assume that $w = 0.5$. To achieve stationarity, the Treasury-bill rate was pre-filtered by taking first differences of natural logs, i.e. δ (log Tbill).[15] Table 3.5 reports the fundamental results.

As reported in Table 3.5 for the 1951–88 period, the lagged values of the FAC index were highly statistically significant in the regression of the Treasury-bill rate on its own past values and the FAC index.[16] This suggests that banker preferences are a statistically significant determinant of monetary policy.

Also as reported in Table 3.5 for the 1951–88 period, the lagged values of the Treasury-bill rate were not significant in the regression of the FAC index on its own past values and the Treasury-bill rate.[17] Taken together with the regressions of the Treasury-bill rate on the FAC index, this suggests that changes in both banker preferences and monetary policy were not being caused by changes in other factors, such as state-of-the-economy variables.

Section 3.4 Summary and Conclusions

In March 1951, the Federal Reserve was given independence from democratic control in order to stabilize the economy at full employment with price stability. There is no dispute in the extant literature that the Federal Reserve failed to achieve its goal during the 1953–4 recession, the first opportunity it had to exercise its mandate. There is controversy, however, concerning why, in 1953–4, the Federal Reserve failed to stabilize the economy at full employment with price stability.

Economists working in both the Monetarist and the Keynesian traditions argue that the Federal Reserve tried, but failed, to stabilize the economy during the 1953–4 recession because of mistaken operating procedures. From the Monetarist perspective, the Federal Reserve failed to stabilize the economy because it was targeting free reserves, rather than a broader measure of reserves, like non-borrowed reserves. From the Keynesian perspective, on the other hand, the Federal Reserve failed to stabilize the economy because of its refusal to buy securities other than Treasury bills.

In contrast to the extant literature, I have argued in this chapter that, because of excessive banker influence, the Federal Reserve did not try to stabilize the economy during the 1953–4 recession. Archival evidence presented in Section 3.2 shows that the Federal Advisory Council (FAC), a group of 12 prominent bankers, lobbied the Federal Reserve for a higher Treasury-bill rate in 1953–4. Econometric evidence presented in Section 3.3 suggests that the Federal Reserve responded to the FAC's lobbying by propping up the Treasury-bill rate. Therefore, the Federal Reserve failed to carry out the mandate it was given in March 1951 to stabilize the economy at full employment with price stability.

Epstein and Schor (1995) demonstrate the decisive role of the U.S. bank cartel in wresting U.S. monetary policy from democratic control in 1951. Consequently, it is not surprising that two years later, in 1953–4, the bank cartel was able to subordinate U.S. monetary policy to its interests.

In short, the archival and econometric evidence presented in this chapter suggests that, until the Federal Reserve is once again made democratically accountable, it is useless to even pose the question of whether or not the Federal Reserve could increase some measure of reserves or purchase some type of securities aggressively enough to stabilize the economy during a recession, unless of course such a result is a side-effect of securing the interests of the U.S. bank cartel.

Notes

1 In Chapter 4, I show that it was in the interests of the U.S. bank cartel for the Federal Reserve to stabilize the economy during the 1969–70 recession, so the Federal Reserve did stabilize it.

2 Free reserves (*FR*) are typically defined as:

$$FR = ER - BR$$

where *ER* is excess reserves, or the amount of reserves banks hold in excess of the reserves they must hold to meet reserve requirements; and *BR* is borrowed reserves, or the amount of reserves that the banks obtain from the Federal Reserve by borrowing at the Federal Reserve's discount rate. Equation 3.1 is obtained by noting that total reserves (*TR*) are defined in the following two ways:

$$TR = NBR + BR$$

and:

$$TR = RR + ER$$

where *NBR* is nonborrowed reserves, *BR* is borrowed reserves, *RR* is required reserves, and *ER* is excess reserves. Setting these two definitions of total reserves equal to each other, rearranging terms, we get:

$$NBR = RR + ER - BR$$

Substituing the definition of free reserves as excess reserves (*ER*) minus borrowed reserves (*BR*) into this equation, we thus get:

$$NBR = RR + FR$$

or:

$$FR = NBR - RR$$

3 In Chapters 5 and 6, I explain how and why this approach to monetary policymaking broke down in the 1960s.
4 Also see, for example, Minsky, 1957; Rousseas, 1960; Kaldor, 1970; Davidson and Weintraub, 1973; Davidson, 1974; Moore, 1979; Moore, 1983; Rousseas, 1986; Moore, 1988; Moore, 1989; Davidson, 1989; Rousseas, 1989; and Pollin, 1991.
5 I use the following archival materials: a) the *Minutes* of the meetings of the Federal Open Market Committee (FOMC *Minutes*); b) the *Minutes* of meetings of the Executive Committee (EC *Minutes*); and c) the *Minutes* of the meetings of the Federal Advisory Council (FAC *Minutes*). In addition, I use the *New York Times*, business magazines, and transcripts of Congressional Hearings to ascertain how monetary policy was being interpreted by contemporaries.

Prior to 1956, the Executive Committee was the policymaking council within the Federal Reserve System. The permanent members of the Executive Committee were Allan Sproul, President of the Federal Reserve Bank of New York, and William McChesney Martin Jr., Chair of the Board of Governors. The other regional-bank presidents and members of the Board of Governors rotated through three seats on the Executive Committee so that, at each meeting, there were five voting members.

Since 1956, the Federal Open Market Committee (FOMC) has been the policymaking council within the Federal Reserve System. The FOMC's permanent members are the seven members of the Board of Governors, or the Federal Reserve Board, and the President of the Federal Reserve Bank of New York. The eleven non-New York regional-bank presidents rotate through four seats on the FOMC so that, at each meeting, there are twelve voting members.

The Federal Advisory Council is the only other significant policymaking council within the Federal Reserve System. The Federal Advisory Council is composed of twelve bankers, one appointed by the Board of Directors of each of the regional banks, who meet with the Board of Governors prior to FOMC meetings four times a year. I provide evidence in Section 3.4 that their recommendations to the Board at these meetings are statistically significant determinants of U.S. monetary policy.
6 The Federal Reserve also controlled short-term interest rates in the 1920s and 1930s. But from the outbreak of the Second World War to March 1951, the Treasury Department determined interest rates, after consulting with the Federal Reserve.

7 Today, the prices of government securities are set in auction markets. But this was not the case in the 1950s, when they were set by the Treasury Department.

8 The boards of directors of the regional Federal Reserve banks are themselves dominated by bankers. That is to say, there are three bankers and three banker-appointed non-bankers on the nine member boards of directors of the twelve regional Federal Reserve banks.

9 There were over 14,000 commercial banks. Less than 500 of the largest commercial banks were also weekly reporting banks.

10 "Business loans" denote all commercial, industrial, and agricultural loans.

11 The banks' selling of one type of asset (e.g. Treasury bills) in order to issue another type of asset (e.g. loans to customers) is called "asset management." Today, banks make loans then look for reserves later by issuing new liabilities, which is called "liability management." The ways in which banks currently acquire required reserves without borrowing from the Federal Reserve or selling other assets (e.g. Treasury bills) through liability management, or through the federal funds, negotiable certificate of deposit, commercial paper, and Eurodollar markets, were not viable sources of funds for the banks during the 1950s (see Chapters 5 and 6; also see Wolfson, 1986).

12 As the dependent variable in Equations 3.2–3.6, and in the subsequent causality tests, I calculate 3-month averages of the monthly data for the Treasury-bill rate in Chapter 1, Section 2, of CITIBASE.

As I explain in Chapter 1, orthodox economists insist that the real interest rate is the best proxy for monetary policy (see, for example, Fazzari, 1993, pp. 40–1, 50–3, 56–8). Aside from the theoretical objections I explain in Chapter 1, in this section I use a nominal short-term interest rate as a proxy for monetary policy because the Federal Reserve controls it directly (see, for example, Khoury, 1990, for a discussion of alternative proxies for monetary policy). In contrast, the Federal Reserve only affects real interest rates indirectly. That is to say, by setting the level of a short-term nominal interest rate, the Federal Reserve affects the level of output and employment. The level of output and employment then affects inflation rates, and thus the level of real interest rates.

Even if the Federal Reserve changes nominal short-term interest rates in response to changing inflation rates in order to sustain a certain level of real interest rates, the level of nominal interest rates remains the Federal Reserve's control variable.

However, there is no archival evidence to support the hypothesis that the Federal Reserve changes short-term nominal interest rates in order to target real interest rates. Rather than targeting real interest rates in order to affect the level of output and employment by affecting the cost of capital and thus the level of investment expenditures, I show in this book that the effects of central banks on the level of real interest rates are, in large part, an unintended consequence of the success or failure of their efforts to organize the banks into cartels that can increase nominal interest rates by restricting the supply of credit (also see Goodhart, 1988).

13 Given that, of the 147 reported values of the FAC index, 85 are zero, the reader is cautioned against reading much into the numerical value of the coefficient of the FAC index. Indeed, the annual average value of the FAC index is reported in Table 3.6.

14 I also used alternative distributed lag structures for differing lengths of time, with no effect on the conclusions drawn in Table 3.5.

15 Following Basil Moore (1988, pp. 150–7), I also used alternative prefiltering techniques, with no effect on the conclusions drawn in Table 3.5.

16 That is to say, the F-ratio (8.53) is greater than its critical value at even a 1 percent level of significance (3.17).

17 That is to say, the F-ratio (1.19) is less than its critical value at even the 5 percent level of significance (2.27).

Table 3.6 Monetary policy preferences of the Federal Advisory
Council, 1951–88 (annual averages)

Date	Index	Date	Index
1951	−0.167	1970	+0.250
1952	0.000	1971	0.000
1953	+0.125	1972	−0.750
1954	−0.500	1973	−0.375
1955	−0.125	1974	+0.375
1956	0.000	1975	+0.625
1957	+0.125	1976	0.000
1958	+0.125	1977	−0.375
1959	−0.250	1978	−1.000
1960	0.000	1979	−0.750
1961	0.000	1980	−0.500
1962	−0.250	1981	−0.500
1963	−0.125	1982	−0.125
1964	−0.500	1983	+0.125
1965	−0.500	1984	+0.125
1966	−0.125	1985	+0.125
1967	−0.375	1986	+0.125
1968	−0.250	1987	−0.125
1969	0.000	1988	0.000

Bibliography

Ahearn, D. S. 1963. *Federal Reserve Policy Reappraised, 1951–59*. New York: Columbia University Press.

Boddy, Raford and James Crotty. 1975. "Class Conflict and Macro-Policy: The Political Business Cycle." *Review of Radical Political Economics*, Vol. 7, No. 1, pp. 1–19.

Brunner, Karl and Allan Meltzer. 1964. *The Federal Reserve's Attachment to the Free Reserve Concept*. Washington, DC: Committee on Banking and Currency, House of Representatives, 88th Congress, 2nd Session.

CITIBASE.

D'Arista, Jane W. 1994. *The Evolution of U.S. Finance, Vol. 1, Federal Reserve Monetary Policy: 1915–1935*. Armonk, NY: M.E. Sharpe.

Davidson, Paul. 1989. "On the Endogeneity of Money Once More." *Journal of Post Keynesian Economics*. Vol. 1, No. 3 (Spring), pp. 488–90.

Davidson, Paul. 1974. "A Keynesian View of Friedman's Theoretical Framework for Monetary Analysis." In *Milton Friedman's Monetary Framework: A Debate with his Critics*. Robert J. Gordon (ed.). Chicago: University of Chicago Press, pp. 90–110.

Davidson, Paul and Sidney Weintraub. 1973. "Money as Cause and Effect." *Economic Journal*, Vol. 83 (December), pp. 1117–32.

Dewald, W. G. and Harry Johnson. 1963. "An Objective Analysis of the Objectives of American Monetary Policy." In *Banking and Monetary Studies*, D. Carson (ed.). Homewood, IL: R.D. Irwin, pp. 171–89.

Epstein, Gerald. 1992. "Political Economy and Comparative Central Banking." *Review of Radical Political Economics*, Vol. 24, No. 1, pp. 1–30.

Epstein, Gerald. 1990. "Prime Rates, Federal Reserve Signaling, and Financial Instability." *Journal of Post Keynesian Economics*, Vol. 12, No. 1, pp. 618–35.

Epstein, Gerald. 1987. "Federal Reserve Behavior and the Limits of Monetary Policy in the Current Economic Crisis." In *The Imperiled Economy: Macroeconomics from a Left Perspective*, R. Cherry (ed.). New York: Union for Radical Political Economics, pp. 247–55.

Epstein, Gerald and Juliet Schor. 1995. "The Federal Reserve Treasury Accord and the Construction of the Postwar Monetary Regime in the United States." *Social Concept*, Vol. 7, No. 1 (July), pp. 7–48.

Epstein, Gerald and Juliet Schor. 1990. "Corporate Profitability as a Determinant of Restrictive Monetary Policy: Estimates for the Postwar United States." In *The Political Economy of American Monetary Policy*, Thomas Mayer (ed.). New York: Cambridge University Press, pp. 51–63.

Epstein, Gerald and Thomas Ferguson. 1984. "Monetary Policy, Loan Liquidation and Industrial Conflict: The Federal Reserve and Open Market Operations in 1932." *Journal of Economic History*, Vol. 64, No. 4, pp. 957–83.

Executive Committee. *Minutes, 1950–1956*. Washington, DC: Board of Governors of the Federal Reserve System.

Fazzari, Steven M. 1994–5. "Why Doubt the Effectiveness of Keynesian Fiscal Policy?" *Journal of Post Keynesian Economics*, Vol. 17, No. 2 (Winter), pp. 231–48.

Fazzari, Steven M. 1993. "Monetary Policy, Financial Structure, and Investment." In Gary A. Dymski, Gerald Epstein and Robert Pollin (eds). *Transforming the U.S. Financial System*. New York: M.E. Shape, pp. 35–64.

Federal Advisory Council. *Minutes, 1950–1988*. Washington, DC: Board of Governors of the Federal Reserve System.

Federal Open Market Committee. *Minutes, 1950–1960*. Washington, DC: Board of Governors of the Federal Reserve System.

Friedman, Milton and Anna Jacobson Schwartz. 1963. *A Monetary History of the United States and Great Britain, 1867–1960*. Princeton, NJ: Princeton University Press.

Goodhart, Charles. 1989. "Has Moore Become Too Horizontal?" *Journal of Post Keynesian Economics*, Vol. 12, No. 2 (Fall), pp. 29–34.

Goodhart, Charles. 1988. *The Evolution of Central Banks*. Cambridge, MA: MIT Press.

Gordon, Robert. 1983. "Using Monetary Control to Dampen the Business Cycle: A New Set of First Principles." National Bureau of Economic Research Working Paper No. 1210.

Guttentag, Jack. 1966. "The Strategy of Open Market Operations." *Quarterly Journal of Economics*, Vol. 80 (February), pp. 1–20.

Havrilesky, Thomas. 1993. *The Pressures on American Monetary Policy*. Boston: Kluwer Academic Publishers.

Havrilesky, Thomas. 1990. "The Influence of the Federal Advisory Council on Monetary Policy." *Journal of Money, Credit, and Banking*, Vol. 22, pp. 38–50.

Kaldor, Nicholas. 1970. "The New Monetarism." *Lloyds Bank Review* (July).

Kalecki, Michal. 1971. "Political Aspects of Full Employment." In *Selected Essays on the Dynamics of the Capitalist Economy: 1933–70*. Michal Kalecki (ed.). Cambridge: Cambridge University Press, pp. 138–45.

Khoury, Salwa S. 1990. "The Federal Reserve Reaction Function: A Specification Search." In *The Political Economy of American Monetary Policy*. Thomas Mayer (ed.). New York: Cambridge University Press, pp. 27–41.

Kolko, Gabriel. 1963. *The Triumph of Conservatism: A Reinterpretation of American History, 1900–1916*. New York: Macmillan.

Lombra, Raymond. 1980. *Controlling Monetary Aggregates III*. Boston: Federal Reserve Bank of Boston.

Lombra, Raymond and Raymond Torta. 1973. "Federal Reserve Defensive Behavior and the Reverse Causation Argument." *Southern Journal of Economics*, Vol. 40, pp. 47–55.

Meigs, James. 1962. *Free Reserves and the Money Supply*. Chicago: University of Chicago Press.

Meltzer, Allan. 2009. *A History of the Federal Reserve*. Volume Two. Chicago: University of Chicago Press.

Meltzer, Allan. 2003. *A History of the Federal Reserve*. Volume One. Chicago: University of Chicago Press.

Meltzer, Allan. 1982. "Comment on Federal Reserve Control of the Money Stock." *Journal of Money, Credit, and Banking*. Vol. 14 (November), pp. 632–40.

Minsky, Hyman P. 1957. "Central Banking and Money Market Changes." *Quarterly Journal of Economics*, Vol. LXXI (May), pp. 171–87.

Moore, Basil J. 1979. "The Endogenous Money Stock." *Journal of Post Keynesian Economics*, Vol. 1, No. 2 (Fall), pp. 479–87.

Moore, Basil J. 1983. "Unpacking the Post Keynesian Black Box: Bank Lending and the Money Supply." *Journal of Post Keynesian Economics*, Vol. 5, No. 3 (Summer), pp. 537–57.

Moore, Basil J. 1988. *Horizontalists and Verticalists: The Macroeconomics of Credit Money*. New York: Cambridge University Press.

Moore, Basil J. 1989. "On the Endogeneity of Money Once More." *Journal of Post Keynesian Economics*, Vol. 11, No. 3 (Spring), pp. 479–87.

New York Times, 1950–60.

Panico, Carlo. 1988. *Interest and Profit in the Theories of Value and Distribution*. New York: St. Martins Press.

Pivetti, Massimo. 1985. "On the Monetary Explanation of Distribution." *Political Economy— Studies in the Surplus Approach*, Vol. 1 No. 2, pp. 73–103.

Pollin, Robert. 1991. "Two Theories of Money Supply Endogeneity." *Journal of Post Keynesian Economics*, Vol. 13, No. 3 (Spring), pp. 366–96.

Romer, Christina D. and David H. Romer. 1993. "Credit Channel or Credit Actions? An Interpretation of the Postwar Transmission Mechanism." In *Changing Capital Markets: Implications for Monetary Policy*. Kansas City, KS: The Federal Reserve Bank of Kansas City, pp. 71–116.

Romer, Christina D. and David H. Romer. 1990. "New Evidence on the Monetary Transmission Mechanism." *Brookings Papers on Economic Activity*, Vol. 1, pp. 121–70.

Rousseas, Stephen W. 1989. "On the Endogeneity of Money Once More." *Journal of Post Keynesian Economics*, Vol. 1, No. 3 (Spring), pp. 474–8.

Rousseas, Stephen W. 1986. *Post Keynesian Monetary Economics*. Armonk, NY: M.E. Sharpe.

Rousseas, Stephen W. 1960. "Velocity Changes and the Effectiveness of Monetary Policy." *Review of Economics and Statistics*, Vol. XLII (February), pp. 27–36.

Schor, Juliet B. 1987. "Class Struggle and the Cost of Job Loss." In *The Imperiled Economy: Macroeconomics from a Left Perspective*. Robert Cherry (ed.). New York: Union for Radical Political Economics, pp. 171–82.

Schor, Juliet B. 1985. "Wage Flexibility, Social Welfare Expenditures, and Monetary Restrictiveness." In *Money and Macro Policy*. Marc Jarsulic (ed.). Boston: Kluwer-Nijhoff Publishing, pp. 135–54.

Weintraub, Sidney. 1978. "A Theory of Monetary Policy Under Wage Inflation." In *Keynes, Keynesians and Monetarists*. Sidney Weintraub (ed.). Philadelphia: University of Pennsylvania Press, pp. 161–81.

Wicker, Elmus. 1990. "Leaning Against the Wind: The Behavior of the Money Stock in Recession and Recovery, 1953–8." In *The Political Economy of American Monetary Policy*. Thomas Mayer (ed.). Cambridge: Cambridge University Press, pp. 269–82.

Wojnilower, Albert M. 1980. "The Central Role of Credit Crunches in Recent Financial History." *Brookings Papers on Economic Activity*, Vol. 2, pp. 277–325.

Wolfson, Martin H. 1986. *Financial Crises: Understanding the Postwar U.S. Experience*. Armonk, NY: M.E. Sharpe.

4 The Federal Reserve's Implacable Opposition to Social Democracy

In March 1951, the Federal Reserve obtained independence from the Treasury Department for the purpose of stabilizing the economy at full employment with price stability. In this chapter, I show that the Federal Reserve used its freedom of maneuver instead to oppose the movement toward social democracy in the U.S., where social democracy is defined as building and sustaining a large and powerful national labor movement aligned with the interests of the unemployed. I provide evidence that the Federal Reserve was constrained in its ability to oppose the movement toward social democracy both by the political context in which it operated and by its primary concern with managing the U.S. bank cartel, as exemplified by the influence on U.S. monetary policy exercised by the Federal Advisory Council, but also by the influence of the twelve banker-controlled Regional Reserve banks. Nonetheless, to the degree that it could, the Federal Reserve's goal was to oppose social democracy by using high interest rates to precipitate then sustain recessions, a goal that it was finally able to achieve during the 1973–5 recession.

As such, I explain U.S. monetary policy from a radical political economic perspective. By a radical political economic perspective I mean one that situates monetary policy in the context of "the capital–labor conflict over the terms of the employment relation" (Dymski, 1990, p. 54; Epstein, 1987). During the 1951–75 period, the terms of the employment relation were determined by what Mike Davis (1986, chapter 2; Gordon *et al.*, 1987, p. 48) calls the Treaty of Detroit, a 1950 agreement of the United Automobile Workers (UAW) to consent to managerial control of investment decisions and of the labor process in exchange for a promise by General Motors to negotiate three-year contracts tying wages (including benefits) to labor productivity and the cost of living, after the expiration of a five-year, no-strike pledge (Lichenstein, 1989, pp. 141–2). Therefore, there were tri-annual rounds of wage negotiations in the automobile industry in 1955, 1958, 1961, 1964, 1967, 1970, and 1973. These rounds of wage negotiations then served as a model for wage negotiations in other industries, especially the steel industry. That is to say, the tri-annual rounds of wage negotiations in the automobile industry were followed by tri-annual rounds of wage negotiations in the steel industry in 1956, 1959, 1962, 1965, 1968, 1971, and 1974. The purpose of this chapter is to show that the Federal Reserve was preoccupied with using high interest rates to strengthen capital against labor in these negotiations.

There are numerous reasons to believe that tight monetary policy strengthens capital against labor (Kalecki, 1971, pp. 138–45; Boddy and Crotty, 1975; Pivetti, 1985; Schor, 1985; Epstein, 1987; Schor, 1987; Panico, 1988; Epstein and Schor, 1990; Epstein, 1992). And the archival research reported in this chapter shows that it was not an effort to stabilize the economy at full employment with price stability but a desire to strengthen capital against labor that explains the Federal Reserve's behavior during the 1951–75 period.

In Chapter 3, I show that, from May 1954 to March 1956, the Federal Reserve did in fact try to stabilize the economy at full employment with price stability. But in Section 4.1, I show that this was only because the UAW's five-year, no-strike pledge was in effect. When the no-strike pledge expired, so did the Federal Reserve's efforts to stabilize the economy, and what took its place in the late 1950s were efforts by the Federal Reserve to use discount-rate increases to neutralize labor's revived use of the strike weapon, by means of what it called a penalty-rate policy.

In Section 4.1, I also show that the efforts of the Kennedy and Johnson administrations to extend social democracy with an incomes policy and capital controls held the Federal Reserve in check until February 1965, after which time it returned to its efforts of the late 1950s to strengthen capital against labor in wage negotiations. I emphasize that the means by which the Federal Reserve hoped to achieve this goal was to precipitate then sustain recessions. However, it changed its operating procedure, from a penalty-rate policy designed to increase the cost of credit to quantity restraints designed to restrict the availability of credit.

In Sections 4.2 and 4.3 respectively, I focus on the Federal Reserve's behavior during the 1970–1 and 1973–75 recessions. In Section 4.2, I explain how the Federal Reserve's duties as manager of the U.S. bank cartel prevented it from raising interest rates to strengthen capital against labor during the 1970–1 tri-annual rounds of wage negotiations in the automobile and steel industries. And in Section 4.3, I explain how the Federal Reserve finally accomplished its goal. On the one hand, my analysis in Section 4.3 is a straightforward extension of my analyses in Sections 4.1 and 4.2 of how the Federal Reserve's behavior is properly understood in terms of the capital–labor conflict over the terms of the employment relation. On the other hand, I also take the opportunity to place my analysis in the context of the orthodox explanations of the Federal Reserve's behavior.

In Section 4.4, I provide a summary and conclusions.

Section 4.1 From a Penalty-rate Policy to Quantity Restraints

As noted above, the Treaty of Detroit was a 1950 agreement between General Motors and the UAW that included a five-year, no strike-pledge and became a model for union contracts in the organized branches of industry, especially the steel industry. In this section, I explain how U.S. monetary policy in the 1950s and 1960s can be understood only in terms of the Treaty of Detroit. In particular, the expiration of the Treaty's no-strike pledge explains the Federal Reserve's change in operating procedures in March 1956, as explained in Chapter 3.

The Treaty of Detroit was designed to put an end to the labor insurgencies that began in 1933, when the industrial proletariat organized itself into a cohesive political force for the first and only time in U.S. history. At the peak of its strength, from the sit-down strikes in Detroit in 1936–7 to the national strikes in the immediate postwar period, the industrial proletariat sought some form of democratic national economic planning to redress mass unemployment (Davis, 1986, chapter 2; Fraser, 1989; Brinkley, 1995, pp. 207, 212–13, 218–19, 224; Katznelson, 2013, pp. 250–74). As Richard Hofstadter (1955, p. 308) puts it: "The demands of a large and powerful labor movement, coupled with the interest of the unemployed, gave the late New Deal a social democratic tinge that had never been present before in American reform movements." And, one might add, a "social democratic tinge" that has not been present since.

However, the need for democratic national economic planning was called into question in 1938 when, for the first time, the government used stabilization policies to pull the economy out of a recession (Brinkley 1995, pp. 83–5). Leading factions of capital, which were virulently opposed to any form of democratic national economic planning (Brinkley 1995, pp. 205, 208), seized upon stabilization policies as a putative solution to the unemployment problem that would not impinge on their prerogatives in the way that democratic national economic planning, or social democracy, would (Weir and Skocpol, 1985; Brinkley 1989, 1995, p. 229).

The opportunity to build upon the potential of stabilization policies to undermine the movement toward social democracy came after the Republicans won the 1946 Congressional elections and passed the Taft–Hartley Act of 1947. After using the Taft–Hartley Act to purge the unions of radical cadre and to prevent inter-union solidarity (Katznelson, 1989, p. 191; Lichenstein, 1989, pp. 133–4; Kotz, 2015, pp. 53–62; McQuaid, 1982, p. 143), General Motors proposed the Treaty of Detroit. General Motors offered to tie wages and benefits to labor productivity and the cost of living if, in return, the UAW would consent to managerial control of investment decisions and of the labor process, as well as a five-year, no-strike pledge (Lichenstein, 1989, pp. 141–2).

In 1948, the UAW rejected the proposed Treaty on the grounds that it was a product of war-induced prosperity, and that some form of democratic national economic planning was still required to solve the unemployment problem in a capitalist economy, not a war. But then, during the 1948–9 recession, the government once again used stabilization policies to ameliorate unemployment and thus, once again, created the impression that social democracy was not necessary to ensure full employment. Consequently, in 1950, the UAW was lulled into accepting the Treaty (Davis, 1986, pp. 52, 85–7; Brinkley, 1989, p. 110; Gerstle and Fraser, 1989, p. xv; Lichenstein, 1989, pp. 123, 142; Brinkley, 1995, pp. 223–4).

Davis (1986, pp. 111–12) reports an editorial in *Fortune Magazine* that interpreted the Treaty of Detroit as

> a basic "affirmation of the free enterprise system." First, the autoworkers accepted "the existing distribution of income between wages and profits as 'normal' if not as 'fair.'" Second, by explicitly accepting "objective economic facts—cost of living and productivity—as determining wages," the contract threw "overboard all theories of wages as determined by political power, and of profit 'as surplus value." Finally, "it is one of the very few union contracts that expressly recognize[s] both the importance of the management function and the fact that management operates directly in the interest of labor."

Following Jackson *et al.* (1972, p. 26; also see Treiber, FOMC *Minutes*, 11 February 1964, pp. 29–30), the three-year contracts envisaged by the Treaty of Detroit can be formalized as follows:

$$(\Delta W/W)^* = (\Delta v/v)^* \tag{4.1}$$

where W is the average real wage (including benefits), * denotes the automobile industry, and v is the value added per worker.

The problem was that the contracts negotiated by the UAW became a model for union contracts in other sectors of the economy, especially the steel industry, without regard for the rates of growth of labor productivity in those sectors, which can be formalized as follows:

$$(\Delta W/W)_i = a_i(\Delta W/W)^*, i = 1, 2, \ldots, n; 0 < a_i < 1 \tag{4.2}$$

where there are n sectors of the economy other than the automobile industry. To the degree that unions in these sectors managed to match the wage and benefit gains of the UAW, a_i had a value close to 1.

Substituting into Equation 4.2 from Equation 4.1, it follows that the average change in the real wage (including benefits) in the ith-industry was some fraction (a_i) of the rate of growth of labor productivity in the automobile industry:

$$(\Delta W/W)_i = a_i(\Delta v/v)^* \tag{4.3}$$

As a result, the Treaty of Detroit had the potential to unleash inflationary pressures. To see why, let p denote the price level in each industry, so that:

$$(\Delta p/p)_i = (\Delta W/W)_i - (\Delta v/v)_i \tag{4.4}$$

Substituting into Equation 4.4 from Equation 4.3, we get:

$$(\Delta p/p)_i = a_i(\Delta v/v)^* - (\Delta v/v)_i \qquad (4.5)$$

The economy-wide price level (P) is the sum of the sectoral price levels, weighted by their share in total value added (V):

$$(\Delta P/P) = \Sigma(\Delta p/p)_i \, V_i/V \qquad (4.6)$$

Substituting into Equation 4.6 from Equation 4.5, it follows that:

$$(\Delta P/P) = \Sigma[a_i(\Delta v/v)^* - (\Delta v/v)_i] \, V_i/V \qquad (4.7)$$

In sum, to the degree that, first, other unions matched the wage and benefit gains of the UAW (i.e. a_i had a value close to 1), and, second, the rate of growth of labor productivity in the automobile industry was greater than the average rate of growth of labor productivity, the three-year contracts negotiated by the UAW unleashed inflationary pressures.

The Federal Reserve was given independence from the Treasury Department in March 1951 as part of the Government's putative effort to deliver on its promise of creating institutions to stabilize the economy at full employment with price stability (Chapter 3; also see Epstein and Schor, 1986, 1995). Unfortunately, no institutional restraints were put in place to hold the Federal Reserve to this goal, which it abandoned in March 1956 to pursue the goal of combatting the inflationary pressures unleashed by the Treaty of Detroit. It was to pursue the latter goal that the Federal Reserve shifted from the stabilization policy pursued between May 1954 and March 1956 to a penalty rate policy in March 1956.

Allan Sproul, President of the Federal Reserve Bank of New York, was architect of the stabilization policy described in Chapter 3. The following statement captures the basic thrust of his defense of the stabilization policy, which he defended throughout 1955, in spite of the fact that the Treaty of Detroit's five-year, no-strike pledge had expired and the UAW was threatening to strike. He argued that prospective discount-rate increases under the penalty rate policy

> raises questions as to whether the central banking system should make credit so dear and difficult to obtain as to cause a decline in production and employment as the lesser of two evils … He [Sproul] was not suggesting that the [Federal Reserve] System disclaim responsibility [for fighting wage-push inflation, as formalized in Equation 4.7]. To the extent that it had the power it should exercise it. But it should face the fact that if we are going to carry through against the claims of organized labor and the acquiescence of big business, we are going to have a real knock-down-and-drag-out fight as to whether monetary policy is to be so severe as to bring on substantial unemployment and reduced income with all that implies … the [Federal

Open Market] Committee would be fooling itself if it thought that it could prevent this wage-cost spiral short of adopting a very severe monetary policy. Whether the [Federal Reserve] System would have the assent of the Government and of the public in such a course seemed to ... be the real question ... he was merely suggesting caution in assuming the System had the answer to the wage-cost spiral ... He was not suggesting that the System not do something. He was arguing that the Committee not be carried away with grandiose ideas of what it might accomplish toward combating a wage-price spiral unless it moved in a very severe way. His view was that we were faced with a much more serious problem than the tools of the central banking system, alone, could be expected to control.

(Sproul, FOMC *Minutes*, 27 March 1956, pp. 32–4;
also see, for example, FOMC *Minutes*, 2 March 1955, p. 65;
FOMC *Minutes*, 2 August 1955, p. 22)

Sproul's arguments became less persuasive after the UAW was successful in using the strike threat to obtain significant concessions from the automobile industry, and after the United Steel Workers, the International Union of Electrical Workers, and other smaller unions subsequently resolved to try and match the UAW's gains (see, for example, *New York Times*, 1 July 1955, pp. 1, 6; *New York Times*, 11 July 1955, pp. 1, 17; FOMC *Minutes*, 2 August 1955, pp. 13–14; FOMC *Minutes*, 23 August 1955, p. 8). Sproul's loss of influence within the Federal Reserve System occurred in March 1956, when a strike threat by the United Steel Workers caused the majority of the members of the Federal Open Market Committee to conclude that a wage-price spiral was in the offing. Just as he had done when the UAW threatened to strike, Sproul, with the support of Governor James Kimble Vardaman Jr., argued for continuing the stabilization policy on the grounds that "it could cause the destruction of the System" if the Federal Reserve "moved to such a degree as would be necessary to stop the wage-price spiral" (FOMC *Minutes*, 27 March 1956, p. 33; also see pp. 9–11). But four other members of the Board of Governors and three regional bank presidents agreed with William McChesney Martin Jr., Chair of the Board of Governors, when he rejected the arguments of Sproul and Vardaman because "the threat of a wage-price spiral was so strong today that the System would be derelict in its duty and obligation if it did not do all that it could do" (Martin, FOMC *Minutes*, 27 March 1956, p. 34).[1]

A new majority of Federal Open Market Committee members thus coalesced behind Martin's call for using the discount rate, rather than open-market operations, as the leading instrument in applying a policy of monetary restraint. As a result, the Federal Reserve increased the discount rate in April 1956 even though the Treasury bill rate had not moved up to equality with it. Since discount-rate increases would no longer appear to be semiautomatic technical adjustments to a rising Treasury-bill rate, the majority of Federal Open Market Committee members hoped that such increases could occur more unexpectedly, more dramatically, and, therefore, with considerable psychological effect on the atmosphere in which wage negotiations were conducted (see, for example, FOMC *Minutes*, 23 August 1955, pp. 10–11). The following statements by Governors James Louis Robertson and Abbot Low Mills Jr., to justify their support for the March 1956 change in operating procedures, illustrate both the Federal Open Market Committee's concern that the wage negotiations in the steel industry would accentuate the wage-price spiral and the Committee's hope that the psychological effect of a discount-rate increase would be to put a damper on the wage-price spiral:

> All in all, the wage-price spiral is showing definite signs of life. Large wage and price increases appear inevitable in steel, and these are likely to spread to other basic industries.
>
> (Robertson, FOMC *Minutes*, 27 March 1956, p. 18)

> if each person at this meeting were to return to his desk and carry out the responsibility set before him, this would mean that in a short time there would be an increase in the discount rate ... and there would be a widespread effort to consult with member banks about their use of the discount window. In combination, the results of such actions could be fearsome in their effects upon the psychology of the market and of the business community.
>
> (Mills, FOMC *Minutes*, 27 March 1956, p. 34)

When Governor C. Canby Balderston spoke to justify his support for the March 1956 change in operating procedures, he not only seconded the concerns and hopes of Robertson and Mills, he also emphasized his belief that the wage-price spiral began as soon as the Treaty of Detroit's five-year, no-strike pledge expired and the UAW began wielding the strike weapon:

> He [Balderston] now wished the [Federal Reserve] System had acted sooner and more vigorously last year [i.e., during the wage negotiations in the automobile industry] when certain commitments were being made by businessmen that were now showing up in business loans, price increases, and in other ways. But it would be a defeatist attitude for the System to argue that those commitments having been made, it cannot take action to influence wage and price movements. In his view, the country now has a wage-price spiral in the making ... the System's actions should be decisive enough to cause businessmen to realize the danger of a wage-price spiral and not abdicate when they face wage negotiations this spring and summer in the way they would if they felt they could simply increase their prices and continue to sell goods. He hoped that labor unions would appreciate the dangers of a wage-price spiral. Translating this to the discount rate ... he would be sympathetic to an increase of ½ percent, to a 3 per cent level.
>
> (Balderston, FOMC *Minutes*, 3 March 1956, pp. 26–7)

Last, the fifth member of the Board of Governors to support the March 1956 change in operating procedures, Charles Noah Shepardson, was particularly clear that it was the Federal Reserve's intention to join forces with capital against labor:

> Recognizing that the [Federal Reserve] System did not have the power without cataclysmic action to stop a wage-price spiral, certainly it should be able to exercise some restraint in the present situation. He [Shepardson] was very much in accord with the views Mr. Balderston had expressed that some definite action on the part of the System would strengthen the hands of industry in wage negotiations coming up. He did not think this would stop wage increases, but it could have a healthy restraining effect.
>
> (Shepardson, FOMC *Minutes*, 3 March 1956, p. 34)

With the votes for a discount-rate increase that would not be signaled by a prior increase in the Treasury-bill rate, caused by contractionary open-market operations designed to gradually reduce free reserves, Martin concluded the 27 March 1956 meeting of the Federal Open Market Committee as follows:

> he [Martin] had tried to emphasize this same point [as Shepardon's] in his remarks. The [Federal Open Market] Committee could not expect monetary policy to achieve all of the task. However, the threat of a wage-price spiral was so strong today that the System would be derelict in its duty and obligation if it did not do all that it could do.
>
> (Martin, FOMC *Minutes*, 27 March 1956, pp. 34–5)

After the Federal Reserve implemented its new operating procedure, in April 1956, of catching the financial markets off-guard with an un-signaled discount-rate increase, the majority of the members of the Federal Open Market Committee believed that it had succeeded in creating an atmosphere that strengthened the hands of industry in wage negotiations. As Martin put it, there was

> a real change in business sentiment ... monetary policy is getting more credit for that change in sentiment than it deserves, but it is so real that some of the people who were saying that monetary policy could have no effect whatsoever are now claiming that it has more effect than it really has.
>
> (Martin, FOMC *Minutes*, 23 May 1956, pp. 9–10;
> also see FOMC *Minutes*, 5 June 1956, p. 17)

Moreover, the majority of members of the Federal Open Market Committee believed that the April 1956 discount-rate increase caused the banks to become more "severe on credit requests" (FOMC *Minutes*, 17 April 1956, 9, 14; also see FOMC *Minutes*, 9 May 1956, p. 14). Nonetheless, there remained the problem, noted in Chapter 3, that the new operating procedure was technically flawed. Open-market operations were supposed to keep the Treasury-bill rate responsive to, but always below, the discount rate. The problem was that, with free reserves negative and the Treasury-bill rate below the discount rate, the banks had an incentive to sell Treasury bills, rather than to borrow from the Federal Reserve, to satisfy their growing need for required reserves during the 1954–7 economic expansion. Consequently, the Federal Reserve had to either offset the banks' sales of Treasury bills with open-market purchases of them or to raise the discount rate "again and again," as Sproul had argued, "say in a period of increased seasonal demand for credit, to keep it in the proper position with respect to the bill rate" (FOMC *Minutes*, 14 September 1955, pp. 23–4).

The Federal Reserve was unwilling to conduct expansionary open-market operations during a period of economic expansion; nor was it willing to keep raising the discount rate every time the banks' sales of Treasury bills pushed the Treasury-bill rate to equality with it. Therefore, the Federal Reserve ended up simply allowing the Treasury-bill rate to move above the discount rate. In other words, the Federal Reserve ended up without a coherent operating procedure.

Given their overriding concern with wage negotiations and their hope that discount-rate increases would strengthen capital against labor, the majority of the members of the Federal Open Market Committee did not consider the incoherence of their operating procedure to be an important issue (see, for example, FOMC *Minutes*, 23 May 1956, pp. 29–31). Rather than trying to work out a coherent operating procedure, the Federal Open Market Committee was initially pre-occupied with the fact that only two regional banks increased their discount rates by one half of a percentage point in April 1956, as Balderston suggested, to 3 percent.[2] The other regional banks increased their discount rates to 2.75 percent and, throughout the spring of 1956, Governors Balderston, Martin, Mills, Robertson, and Shepardson argued that they should go to 3 percent because, as Balderston put it, "an increase [in the discount rate] to 3 per cent in one or two additional districts might induce prudence in impending steel industry moves to raise wages and prices" (FOMC *Minutes*, 9 May 1956, p. 14).

When an ultimately successful steel strike began on 17 July 1956, these five governors insisted that not just "one or two additional districts" but all the districts should increase their discount rates to 3 percent (see, for example, *FOMC Minutes*, 17 July 1956, pp. 7, 30, 34). On 3 August 1956, they got their way, largely because Sproul's refusal to go along with the discount-rate increases, and the reluctance of some non-New York regional banks to move before the Federal Reserve Bank of New York did, cost him his job. Alfred Hayes, the new president of the Federal Reserve Bank of New York, then became a resolute advocate of monetary restraint to fight wage-push inflation. Upon taking office, Hayes increased the New York bank's discount rate to the level of the other reserve banks. At his first meeting of the Federal Open Market Committee, Hayes explained his decision to increase the discount rate on the grounds that "the sizeable increases in steel workers' wages and steel prices are likely to start a chain reaction in other industries":

> The tendency toward price increases ... results primarily from recent wage increases rather than capacity limitations or demand pressures.

Eventual offsets to rising costs through increasing productivity are only a long range possibility and are no remedy for the inflationary threat in the near future.

(Hayes, FOMC *Minutes*, 21 August 1956, pp. 11–12)

The majority of members of the Federal Open Market Committee welcomed the 1957–8 recession as an opportunity to break the chain reaction of higher wages and prices that resulted from labor's redeployment of the strike weapon. The Committee's majority believed that the wage and benefit gains of the UAW in 1955 and of the United Steel Workers in 1956 caused the 1957–8 recession because, after being passed on in higher prices, they depressed aggregate demand (see, for example, FOMC *Minutes*, 14 September 1955, pp. 23–4; FOMC *Minutes*, 7 May 1957, pp. 40–1). The Committee's majority thus concluded that the economy should be revived by means of "a complete reversal of price increases already in effect and reflecting past wage increases" (FOMC *Minutes*, 7 January 1958, p. 32).

The Federal Open Market Committee's analysis of the cause of, and the solution to, the 1957–8 recession implied that stabilization policies would prolong the economy's stagnation. That is to say, by creating "the feeling on the part of industry that we [the Federal Open Market Committee] will provide all the money necessary to enable it to pass on to the consumer the amount of additional costs resulting from wage negotiations" (FOMC *Minutes*, 16 April 1957, p. 11), and thereby creating the kind of climate which "encourages management to accede to wage demands" (FOMC *Minutes*, 11 February 1958, p. 19), an easing of monetary policy in response to the 1957–8 recession would contribute to a postponement of the downward wage and price adjustments which were necessary, according to the Committee's majority, for economic recovery.

Instead of stabilization policies, the economic analysis of the cause of the 1957–8 recession by the majority of the members of the Federal Open Market Committee implied that implacable monetary restraint was the best way to shorten the period of stagnation of the economy. The Federal Reserve thus decided to increase the discount rate, when the recession began in August 1957, to "maintain as far as possible the kind of climate that would hold some restraint against wage moves" (FOMC *Minutes*, 1 October 1957, p. 23), or in order to maintain the kind of climate where wage negotiations would be conducted "without the illusion on either side as to the possibility of wage increases being passed on as price increases" (FOMC *Minutes*, 7 January 1958, p. 47). Indeed, during the first recession after the Treaty of Detroit's five-year no-strike pledge had expired, in 1957–8, Balderston went so far as to define

the mission of the Federal Reserve [as] control[ling] the money supply so effectively that inflationary tendencies might be curbed until such time as excess capacities serve as a break on cost increases and wage increases.

(Balderson, FOMC *Minutes*, 7 May 1957, pp. 35–6)

Balderston was not alone in his opinion. The following statement, that Martin had the chief economist of the Board of Governors (Allyn Young) read for him, sums up the general attitude of the Federal Reserve System toward the 1957–8 recession:

> Had not monetary policy validated the immediate postwar price level? Had not the post-Korean price level also been substantially validated? Had not monetary action aggressively met the threat of serious recession in 1953–54? ... Monetary policy is now getting under pressure to demonstrate once again its flexibility to prompt adaptation to relaxed output, employment, and credit market tensions. If credit ease is permitted to develop, or is actively fostered on the grounds of uncertainties, before more competitive conditions emerge in those markets experiencing the greatest expansion of demand, the only conclusion for the business and consumer community to reach is that the dollar depreciation of the past year and a half is to be validated.
>
> (Young, FOMC *Minutes*, 26 March 1957, pp. 13–16)

The majority of the members of the Federal Open Market Committee believed that its efforts to sustain a high discount rate during the 1957–8 recession strengthened capital against labor. For example, Shepardson noted a

> report in the newspapers this morning of a proposal by a leader of the AFL-CIO Building and Construction Trades Department for a moratorium on demands for wage increases. ... While this leader might not be speaking for labor generally, he [Shepardson] hoped there would not be any easing of the situation that would cause a cessation of this kind of thinking on the part of labor organizations.
>
> (Shepardson, FOMC *Minutes*, 3 December 1957, p. 30)

However, the Federal Reserve's ability to strengthen capital against labor was constrained by the fact that it was given independence from the Treasury Department in March 1951 in order to stabilize the economy, which was widely understood to mean attempting to counteract recessions as well as inflationary booms. Therefore, "the main problem" with the high discount-rate policy during the 1957–8 recession was one "of public relations in dealing with the feeling in some quarters that central banking policy was seeking a depression" (FOMC *Minutes*, 1 October 1957, pp. 23–4). This problem proved insurmountable and the Federal Reserve ended up easing policy and, thus, in the majority opinion of members of the Federal Open Market Committee, "creating demand by simply pumping up credit" (FOMC *Minutes*, 7 May 1956, pp. 40–1), or "putting out funds in the hope of creating employment where there was not consumer demand" (FOMC *Minutes*, 3 March 1959, p. 47).[3]

External pressures on the Federal Reserve for an easy monetary policy dissipated in 1958 when, for the first time, cheap foreign cars like the Volkswagen were imported on a significant scale and steel imports exceeded steel exports. In the face of such sobering signs of international competition, the automobile industry formed a united front against the UAW and spoke openly of a general lockout when the three-year contract came up for renewal in autumn 1958. In 1959, the steel industry also formed a united front, and U.S. Steel head, Roger Blough, called for "rolling back unionism" (Strauss, 1962, pp. 81–3; Davis 1986, p. 123).

At the same time that the outbreak of serious international competition thus enhanced the solidarity of capital, it eroded the solidarity of labor. For example, in the *New York Times* (28 October 1958, p. 29), A. H. Raskin wrote that workers, "amazingly," had come to

> mimic the position of the business community that higher wages were causing inflation. One unemployed worker suggested that firms would not produce goods in the United States with wages 50 cents an hour lower in foreign countries. He concluded that unions had to start worrying about creating jobs and stop worrying about getting higher wages for people who already had jobs.
> (Raskin, *New York Times*, 28 October 1958, p. 29)

The majority of the Federal Open Market Committee wanted to strengthen industry by encouraging this kind of thinking among workers. Consequently, the discount rate was increased to 2 percent at four regional banks in August 1958[4] because, as Martin put it, it was unclear "what was going to happen with regard to the current negotiations in the automobile industry" (FOMC *Minutes*, 9 September 1958, pp. 49–51, 54; see also Davis, 1986, p. 54). However, the other regional banks did not increase their discount rates because they were waiting for the Federal Reserve Bank of New York to act, and the Federal Reserve Bank of New York had returned to Sproul's position of dissenting from the use of tight monetary policy against wage-push inflation. For example, Hayes pointed out, quite correctly, that an incomes policy was more appropriate than monetary policy for coping with inflationary pressures:

> I [Hayes] would be the last to deny that inflation is a serious long-term problem, primarily because of the tendency of wage increases in key industries, in good times and bad, to exceed a reasonable share of national productivity gains. But I cannot see any justification for combatting this long-term threat by means of a rapid shift in monetary policy. ... Just what is the right remedy for this long-term wage-push inflationary threat, I am not sure. It may be some form of concentrated Government effort to discourage or prevent wage increases in excess of a reasonable share of national over-all productivity gains.
> (Hayes, FOMC *Minutes*, 9 September 1958, pp. 10–12;
> also see FOMC *Minutes*, 30 September 1958, p. 16;
> FOMC *Minutes*, 21 October 1958, p. 20)

To quell rumors of dissent within the Federal Reserve System, all the regional banks moved their discount rates to 2 percent in September 1958, thereby clearing the way for the majority of the Board of Governors to call for a discount-rate increase to 2.5 percent. But, again, the Federal Reserve Bank of New York balked, so only eight banks responded with discount-rate increases in October.[5] It was not until the AFL-CIO announced plans to expand its struggle against capital beyond the confines of collective bargaining and into the political arena, on 7 November 1958, that the Federal Reserve Bank of New ended its opposition to the use of tight monetary policy against wage-push inflation (*New York Times*, 8 November 1958, p. 1; FOMC *Minutes*, 10 November 1958, p. 14).

The Federal Reserve did nothing in winter 1958–9 because "all automobile manufacturers except Studebaker Packard had their labor contract dilemma behind them" (FOMC *Minutes*, 10 November 1958, p. 21). Nonetheless, the fact that all dissent within the Federal Reserve System to an anti-labor monetary policy dissipated in November 1958 permitted the Federal Reserve to increase the discount rate in March and May 1959. These increases were implemented, when the three-year contract signed by the United Steel Workers in 1956 came up for renewal, because "it appeared that the forthcoming wage negotiations were apt to set the stage for further acceleration" of the wage-price spiral (FOMC *Minutes*, 5 May 1959, p. 23). Hayes made the following statement to justify the March and May 1959 discount-rate increases:

> Numerous producers of manufactured goods are reported to be eager to raise their prices in view of the improved demand situation and to be only waiting for the expected rise in steel prices, following the current wage negotiations, before announcing increases for their own products. Thus the steel negotiations take on even more than usual significance in terms of probable widespread repercussions throughout the economy. ... The time has come for a decisive signal of the Federal Reserve System's determination to do its part to check inflationary trends. The discount rate is of course the most obvious instrument for giving such a signal.
>
> (Hayes, FOMC *Minutes*, 26 May 1959, pp. 16–17)

With the principal representative of "liberal" opinion within the Federal Reserve System thus parroting what had been the "conservative" position, the conservatives were able to become more extreme in their own opinions. For example, Shepardson justified his support for the discount-rate increases in March and May 1959 by attacking the principal plank of the Treaty of Detroit—namely, the link between real wages and labor productivity:

> He [Shepardson] was ... concerned by the line of thinking which held that as long as wage increases did not exceed productivity the situation might be all right. This, he felt, was a fallacy, and he saw no basis for agreement with the idea that wages should take all of the increased productivity. As he saw it, to accept such a view would mean automatically accepting the idea of inflation.
>
> (Shepardon, FOMC *Minutes*, 5 May 1959, p. 23)

Throughout the summer of 1959, the Federal Reserve wanted to continue increasing the discount rate to support the industrial bourgeoisie's efforts to prevent "an excessive wage settlement in the steel industry, and the probable impact of such a settlement in other industries" (FOMC *Minutes*, 16 June 1959, p. 10; FOMC *Minutes*, 28 July 1959, pp. 24–5). However, the Federal Reserve did nothing because of an overriding desire to see a 4.5 percent ceiling on new issues of government bonds removed. Throughout the summer, legislation to remove the interest-rate ceiling was under consideration in Congress. But opposition to higher interest rates had been building in Congress ever since the Federal Reserve began raising them in August 1958, and yet another discount-rate increase would have undermined whatever chances there were of passing the legislation (FOMC *Minutes*, 26 May 1959, p. 51). Martin expressed this constraint on U.S. monetary policy in summer 1959 as follows:

> The last thing he [Martin] would want to suggest ... would be to ease [Federal Reserve] System policy simply to obtain legislation to eliminate the interest rate ceiling on Treasury bonds. ... However, ... he felt it necessary to be careful that the System did not conduct itself in a way that might look like deliberate action to nettle people. Interest rates were now a major issue politically. They might be a national issue in 1960 or during the next few months, and at the moment he was not sure it would be possible to get a bill on the interest rate ceiling through Congress. ... At the moment the System was in the midst of a struggle to prevent the writing of policy into law.
>
> (Martin, FOMC *Minutes*, 7 July 1959, pp. 37–8)

On 18 August 1959, the House Ways and Means Committee voted a bill onto the House floor that would have eliminated the interest-rate ceiling on government bonds for three years. But the Ways and Means Committee immediately reversed itself, putting the issue off until the next session of Congress (FOMC *Minutes*, 18 August 1959, pp. 32–3).

As soon as the legislation to remove the interest-rate ceiling on government bonds died in committee, the Federal Reserve increased the discount rate one final time, to 4 percent in September 1959, because "a real showdown is in process in the current struggle in the steel industry" (FOMC *Minutes*, 22 September 1959, p. 12). As Martin put it:

> he found it difficult to separate the monetary politics from the economics of the situation. ... he was no better informed than the other members of the [Federal Open Market] Committee concerning what might happen with respect to the interest rate ceiling legislation. However ... he now questioned whether the [Federal Reserve] System could be in a situation of ... continuing to sit on the sidelines, as it had been doing for some time.
>
> (Martin, FOMC *Minutes*, 1 September 1959, p. 39)

There were no more discount-rate increases in 1959 because, when the depletion of steel inventories turned the steel strike in the proletariat's favor, President Dwight Eisenhower invoked the back-to-work provisions of the Taft–Hartley Act to end the strike. When the depletion of steel inventories began to turn the tide in the proletariat's favor, Kaiser Steel and other small producers broke ranks with the major steel producers and agreed to a 5 percent increase in total payroll. After President Eisenhower invoked the Taft–Hartley Act to force the United Steel Workers back to work, the major steel producers were able to compel their workers to settle for a 3.5 percent increase in wages and benefits (FOMC *Minutes*, 12 January 1960, p. 25; Davis, 1986, p. 123).

There were no more discount-rate increases in 1960, either, in spite of the fact that the Federal Reserve wanted to use them to support a concerted assault by capital on labor. The most important results of the industrial bourgeoisie's 1960 offensive were the loss of cost-of-living adjustments by the railroad and electrical-machinery workers, two defeats of the UAW in the aerospace industry (leading to the decertification of the union at Sikorsky), and a successful effort by General Electric to both reduce its cost of living adjustments and reintroduce incentive pay (Davis, 1986, p. 124). Shepardson, without dissent from his colleagues on the Federal Open Market Committee thus argued for continuing monetary restraint despite the 1960 recession, as follows:

> The country was going through some wholesome and salutary adjustments, painful to be sure, but adjustments that were needed for some time. ... Some of the price movements and some of the indications of a little more restraint in wage negotiations were sound and constructive developments.
>
> (Shepardson, FOMC *Minutes*, 13 December 1960, pp. 16–17)

Nonetheless, the Federal Reserve was forced to sit on the sidelines because the interest-rate ceiling on government bonds neutralized its ability to use discount-rate increases to strengthen capital against labor. Moreover, the Federal Reserve was under pressure from the Eisenhower administration not to derail Vice-President Richard Nixon's bid for the presidency.

After the 1960 presidential election, the Federal Reserve faced two new constraints on its ability to use discount-rate increases to strengthen capital against labor. The first constraint was the implementation of an incomes policy by the Kennedy administration. Aware of the inflationary pressures unleashed by the Treaty of Detroit during the 1961–2 rounds of wage negotiations in the automobile and steel industries, the Kennedy administration prescribed wage increases greater than the growth of labor productivity where they were low "because the bargaining position of workers had been weak" and wage increases less than the growth of labor productivity in industries where they had been high "because the bargaining position of workers had been especially strong" (Council of Economic Advisors, 1962, p. 189; also see Ackley 1966, p. 71, *passim*; Shultz and Aliber, 1966, p. 3; Solow, 1966, p. 42; Ross, 1966, pp. 119, 122, 124–5).

Leading factions of capital, adamantly opposed to this renewal of the movement toward social democracy, responded with capital flight. After all, an effective incomes policy ultimately implies a state bureaucracy to manage wages and prices in a way that undermines the fundamental tenet of a free-enterprise system—namely, the capacity of capitalists to make profits by charging whatever prices for their goods and services the market will bear. Consequently, any revival of the movement toward social democracy in the form of an incomes policy must be accompanied by capital controls.

The Kennedy administration postponed this logical implication of its income policy by means of the expedient called "operation twist"—the second constraint on the Federal Reserve's ability to use discount-rate increases to strengthen capital against labor. Operation Twist meant that the Federal Reserve could sell all the Treasury bills it wished, the key component of its tight monetary policy in the late 1950s. However, rather than restricting the supply of bank reserves (e.g. making free reserves negative), the Administration compelled the Federal Reserve to offset the sales of Treasury bills by purchases of long-term government bonds of equal value. The Administration hoped the sales of Treasury bills would put upward pressure on short-term interest rates, and thus staunch the capital flight, while the purchases of government bonds would put downward pressure on long-term interest rates, and thus stimulate domestic investments.

Unfortunately, Operation Twist did not affect the implacable logic of the revival of the movement toward social democracy, according to which the incomes policy would have to be either abandoned or complemented with capital controls. President Kennedy confronted this logic head-on in April 1962 when he forced Roger Blough, Chair of U.S. Steel, to rescind an announced steel-price increase. He then tried to change the subject with Operation Twist, leaving it to President Johnson, during the 1964–5 rounds of wage negotiations in the automobile and steel industries, to enact capital controls—namely, the Voluntary Foreign Credit Restraint Program of January 1965. It was at this point that the Federal Reserve revolted.

In 1964–5, as noted above, five members of the Board of Governors (C. Canby Balderston, Abbot Low Mills Jr., William McChesney Martin Jr., James Louis Robertson, and Charles N. Shepardson) were already committed to strengthening capital against labor by using high interest rates to precipitate then sustain a recession, and, even before the Johnson administration announced capital controls in January 1965, Alfred Hayes, President of the Federal Reserve Bank of New York, was rallying the rest of the Federal Open Market Committee to join the struggle. For example, in February 1964, Hayes had the First Vice-President of the Federal Reserve Bank of New York (William F. Treiber), present the following statement to the Federal Open Market Committee:

> There are indications that ... the United Automobile Workers will press for substantial wage increases, citing large increases in productivity and large profits in their ... industry[y]. ... While large wage increases in industries that have had above average increases in productivity may be absorbed without increases in prices in those industries, the large wage increases are

likely to foster corresponding wage increases elsewhere and push up wages generally faster than the increase in over-all productivity. The consequence could be a cost-push on prices.

(Treiber, FOMC *Minutes*, 11 February 1964, pp. 29–30)

In September 1964, after the tri-annual round of wage negotiations in the automobile industry was completed, Hayes then weighed in with this assessment of the situation:

The long record of price stability may now be in more serious jeopardy than at any time in recent years. . . . Although the auto industry itself apparently intends to absorb the higher costs without raising prices, there remains a grave danger that the generous settlements may have pervasive cost and price effects in other areas. The settlements, which were apparently in the range of 4½ percent per annum, exceeded both the 3.2 percent guideline [set by the Johnson administration] and the increases of somewhat over 3½ percent gained in each of the 1958 and 1961 [rounds of wage negotiations in the automobile industry] . . . With much of the latest increase taking the form of fringe benefits, it is not clear just how strong the influence will be on labor settlements in other industries, where fringes may tend to differ in nature and where there may be greater resistance on the part of managements. I should add, however, that greater resistance might result in serious strikes as an alternative to excessive cost increases, and the prospect of hard bargaining in the steel industry is nor reassuring. Furthermore, apart from labor cost effects, the auto settlements may have significant psychological influences on the direction of inflation. This could show up in greater willingness in other industries to attempt price increases, greater interest in inventory accumulation, and higher raw material prices.

(Hayes, FOMC *Minutes*, 29 September 1964, p. 20)

As a result of the tone set within the Federal Reserve System by these and similar statements, there was only one voice of dissent in February 1965, that of Governor George W. Mitchell, when the Federal Reserve moved to defy the Johnson administration's extension of the movement toward social democracy with the Voluntary Foreign Credit Restraint Program by once again implementing the form of monetary restraint designed in 1954–6—namely, open-market sales of Treasury bills to make free reserves negative, push the Treasury-bill rate above the discount rate, and thus trigger a "technical adjustment" of the latter to a higher level.

The large New York banks demanded this tight monetary policy in exchange for their submission to the Voluntary Foreign Credit Restraint Program, and Mitchell objected to tightening policy for this reason, arguing that, since only "a relatively small number of banks were foreign lenders," such a "*quid pro quo*" "was difficult to justify in a democracy" (FOMC *Minutes*, 12 January 1965, p. 11; FOMC *Minutes*, 15 June 1965, p. 49).

Nonetheless, Mitchell did not object in May 1965 when Robertson argued that:

> There was no gainsaying the possibility that an outsize steel wage contract and accompanying price increase might give rise to ramifying wage and price advances in numerous sectors of the economy.
>
> (Robertson, FOMC *Minutes*, 13 April 1965, p. 55)

> A significant and overt tightening action by the Federal Reserve would be called for as part of a vigorous program of counter-inflationary public action ... [if] ... business and labor expectations of inflation are so whetted as to start something of an administered wage-price spiral.
>
> (Robertson, FOMC *Minutes*, 11 May 1965, p. 46)

In June 1966, Mitchell overcame his initial reluctance and favored tight monetary policy because he too "was disturbed by the possibility of overly generous wage settlements" (FOMC *Minutes*, 28 June 1966, p. 50).[6]

The problem was how to implement such a tight monetary policy. In February 1965, aware that the penalty-rate policy had driveled into incoherence, and not being able to imagine an alternative, the Federal Reserve simply resorted to the tight monetary policy it had conducted between May 1954 and March 1956. It began with open-market sales of Treasury bills with the objective of moving free reserves "within $50 million of zero" (FOMC *Minutes*, 2 February 1965, p. 82). In March, the free-reserve target was lowered to "more often below zero than above" (FOMC *Minutes*, 2 March 1965, p. 61). By September, when net borrowed reserves were allowed to fluctuate "between $100 and $200 million on a weekly basis" (FOMC *Minutes*, 28 September 1965, p. 20), Hayes charted the future course of monetary policy as follows:

> We should try to move more decisively than we have done in recent months to check the excessive credit growth; and for this purpose an overt move seems required, combining a discount rate increase with some further increase in net borrowed reserves to the $200 to $250 million level. An increase in the prime rate[7] would almost certainly follow immediately. ... The ceilings under Regulation Q[8] would certainly have to be adjusted upward in the event of the policy move contemplated.
>
> (Hayes, FOMC *Minutes*, 28 September 1965, pp. 36–7)

Following Hayes's recommendation, net borrowed reserves were increased to the $200–$250 million range, triggering a discount-rate increase in December 1965. Nonetheless, Hayes's insistence that "the ceilings under Regulation Q would certainly have to be adjusted upward" with the discount-rate increase meant that the Federal Reserve failed to achieve its target of checking "the excessive rate of credit growth," for increasing the Regulation Q ceilings permitted banks to offer a yield on large-denomination certificates of deposit (CDs) that was higher than the yield on Treasury bills. The banks could thus obtain all the funds they wanted by giving firms an incentive to switch working capital from Treasury bills to CDs.[9]

What is more, as I explain in Chapter 5, the 1965 discount-rate increase unleashed a wave of price increases, since it allowed firms to defy the Johnson administration's incomes policy on the grounds that higher borrowing costs justified higher prices.

Hayes may have hoped that higher interest rates would reduce the demand for credit. But by early 1966 it was evident to most members of the Federal Open Market Committee that the demand for credit was interest-rate inelastic. Mitchell and Governor Arthur F. Brimmer, who replaced Balderston on the Board in 1966, thus took the lead in arguing that the Federal Reserve should restrict the supply of credit instead. To do this, they argued for open-market sales of Treasury bills designed to increase their yield above the Regulation Q ceilings on large-denomination CDs:

> The [Federal Open Market] Committee should have less implicit and explicit concern with the rate structure and more concern with availability ... the banking system was not doing all that it could to restrain the exuberance of its customers. That was because bankers were not sure just how far the Committee would go in permitting them to accommodate loan demands.
>
> (Mitchell, FOMC *Minutes*, 1 March 1966, pp. 79–80;
> also see FOMC *Minutes*, 10 May 1966, p. 67;
> FOMC *Minutes*, 7 June 1966, p. 86)

> it was important ... to let the market—and especially the larger banks—know that the [Federal Open Market] Committee did not subscribe to a pattern of activity in which those banks competed actively for funds to relend to their customers.
>
> (Brimmer, FOMC *Minutes*, 28 June 1966, p. 75)

> If the [Federal Reserve] System wanted to firm further it could get a considerable amount of restraint by reducing the ceiling rate on large-denomination CDs by as little as one-eighth of a percentage point. It was the anticipation of lenders that they might not be able to get funds in the future that was holding down the operations of financial intermediaries in general.
>
> (Mitchell, FOMC *Minutes*, 3 October 1967, p. 76)

In March 1966, the Federal Reserve decided to shift to this new operating procedure, based on restricting the availability of credit rather than increasing its cost. At that time, the reserve-bank presidents were told to have "informal discussions" with the "individual bankers in their Districts" to inform them that restraint on credit extensions was required at present, that it was not desirable to meet all demands for credit, and that the System did not intend to supply the reserves that would be needed to do so (Martin, FOMC *Minutes*, 1 March 1966, p. 96).

The first test of the new operating procedure came in the wake of the autumn 1967 tri-annual round of wage negotiations in the automobile industry, and whether or not they would serve as the model for a settlement in the steel industry during the 1968 tri-annual round of wage negotiations there. The following statements by Sherman Maisel (who replaced Mills on the Board in 1965), Robert Sherrill (who replaced Shepardson on the Board in 1967), and Robertson illustrate that the new operating procedure had ample support:[10]

[Do not increase the Regulation Q ceilings because] he [Maisel] feared a replay of the first four months of 1966 when, because of a concentration on marginal reserves, the System had allowed bank credit to expand at an inflationary rate in order to meet the greater demands for reserves from the banks as they expanded their time deposits with the aid given by the increase in the Q ceilings in December 1965.

(Maisel, FOMC *Minutes*, 5 March 1968, p. 99)

Bank managements viewed the level of the Q ceilings as an important determinant of the availability of funds to them, and the possibility that the ceilings might not be raised could have significant effects on their policies. To increase the ceilings before it was clearly necessary to do so would be to sacrifice an important psychological means for effecting restraint.

(Sherrill, FOMC *Minutes*, 5 March 1968, p. 104)

I [Robertson] would not favor lifting ceilings for the purpose of enabling large banks to expand their CDs in order to expand their loans and thus contradict the very purpose of restrictive monetary policy.

(Robertson, FOMC *Minutes*,
2 April 1968, p. 88)

In Chapter 6, I explain why this operating procedure failed to affect the 1967–8 rounds of wage negotiations in the automobile and steel industries. Indeed, unlike in the late 1950s, members of the Federal Open Market Committee did not even claim among themselves that they had had any affect. But this only hardened their resolve to clamp down further by means of the same operating procedure in anticipation of the 1970–1 rounds of wage negotiations. Sherrill, for example, proved a worthy successor to Shepardson. He greeted the first recession since 1960–1, which lasted from December 1969 to November 1970, with the following statement:

the economic expansion was slowing, although perhaps not as rapidly as might be necessary [for] ... business attitudes [to] ... be sufficiently affected by the time of the next round of wage negotiations to produce substantial resistance to demand for large increases. If such demands were not resisted inflationary conditions were likely to prevail for a long time ... it [was thus] ... important to avoid giving any indication of easing.

(Sherrill, FOMC *Minutes*, 25 November 1969, p. 76;
also see FOMC *Minutes*, 10 February 1970, pp. 58–9)

In anticipation of this opportunity to fight the inflationary pressures unleashed by the Treaty of Detroit by precipitating then sustaining a recession, Sherrill had thus embraced the new operating procedure adopted by the Federal Reserve in March 1966:

> Given continuation of the current Regulation Q ceilings, firming action of the type he [Sherrill] favored probably would trigger a sizeable amount of disintermediation. ... As pressure increased, bankers undoubtedly would begin to probe to discover the [Federal Reserve] Board's attitude concerning Q ceilings; and if it became clear that the Board was not disposed to raise the ceilings, their expectations would change rapidly. Bankers would in turn communicate their views to businessmen.
>
> (Sherrill, FOMC *Minutes*, 17 December 1968, p. 62)

> recent developments suggested that high interest rates alone were not the solution. ... Tight control over the availability of credit was likely to be the best approach; growth in bank credit had to be curbed.
>
> (Sherrill, FOMC *Minutes*, 14 January 1969, p. 59)

In the same way, Brimmer proved to be a worthy successor to Balderston. He greeted the 1969–70 recession with the following statement:

> the economy was slowing. Since that had been the Committee's objective ... it did not argue for providing banks with resources that would be used to finance greater spending ... the [Federal Open Market] Committee should be prepared to accept ... a decline in real GNP in maintaining present policy.
>
> (Brimmer, FOMC *Minutes*, 25 November 1969, p. 75;
> also see FOMC *Minutes*, 10 February 1970, pp. 59–60;
> FOMC *Minutes*, 20 October 1970, p. 54)

Also like Sherrill, Brimmer embraced the new operating procedure for fighting the inflationary pressures unleashed by the Treaty of Detroit by precipitating then sustaining a recession:

> He [Brimmer] was prepared to see the money market banks lose a substantial portion of their CDs. He hoped that such losses would lead banks to curtail loans to business customers.
>
> (Brimmer, FOMC *Minutes*, 14 January 1969, p. 58)

> the ceilings had been the cutting edge of policy recently. ... If they [i.e., the banks] were able to attract a substantial volume of time deposits as a result of an increase in the ceilings he [Brimmer] would expect them promptly to increase the rate at which they were making loan commitments. He favored no change in Q ceilings at this time.
>
> (Brimmer, FOMC *Minutes*, 24 June 1969, p. 82)

Sherrill and Brimmer were only joining the choir, led by Robertson, Mitchell, and Hayes. Robertson greeted the 1969–70 recession by saying that "holding on to general restraint for too long runs the risk of courting a significant recession. But I ... am not afraid of the spectre of recession (FOMC *Minutes*, 10 February 1970, p. 83). And of course by "general restraint" Robertson meant not increasing the Regulation Q ceilings because "the all too likely consequence" of doing so "would be to raise interest rates another notch, without any restraint on availability. Indeed, a Q ceiling increase could well let more funds flow through the banks, thus creating a more accommodative atmosphere" (FOMC *Minutes*, 1 April 1969, p. 102).

Mitchell also welcomed the 1969–70 recession by saying that monetary restraint "could slow" the inflationary pressures unleashed by the Treaty of Detroit "by creating and maintaining a climate of slow growth, low corporate profits, and underemployment of resources" (Mitchell, FOMC *Minutes*, 7 April 1970, p. 61). And by monetary restraint he also meant "the curtailment of bank credit expansion by fostering a continuing run-off of CDs at large banks" (FOMC *Minutes*, 4 February 1969, pp. 38, 64).

For his part, Hayes continued to rally the Federal Open Market Committee with statements like the following ones:

> the General Motor's settlement ... points to no diminution of upward wage pressures ... unemployment for a fairly extended period in the 5 to 5 ½ percent range might be a reasonable price to pay for checking the inflationary spiral.
>
> (Hayes, FOMC *Minutes*, 17 November 1970, p. 44)

> there would seem to be a serious risk that the business slowdown will be aborted, before it can have much effect on prices and wages. ... The outlook for major wage negotiations in 1970 is disturbing ... some moderate rise in unemployment is a necessary condition to checking the inflationary spiral. This is another way of saying "the slowdown is what we have been desperately trying to achieve. Let's not reverse it before it has had some results.
>
> (Hayes, FOMC *Minutes*, 10 February 1970, pp. 45–6;
> also see FOMC *Minutes*, 10 February 1970, pp. 46–7;
> FOMC *Minutes*, 20 October 1970, p. 41)

Indeed, Governor J. Dewey Daane was the only hold-out in the late 1960s for a stabilization policy, rather than a policy designed to fight the inflationary pressures unleashed by the Treaty of Detroit by precipitating then sustaining a recession—and even he came around (see, for example, FOMC *Minutes*, 10 February 1970, p. 16, 63), a conversion blandly noted by Hayes with the comment that he was "inclined to agree with Mr. Daane that a rather prolonged policy of monetary restraint will be ... necessary [to ensure] ... that the slowdown will ... last long enough to make a serious dent in the problem of inflation" (Hayes, FOMC *Minutes*, 25 November 1969, pp. 51–2).[11] So what went wrong? Why was it not until the 1973–5 recession that the Federal Reserve actually sustained its policy of monetary restraint? This is the topic of the next section.

Section 4.2 The Federal Reserve's Low-interest-rate Policy of 1970–2: Determinants and Constraints

In Section 4.1, I presented evidence that the principal goal of the Federal Reserve in the late 1960s was to fight wage-push inflation by supporting capital against labor in tri-annual rounds of wage negotiations in the automobile and steel industries, and that precipitating then sustaining a recession was their means. It looked as if the Federal Reserve had finally accomplished its purpose with the tight monetary policy in place at the onset of the recession, which lasted from December 1969 until November 1970, just as the 1970–1 wage negotiations in the automobile and steel industries were getting underway.

Nonetheless, the Federal Reserve eased monetary policy in February 1970, and kept it easy until February 1972, as represented, for example, by a fall in the federal funds rate[12] from about 9 percent in February 1970 to about 3.3 percent February 1972.

Arthur F. Burns, who replaced William McChesney Martin Jr. as Chair of the Board of Governors of the Federal Reserve System on 30 January 1970, eased monetary policy at his first meeting of the Federal Open Market Committee (FOMC Minutes, 10 February 1970, pp. 3, 83–4) even though the following nine members of the Federal Open Market Committee argued for continued restraint: 1) Bopp (FOMC *Minutes*, 10 February 1970, pp. 53–4); 2) Brimmer (FOMC *Minutes*, 10 February 1970, pp. 59–60); 3) Coldwell (FOMC *Minutes*, 10 February 1970, pp. 76, 80); 4) Daane (FOMC *Minutes*, 10 February 1970, p. 63); 5) Hayes (FOMC *Minutes*, 10 February 1970, pp. 46–7); 6) Kimbrel (FOMC *Minutes*, 10 February 1970, p. 95); 7) Morris (FOMC *Minutes*, 10 February 1970, p. 81); 8) Robertson (FOMC *Minutes*, 10 February 1970, pp. 82–3); and 9) Sherrill (FOMC *Minutes*, 10 February 1970, pp. 58–9).

Only Sherman Maisel (FOMC *Minutes*, 10 February 1970, p. 61) and George F. Mitchell (FOMC *Minutes*, 10 February 1970, p. 64) supported Burns' decision to ease. The following statements are representative of the majority opinion:

> Those present were almost unanimously of the view that the Federal Reserve should not ease its stance at this time.
>
> (Daane, FOMC *Minutes*, 10 February 1970, p. 16)

> the [Federal Open Market] Committee was ... at a crucial turning point; if it backed away, all its efforts and the costs already paid could prove to have been in vain.
>
> (Coldwell, FOMC *Minutes*, 10 February 1970, p. 76)

> It took a great deal of effort to achieve the current degree of fiscal and monetary restraint. If we let go now ... I [Robertson] think general

stabilization tools will have been discredited and the country could be drawn to a whole new set of harsh and arbitrary controls. That eventuality I [Robertson] regard as so damaging to our long-run national interest that we must be very careful not to trigger it.

(Robertson, FOMC *Minutes*, 10 February 1970, p. 83)

This period of easy monetary policy has become paradigmatic among ortho-dox monetary theorists (i.e. Monetarists, New Classical economists, and New Keynesians)[13] of how attempts by the Federal Reserve to stabilize the economy at full employment simply create the conditions for higher inflation in the future. John T. Woolley (1984, chapter 8), Steven M. Goldfeld and Lester V. Chandler (1985, p. 575), and Donald F. Kettl (1986, chapter 5) add the twist that, by easing monetary policy in 1970–2, the Federal Reserve not only attempted to counteract the recession but also tried to help re-elect President Nixon in November 1972. Rather than the Nixon administration convincing the Federal Reserve to lower interest rates as part of Nixon's re-election strategy, I show in this section that the Federal Reserve used temporary increases in the federal funds rate to convince the Administration to take actions to hold wages down. In other words, during the 1970–1 period, effective pressure was exerted by the Federal Reserve on the Administration, not by the Administration on the Federal Reserve.

My thesis is that the Federal Reserve's role as manager of the U.S. bank cartel prevented it from engaging in the class struggle in the 1970–1 period, in spite of its desire, documented in Section 4.1, to let the recession weaken labor during the 1970–1 wage negotiations in the automobile and steel industries. In other words, the Federal Reserve eased monetary policy to protect the liquidity of the U.S. bank cartel, thereby subordinating the long-term interests of capital as a whole, as it perceived them, to the short-term interests of a particular faction of capital.

In the late 1960s, the U.S. bank cartel secured its liquidity by issuing large-denomination CDs, Eurodollar deposits, and commercial paper. In Section 4.1, I provided evidence that in the late 1960s the Federal Reserve decided to use Regulation Q ceilings to close the banks off from the CD market. In Chapter 6, I show that, by the end of 1969, it had also closed the U.S. bank cartel off from the Eurodollar market. The bank cartel was thus compelled to secure its liquidity positions in the commercial-paper market (see, for example, FOMC *Minutes*, 12 August 1969, p. 23).

However, Congress considered it unjust that the U.S. bank cartel was able to secure its liquidity positions while the Federal Reserve used contractionary open-market operations and high interest rates to squeeze the liquidity out of the thrift industry, and thus out of the housing market. Consequently, Congress passed legislation authorizing the Federal Reserve to put interest-rate ceilings and reserve requirements on bank issues of commercial paper. To compel the Federal Reserve to use its new authority, the House of Representatives also passed legislation that, among other things (noted below), posed a direct threat to the Federal Reserve's independence by instructing it to sustain a 4 percent annual rate of growth of the money supply, narrowly defined as M_1 (*New York Times*, 8 February 1970, p. 18; *New York Times*, 24 March 1970, p. 63; *New York Times*, 10 May 1970, section 3, p. 7).[14]

Ironically, Milton Friedman (1962, p. 188, *passim*), alone among prominent monetary economists, was arguing in the late 1960s that the Federal Reserve was using its independence to manage the U.S. bank cartel rather than stabilize the economy at full employment with price stability. His argument, which carried the day in late 1969, was that Federal Reserve independence should be ended in favor of a Congressionally mandated money-supply rule. I return to this issue in Chapter 7, where I argue that an interest-rate rule would be more effective.

To thwart the danger that monetary policy would be written into law in this way, the Federal Reserve was compelled to announce on 29 October 1969, effective 2 December, interest-rate ceilings on bank issues of commercial paper. As Martin put it, the Federal Reserve was going "to apply Regulation Q to funds received by member banks from the issuance of commercial paper or similar obligations by bank holding companies or collateral affiliates" (Martin, FOMC *Minutes*, 25 November 1969, p. 5).

The Manager of the Federal Reserve's Open Market Account (Holmes) summarized for the Federal Open Market Committee the effect of this new rule on market participants as follows:

> the Board [of Governors]'s proposed ruling with respect to commercial paper outstanding was generally regarded—particularly by those banks with paper outstanding—as an indication of the [Federal Reserve] System's intention to pursue a policy of relentless pressure on the banking system.
>
> (Holmes, FOMC *Minutes*, 25 November 1969, p. 32)

In response, the U.S. bank cartel insisted that restrictions on their ability to issue commercial paper be accompanied by increases in the interest-rate ceilings on CDs (FOMC *Minutes*, 16 December 1969, pp. 50, 63, 80, 85; FOMC *Minutes*, 15 January 1970, pp. 38, 95; *New York Times*, 12 January 1970, p. 38; *New York Times*, 21 January 1970, p. 1).

Higher interest-rate ceilings on CDs would allow the U.S. bank cartel to bid more funds away from the thrift industry and thus the housing market. Therefore, on 18 January 1970, the National Association of Homebuilders, the most influential Congressional lobby at the time, adopted a resolution against higher interest-rate ceilings on CDs (*New York Times*, 19 January 1970, p. 75). It thus came as no surprise that, after the Federal Reserve announced increases in the interest-rate ceilings on CDs on 20 January (*New York Times*, 21 January 1970, p. 58), the Democratic caucus of the House of Representatives unanimously adopted a resolution urging the "appropriate committees" to "draft a specific program to combat high interest rates and to bring about a more equitable and effective monetary policy for the nation" (Edwin L. Dale, *New York Times*, 22 January 1970, p. 49). In addition, Senator William Proxmire, Democrat from Wisconsin, attached an amendment to an omnibus housing bill that was designed to force the Federal Reserve to lend directly to the housing industry (see, for example, FOMC *Minutes*, 7 April 1970, pp. 51–2).

In short, Congress would not allow the Federal Reserve to continue its tight monetary policy unless it was applied to the U.S. bank cartel as well as to the thrifts and the housing industry. On the other hand, the U.S. bank cartel would not allow the Federal Reserve to jeopardize their liquidity positions. Caught between a rock and a hard place, the Federal Reserve eased monetary policy (see, for example, FOMC *Minutes*, 15 January 1970, pp. 35–6, 90; *New York Times*, 8 February 1970, pp. 1, 18; *New York Times*, 10 February 1970, p. 55).

Even though interest rates (e.g. the federal funds rate) fell precipitously from February 1970 to February 1972, the Federal Reserve remained preoccupied with weakening labor in the 1970–1 tri-annual rounds of wage negotiations in the automobile and steel industries. The contradictory pressures from Congress and the U.S. bank cartel prevented the Federal Reserve from using high interest rates to weaken labor on its own. Nonetheless, twice during the 1970–1 wage negotiations the Federal Reserve increased interest rates long enough to compel the Nixon administration to take actions to hold wages down.

The first time the Federal Reserve increased interest rates, with the aim of pressuring the Administration to hold wages down, was in April 1970. As the following statements by Governors James Louis Robertson and Arthur Burns (who replaced Martin as Chair of the Board of Governors in February 1970) illustrate, the Federal Reserve increased interest rates in April 1970 because an unexpected postal workers' strike prompted Congress and the Administration to legislate retroactive pay raises (also see, for example, FOMC *Minutes*, 7 April 1970, pp. 27, 35, 40, 44; FOMC *Minutes*, 5 May 1970, p. 44):[15]

> the whole business picture had changed ... because of the way the Government had given in to the demands of postal workers and was proposing to pass the costs on to consumers in the form of price increases. He [Robertson] thought that would have important implications for the way in which businesses reacted to wage demands.
>
> (Robertson, FOMC *Minutes*, 7 April 1970, p. 48)

> There had been an insurrection against the Government, and the Government had dealt with it in a manner that resulted in a very sharp increase in the pay of Government employees. ... Many people had been hoping that the Government would set an example of moderation for private industry. ... It now appeared, however, that the Government might be leading the wage parade. ... he [Burns] was distressed by the fact that the Government had set an example of pushing up wages and had lost its strong moral position in its effort to keep wages under restraint.
>
> (Burns, FOMC *Minutes*, 7 April 1970, pp. 49–50)

As the Federal Reserve feared, the success of the postal workers galvanized private-sector workers.[16] The Federal Reserve was most concerned with the wage negotiations in the automobile industry. When they began in mid-September, the UAW planned to demand cost-of-living adjustments.[17]

Congressional pressures prevented the Federal Reserve from acting on its own to help the automobile industry in its struggle with the UAW. For example, the Federal Reserve's April 1970 increase in interest rates in response to the postal workers' strike prompted a subcommittee of the House Banking Committee to recommend a National Development Bank (see, for example, *New York Times*, 13 May 1970, p. 72).[18] In addition, on 12 May 1970, the Senate Banking Committee began hearings on the legislation that the House of Representatives passed in October 1969. The House version of the bill not only dictated the rate of growth of M_1, as noted above, it also dictated how the banks could use the funds deposited with them. Along with the National Development Bank, this legislation thus posed the most serious threat since the New Deal in the early 1930s to the prerogatives of the U.S. bank cartel. As an analysis in the *New York Times* put it, the legislation posed

> the basic question ... [of] whether a decentralized system of economic decision-making will be preserved or whether, reflecting Governmental impatience at the difficulty of solving intractable social problems, the capital markets will increasingly be made subject to centralized control aimed at accomplishing a variety of public policy objectives.
>
> (*New York Times*, 10 May 1970, section 3, p. 7)

The only way to stop the legislative momentum toward greater governmental control of capital was to make money and credit readily available at low interest rates. Yet the Federal Reserve managed to avoid this inevitability until 17 June 1970, when President Nixon caved in to the Federal Reserve's increasingly shrill demands for an incomes policy (see, for example, FOMC *Minutes*, 7 April 1970, pp. 44–5, 49; FOMC *Minutes*, 21 July 1970, p. 49; FOMC *Minutes*, 18 August 1970, p. 66; *New York Times*, 5 May 1970, p. 72; *New York Times*, 6 May 1970, p. 65; *New York Times*, 9 May 1970, p. 35; *New York Times*, 10 May 1970, section 3, p. 1; *New York Times*, 15 May 1970, p. 51; *New York Times*, 17 May 1970, section 3, pp. 1, 5; *New York Times*, 18 May 1970, p. 47).

This flurry of prominent newspaper coverage in May 1970 reflected the turmoil in financial markets as the U.S. bank cartel panicked, just as it had in August 1966, in the face of the Federal Reserve's advocacy of an incomes policy, rather than monetary policy, to cope with the wage-price spiral. Indeed, May 1970 is interpreted in the extant literature (e.g. by Minsky 1986; Wolfson, 1986) as the second postwar financial crisis. And just as with the first postwar financial crisis in August 1966, it is not understood as a political question but as a problem of financial instability. I return to this topic in Chapter 5.

The second time the Federal Reserve increased short-term interest rates (i.e. the federal funds rate), with the aim of pressuring the Administration to hold down wages, during the general downward trend in interest rates from February 1970 to February 1972, was in March 1971. The trigger this time was the Federal

Reserve's frustration with President Nixon's hapless efforts to implement the incomes policy, announced in June 1970. The majority of members of the Federal Open Market Committee thought the Administration's incomes policy had failed in November 1970, when General Motors granted the UAW cost-of-living adjustments as well as a 12.5 percent first-year wage increase. Nonetheless, it was not until March 1971, when the Administration made public, but futile, efforts to hold down wages in the construction industry, that the Federal Reserve decided to raise the federal funds rate because "more had to be done in the general area of incomes policy" (FOMC *Minutes*, 9 March 1971, p. 39; also see FOMC *Minutes*, 17 November 1970, pp. 10, 43–6, 52, 54–5, 65, 101; FOMC *Minutes*, 15 December 1970, pp. 49, 77; FOMC *Minutes*, 9 February 1971, pp. 43, 50; FOMC *Minutes*, 6 April 1971, p. 36).

The Federal Reserve continued to increase the federal funds rate until President Nixon announced a wage and price freeze in August 1971 (see, for example, FOMC *Minutes*, 27 July 1971, pp. 5, 55–6; FOMC *Minutes*, 24 August 1971, p. 4). That is to say, the federal funds rate rose from about 3.5 percent in March 1971 to about 5.5 percent in August 1971, before trending downwards again to about 3.3 percent in February 1972. The following statement by the Chair of the Board of Governors, Arthur Burns, illustrates not only that the Federal Reserve increased the federal funds rate in March 1971 in order to influence government economic policy, but also the Federal Reserve's underlying preoccupation with class struggle:

> the Administration had been much too slow to recognize the need for an effective incomes policy. .... Years ago, when business activity turned down, prices would respond—with some lag—not by rising more slowly but by declining; and wages would follow. That response had become progressively weaker after World War I, and of late one found that at a time when unemployment was increasing prices continued to advance at an undiminished pace and wages rose at an increasing pace ... one element in the (new) situation was the expansion of trade unionism in the public sector over the past decade. There had been numerous strikes of public service employees—strikes against the Government—and most of them had been successful in the sense that the wage demands had been met. That ... had a profound influence on the entire labor movement; in light of the evidence, it was judged that the Government lacked the power or the will to curb abuses in the market place. Hence, trade unions have become bolder.
>
> (Burns, FOMC *Minutes*, 8 June 1971, pp. 49–51, 53)

Burns mentioned other factors strengthening labor, such as the expansion of welfare programs, which Burns considered a government subsidy of strikers, before concluding that any efforts by the Federal Reserve to weaken labor "would lead many observers to wonder about the nature and purposes of the [Federal Reserve] System and would produce strongly negative reactions in Congress and the Administration" (FOMC *Minutes*, 8 June 1971, p. 75). In short, the Federal Reserve had to content itself with increasing the federal funds rate until the

Administration could be convinced to announce a wage and price freeze—not until recession broke organized labor.

In summary, the Federal Reserve was preoccupied with the struggle between capital and labor over the terms of the employment relation. But its role as manager of the U.S. bank cartel forced it to subordinate this preoccupation to the imperative of guaranteeing the liquidity positions of the U.S. bank cartel. Its advocacy of an incomes policy, and thus the two upward spikes of the federal funds rate during 1970–1, when its trend was downward, resulted from this preoccupation.

When Congress adjourned in late 1971 without passing the legislation noted above, the Federal Reserve returned to its policy of the 1950s and 1960s of trying to weaken labor by increasing interest rates. Its effective advocacy of an incomes policy thus came to an end, as did the incomes policy.

Section 4.3 The Federal Reserve's Tight Monetary Policy during the 1973–5 Recession

During the 1973–5 recession, the Federal Reserve broke with its perceived practice of easing monetary policy during recessions in order to raise short-term interest rates. It was this unprecedented decision to tighten monetary policy that makes the Federal Reserve's behavior during the 1973–5 recession especially useful for differentiating the radical political economic approach, which analyzes monetary policy in terms of class and intra-class conflicts, from the orthodox approaches to the analysis of monetary policy. In this section, I show that the orthodox approaches try, but fail, to account for the tightening of monetary policy during the 1973–5 recession as an effort to stabilize the economy at full employment with price stability. I then show that the radical political economic approach accounts for the tightening of monetary policy as an effort to weaken labor during the 1973–4 tri-annual rounds of wage negotiations in the automobile and steel industries.

Table 4.1 is designed to show the singularity of the Federal Reserve's tight monetary policy during the 1973–5 recession.

Column two of Table 4.1 shows the level of the short-term interest rate controlled by the Federal Reserve at the beginning of the recessions in the U.S. since March 1951, when the Federal Reserve obtained control of short-term interest rates.[19] During the recessions reported in the first three rows of Table 4.1, the Treasury-bill rate was the Federal Reserve's control variable. During the recessions reported in rows four through eight, the Federal Reserve controlled the federal funds rate (the interbank lending rate).

Column three of Table 4.1 reports the highest level of the Federal Reserve's control variable during each recession. And column four reports the months that elapsed between the beginning of the recession and the highest level of the Federal Reserve's control variable.

Note that in four of the eight recessions the highest level obtained by the Federal Reserve's control variable was its level at the beginning of the recessions. That is to say, in July 1953, December 1969, July 1981, and June 1990,

Table 4.1 The Federal Reserve's control variable during the last eight recessions (percent per annum)

(1)	(2)	(3)	(4)	(5)
Recession	*Level at the cyclical peak*	*Highest level during the recession*	*Months from (2) to (3)*	*Months to level below (2)*
1) July 53/May 54	2.1	2.1	0	1
2) Aug. 57/Apr. 58	3.4	3.6	1	3
3) Apr. 60/Feb. 61	3.2	3.4	1	2
4) Dec. 69/Nov. 70	9.0	9.0	0	3
5) Nov. 73/Mar. 75	**10.0**	**12.9**	**8**	**12**
6) Jan. 80/July 80	13.8	17.6	3	4
7) July 81/Nov. 82	19.0	19.0	0	1
8) June 90/Mar. 91	8.3	8.3	0	1

Sources: CITIBASE and the National Bureau of Economic Research.
Note: The Treasury-bill rate was the Federal Reserve's control variable in the 1950s and the early 1960s. Since the late 1960s, the Federal Reserve's control variable has been the federal funds rate.

the Federal Reserve either decided or was compelled to ease monetary policy as soon as the recessions began.

In two of the remaining four recessions, which began in August 1957 and April 1960, the Federal Reserve continued to raise its control variable for only one month after the cyclical peak in the economy. Again, it appears indisputable that the Federal Reserve either decided or was compelled to ease monetary policy as soon as the recessions began.

In contrast, row five of column four shows that the Federal Reserve did not stop raising its control variable (i.e. the federal funds rate) until the eighth month of the 1973–5 recession. That is to say, the Federal Reserve raised the federal funds rate to 12.9 percent in July 1974, almost three percentage points higher than its 10 percent level at the beginning of the recession, in November 1973.

The 1980 recession is the only other recession during which the Federal Reserve raised its control variable more than a couple of tenths of a percentage point above its level at the beginning of the recession. That is to say, the Federal Reserve raised the federal funds rate to 17.6 percent in April 1980, almost four percentage points higher than the 13.8 percent level of the federal funds rate at the beginning of the recession, in January 1980. Nonetheless, the Federal Reserve increased the federal funds rate for over twice as long during the 1973–5 recession than during the 1980 recession: for eight months as opposed to three (see rows five and six of column four). What is more, whereas the Federal Reserve reversed course during the fourth month of the 1980 recession and reduced the federal funds rate below its level at the beginning of the recession, the Federal Reserve kept the federal funds rate above its level at the beginning of the 1973–5 recession for a full year (see rows five and six of column five). Figure 4.1 illustrates the mainstream explanations of why the Federal Reserve pursued this singularly tight monetary policy despite the 1973–5 recession.

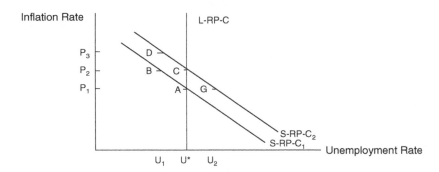

Figure 4.1 Phillips-curve (P-C) analyses of the effects of monetary policy, in both the short-run and the long-run.

Orthodox monetary theorists (i.e. Monetarists, New Classical economists, and New Keynesians)[20] assume a short-period trade-off between the inflation rate and the unemployment rate, represented by the negatively sloped short-period Phillips curve.[21] However, in the long-period, as explained in Chapter 1, orthodox monetary theorists assume that the forces of demand and supply in the labor market cause the real wage to adjust to the full employment level, represented in Figure 4.1 by the vertical long-period Phillips curve at the full-employment level of the unemployment rate (U^*). Anyone unemployed at U^* is deemed by orthodox monetary theorists to be voluntarily unemployed. That is to say, they are assumed to be unwilling to accept employment at the real wage which clears the labor market.

For orthodox monetary theorists, point A in Figure 4.1 represents a Golden Age of full employment with price stability before the mid 1960s, when President Johnson launched his budget-busting wars on poverty at home and communism abroad. Monetarists and New Classical economists allege that the Federal Reserve accommodated Johnson's budget deficits by increasing the rate of growth of the stock of money (e.g. M_1), which is represented by a movement along the first short-period Phillips curve, from point A to point B.

Given that there was full employment at point A, by moving the economy to point B, the Federal Reserve's accommodation of the government's budget deficits caused excess aggregate demand, and thus an increase in the inflation rate, from P_1 to P_2. Monetarists account for the fall in the unemployment rate, despite their claim that U^* represents full employment, by arguing that corporations, still willing to pay the same real wage, offered their workers higher money wages to compensate for the higher prices. But the workers, plagued with adaptive rather than rational expectations, confused the money-wage increases offered by corporations with real-wage increases, and thus increased the supply of labor, from U^* to U_1. When workers realized their mistake, they withdrew the additional labor, which is represented by a shift-out of the short-period Phillips curve, and by the economy moving from point B to point C. In short, for Monetarists, the Federal Reserve's accommodation of the government's budget deficits caused a short-period fall in the unemployment rate, but in the long-period all that remained was a higher inflation rate.

New Classical economists agree with the Monetarists about everything except how long it takes workers' inflationary expectations to catch up with the actual inflation rate, and thus how long it takes the short-period Phillips curve to shift out. Whereas Monetarists argue that the Federal Reserve's accommodation of the government's budget deficits reduces unemployment long enough to explain a political business cycle during Nixon's re-election campaign (see, for example, Willet, 1988), New Classical economists argue that the adjustment back to the long-period Phillips curve is more or less instantaneous (see, for example, Fellner, 1978, 1980).

No matter how long it took the economy to get to point C in Figure 4.1, Monetarists and New Classical economists agree that the only way the Federal Reserve could restore the economy to its original position of full employment with price stability at point A was to stop accommodating the government's budget deficits. The Federal Reserve allegedly took this advice during the 1973–5 recession by resolving to slow down the rate of growth of the money supply (M_1). In terms of Figure 4.1, the Federal Reserve thus resolved to move the economy along the second Phillips curve, from point C to point G. Interest rates increased in the short-period, thereby causing unemployment to rise from U^* to U_2. But as soon as workers realized that the rate of growth of the stock of money had slowed down, and that the inflation rate had thus fallen from P_2 to P_1, the short-period Phillips curve would shift back in so that the economy would move from point G to point A.

As can be seen in Table 4.2—which presents data on the midpoint of the Federal Reserve's target ranges for the rate of M_1 growth (column two), the estimated rate of M_1 growth (column three), and the federal funds rate (column four)—it is plausible to argue that, from February to June 1974, the rise in the federal funds rate was an unfortunate but necessary price to pay for regaining control of the rate of growth of the stock of money (M_1).

However, the Federal Reserve's behavior from July 1974 to February 1975 is inexplicable from a Monetarist or New Classical perspective. Monetarist and New Classical monetary theories prescribe that the Federal Reserve should have decreased the federal funds rate by however much was necessary to prevent M_1 growth from falling short of the midpoint of its targeted growth rate. Yet there is overwhelming archival evidence that the Federal Reserve failed to decrease the federal funds rate sufficiently to increase the rate of growth of M_1 during the summer and fall of 1974 because "it really wanted a very tight policy" regardless of the rate of M_1 growth (Mayer, 1981, p. 65; also see, for example, Lombra, 1988, p. 360; FOMC *Minutes*, 18 June 1974, p. 52; FOMC *Minutes*, 16 July 1974, pp. 33, 37; FOMC *Minutes*, 20 August 1975, p. 87). For example, there were no objections in June 1974 when George Mitchell, a member of the Board of Governors, told his colleagues on the Federal Open Market Committee that "a slowing of M_1 ... no matter how large, should be accepted (FOMC *Minutes*, 18 June 1974, p. 69).

Table 4.2 Targeted and estimated M_1[1] growth rates

(1)	(2)	(3)	(4)
Year and month	*Midpoint of range for M_1 growth*	*Estimated rate of M_1 growth*[2]	*Federal funds rate*
73.11	5.5	6.4	10.0
73.12	4.5	4.9	10.0
74.1	4.5	4.0	9.6
74.2	0	11.8	9.0
74.3	7.0	9.2	9.4
74.4	5.0	6.5	10.0
74.5	5.0	6.7	11.0
74.6	5.5	8.3	11.9
74.7	4.0	3.2[3]	12.9
74.8	5.75	2.6	12
74.9	4.5	1.7	11.3
74.1	6.0	5.6	10.1
74.11	8.0	6.4	9.4
74.12	6.0	1.1	8.5
75.1	5.0	−2.3	7.1
75.2	6.5	7.0	6.2

Sources: CITIBASE and Mayer (1981: 63).

[1] M_1 is defined as currency in circulation and demand deposits.

[2] As given at the next Federal Open Market Committee meeting.

[3] The series was revised.

New Keynesian monetary theorists use Okun's Law—which states that a real growth rate greater (less) than 2.25 percent causes the unemployment rate to fall (rise) (see, for example, Dornbusch and Fisher, 1994, pp. 17–18)—to explain why the Federal Reserve wanted a tight monetary policy during the 1973–5 recession regardless of the rate of M_1 growth. New Keynesians define U^* in Figure 4.1 as the unemployment rate which corresponds to a 2.25 percent real growth rate, and thus call U^* the non-accelerating inflation rate of unemployment (NAIRU). They attribute the movement along the short-period Phillips curve, from point A to point B, to the Federal Reserve's decision, during the late 1960s and early 1970s, to keep the federal funds rate so low that the real growth rate exceeded 2.25 percent. The short-period Phillips curve shifted out, according to New Keynesians, because the excess aggregate demand pressures caused by this low-interest-rate policy created conditions under which workers obtained changes in social programs that improved their standard of living (i.e. the social programs increased the real wage, broadly defined, and made it downwardly inflexible).[22] The economy then moved from point B to point D because the Federal Reserve sustained its low-interest-rate policy despite the new social programs.

Once the economy had moved to point D, New Keynesians allege that raising the federal funds rate to a level corresponding to a 2.25 percent real growth rate would only move the economy to point C in Figure 4.1. Therefore, the only way the Federal Reserve could restore the economy to full employment with price stability, at point A, was to raise the federal funds rate high enough to move the economy along the second short-period Phillips curve, from point D to point G, then keep the economy at point G until the higher unemployment rate of U_2 compelled workers to give up their earlier gains. It is plausible to argue that this is what the Federal Reserve was trying to do during the 1973–5 recession (see, for example, Lombra and Moran, 1980; Lombra, 1988, pp. 349–50).

The problem with the New Keynesian explanation of U.S. monetary policy during the 1973–5 recession is the overwhelming archival evidence that the Federal Reserve lowered the federal funds rate during the second part of the 1973–5 recession not in order to stabilize the economy at point A in Figure 4.1, but because of its desire to put a damper on public discussions of the need for fiscal programs that would be far more difficult than lower interest rates to reverse in the future. As Frank E. Morris, President of the Federal Reserve Bank of Boston, put it:[23]

> In order to restrain the contraction in business activity to the sort of mild recession that would be productive in reducing the rate of inflation over the longer run ... monetary policy had to be formulated on the assumption that the deeper the recession proved to be, the greater were the probabilities that Government policies adopted to combat it would produce too sharp a recovery.
>
> (Morris, FOMC *Minutes*, 15 October, 1974, p. 69)

Rather than trying to stabilize the economy at full employment with price stability, at point A in Figure 4.1, the Federal Reserve was preoccupied during the 1973–5 recession with the implications for U.S. corporations and banks of the successful formation of the oil cartel, the Organization of Petroleum Exporting Countries (OPEC), which quadrupled the price of oil, right after a series of natural calamities and synchronized cyclical expansions in the advanced capitalist countries caused the prices of other primary commodities and food to soar. In October 1974, *Business Week* summed up the situation confronting U.S. capital as follows:

> It is inevitable that the U.S. economy will grow more slowly. ... Some people will obviously have to do with less. ... The basic health of the U.S. is based on the basic health of its corporations and banks. ... Yet it will be a hard pill for many Americans to swallow—the idea of doing with less so that big business can have more.
>
> (quoted in Steinberg *et al.*, 1978, p. 6)

Because of its independence from democratic accountability, the Federal Reserve took the lead in trying to convince "many Americans" that they would have to do "with less so big business can have more." First, in September 1973, the Federal Reserve raised the federal funds rate to the unprecedented level of 10.8 percent in order to have a psychological effect on labor negotiations then coming to a head in the automobile industry. The Federal Reserve judged, correctly it turned out, that the UAW would not be able to protect their real wage from rising prices, of food in particular, in a situation dominated by public discussions of the unprecedentedly high interest rates. It was only after the UAW accepted defeat, and settled for a 6.2 percent money-wage increase in the first year of a three-year contract, that the Federal Reserve lowered the federal funds rate (see, for example, FOMC *Minutes*, 21 August 1973, p. 34; FOMC *Minutes*, 18 September 1973, p. 20; FOMC *Minutes*, 2 October 1973, pp. 21–6; FOMC *Minutes*, 17–18 December 1973: p. 73).

The Federal Reserve's decision to start raising the federal funds rate again in February 1974 also resulted from its desire to convince "many Americans" that they would have to do "with less so that big business can have more." That is to say, the Federal Reserve started raising the federal funds rate because retired workers in the aluminum industry succeeded in protecting themselves from the rising prices by negotiating cost-of-living adjustments (COLAs). The Federal Reserve hoped that a public discussion of the higher interest rates despite stagnate growth would dampen the exuberance of the United Steel Workers at the prospect of replicating, in negotiations just beginning, the success of the retired workers in the aluminum industry (see, for example, FOMC *Minutes*, 20 February 1974, p. 40; FOMC *Minutes*, 18–19 March 1974, p. 147).

In the event, the Federal Reserve's efforts to undermine labor with higher interest rates were dwarfed by the effects of the expiration of the government's price controls on 30 April 1974, which the Nixon administration had implemented in August 1971. The expiration of price controls convinced the steel industry that higher money wages could be passed on in higher prices. Therefore, it jumped at the chance to avoid a strike by granting COLAs to the United Steel Workers. At the same time, the expiration of the Government's price controls caused the speculative hoarding of inventories for the first time since the Korean War, and on a scale that had not been seen since 1920. Taken together, labor's willingness to accept COLAs instead of money-wage increases and the speculative hoarding of inventories explain why the Federal Reserve administered a tight monetary policy during the 1973–5 recession. The COLAs cut both ways. If the Federal Reserve made the carrying cost of inventories high enough to force a liquidation of the hoarded goods, then a collapse of raw materials prices would reduce the real wage (see, for example, FOMC *Minutes*, 15–16 April 1974, pp. 36–8, 56, 59, 80–2, 90–1; FOMC *Minutes*, 20 August 1974, p. 43).

In summary, the Federal Reserve's tight monetary policy during the 1973–5 recession was not an effort to stabilize the economy at full employment with price stability (i.e. at point A in Figure 4.1). It was rather an effort to force a distress liquidation of inventories, and thus force workers, who had just tied their livelihoods to the price indexes, to absorb the real-income losses. It follows that, in order to understand monetary policy, the orthodox monetary theories should be replaced with the radical political economic approach.

Section 4.4   Summary and Conclusions

In March 1951, the Federal Reserve obtained independence from the Treasury Department for the purpose of stabilizing the economy at full employment with price stability. Most monetary theorists, from New Classical economists on the right to Post Keynesians on the left, explain U.S. monetary policy in the 1951–75 period as a (failed) effort to accomplish this goal. There has been considerable debate over the appropriateness and efficacy of the Federal Reserve's "stabiliz- ation policies." Consequently, there has been little recognition of the fact that the principal issue of concern to policymakers within the Federal Reserve System between 1951 and 1975 was not stabilizing the economy but the capital–labor conflict over the terms of the employment relation.

The Federal Reserve did try to stabilize the economy at full employment with price stability between May 1954 and March 1956, but only because the leading sections of the industrial proletariat had agreed, in 1950, to a five-year, no-strike pledge. This stabilization policy took the form of contractionary open-market operations to reduce free reserves, in the hope of putting the banks under pressure to ration credit. However, the contractionary open-market operations also put upward pressure on the Treasury-bill rate, as the banks responded to the loss of free reserves, not by rationing credit, but by selling Treasury bills in order to use the funds thus obtained to make new loans. When the Treasury-bill rate was pushed to equality with the discount rate, the Federal Reserve would increase the latter out of a per- ceived need to prevent the banks from borrowing from it to buy Treasury bills.

However, when the five-year, no-strike pledge expired, so did the Federal Reserve's efforts to stabilize the economy. Starting in 1955–6, there were tri- annual rounds of wage negotiations in the automobile and steel industries and, after March 1956, the Federal Reserve supplanted its stabilization policy with policies designed to strengthen capital against labor in these wage negotiations. In the late 1950s, the Federal Reserve tried to achieve this goal by means of a penalty-rate policy of discount-rate increases that would have a greater psycho- logical effect on the business climate because they could not be anticipated by the Treasury-bill rate rising to equality with it. The Federal Reserve thus increased the discount rate in April and August 1956, and in March, May, and September 1959, in an effort to neutralize the United Steel Workers' use of the strike weapon to obtain higher wages and benefits. The Federal Reserve also increased the discount rate in August and October 1958 in an effort to neutralize the UAW's threatened use of the strike weapon.

Nonetheless, in retrospect, the discount-rate increase in August 1957 is the most interesting one undertaken in the late 1950s because it was made as the economy collapsed into the 1957–8 recession. The August 1957 discount-rate increase was not directly related to a specific strike threat by a leading section of the industrial proletariat. Yet this discount-rate increase remained a component of an explicitly anti-labor monetary policy, the goal of which was neutralizing labor's revived use of the strike weapon. Both the UAW in 1955 and the United Steel Workers in 1956 made significant wage and benefit gains. For the policymakers within the Federal Reserve System, the August 1957 discount-rate increase would exacerbate the 1957–8 recession and thus help the industrial bourgeoisie in its efforts to reverse those gains. With the same arguments that were repeated during the recessions of 1960–1, 1969–70, and 1973–5, the Federal Reserve increased the discount rate in August 1957, just as the 1957–8 recession began, to "maintain as far as possible the kind of climate that would hold some restraint against wage moves" (FOMC *Minutes*, 1 October 1957, p. 23), or to maintain the kind of climate where wage negotiations would be conducted "without the illusion on either side as to the possibility of wage increases being passed on as price increases" (FOMC *Minutes*, 7 January 1958, p. 47).

Even though the goal of monetary policy remained the same during the 1956–75 period, its operating procedures did not. In particular, the penalty-rate policy introduced in March 1956, which replaced the stabilization policy introduced in May 1954, had a fundamental technical flaw. Whereas under the stabilization policy, discount-rate increases were semiautomatic technical adjustments to a rising Treasury-bill rate, designed to keep the banks from having a profit opportunity to borrow from the Federal Reserve in order to purchase Treasury bills, the penalty-rate policy was designed to give the Federal Reserve the flexibility to increase the discount rate regardless of the level of the Treasury-bill rate. The penalty-rate policy assumed that open-market operations would be used to keep free reserves negative. Otherwise, the banks would not be under pressure to reduce, or at least restrain the rate of growth of, their lending, sell Treasury bills, or borrow from the Federal Reserve, and the discount rate would be of little consequence. But with free reserves negative and the discount rate greater than the Treasury-bill rate, the banks would sell Treasury bills relentlessly. Consequently, the only way the Federal Reserve would be able to keep the discount rate greater than the Treasury-bill rate would be either to allow free reserves to become positive or to increase the discount rate over and over again.

The Federal Reserve was unwilling to conduct expansionary open-market operations during a period of economic expansion. Nor was the Federal Reserve willing to keep raising the discount rate every time the banks' sales of Treasury bills pushed the Treasury-bill rate to equality with it. Therefore, the Federal Reserve ended up simply allowing the Treasury-bill rate to move above the discount rate. In other words, the Federal Reserve ended up without a coherent operating procedure.

Given their overriding concern with wage negotiations and their hope that discount-rate increases would strengthen capital against labor, the majority of members of the Federal Open Market Committee in the late 1950s did not consider the incoherence of their operating procedure to be an important issue. However, after a five-year hiatus, when the Federal Reserve was once again ready to implement a tight monetary policy, in February 1965, the composition of the Federal Open Market Committee had changed and the new members were not inclined to embrace a flawed operating procedure. Therefore, the Federal Reserve reverted back to the stabilization policy pursued between May 1954 and March 1956.

However, by the mid 1960s, the underlying financial situation had changed. Whereas in the late 1950s, the banks obtained funds for new loans by selling Treasury bills (asset management), in the mid 1960s they did so by issuing large-denomination negotiable CDs (liability management). By the end of the tight monetary policy from February 1965 to October 1966, its cutting edge had thus become forcing bank disintermediation by pushing the market yields on CDs above the their interest-rate ceilings. And the effort to impose quantity restraints on the banks in this way remained the cutting edge of the tight monetary policy from May 1968 to February 1970.

With Martin's retirement as Chair of the Federal Reserve Board, on 30 January 1970, the Federal Reserve's approach to monetary restraint changed dramatically. First, free reserves were dropped as the gauge of the degree of pressure the Federal Reserve was putting on the supply of bank reserves, to be replaced by a series of experiments with other measures (i.e. borrowed reserves, nonborrowed reserves, and total reserves). Second, the interest-rate ceilings on CDs were eliminated in May 1970, effectively ending the Federal Reserve's efforts to impose quantity restraints on the banks, in favor of simply targeting the level of short-term interest rates. Third, the level of short-term interest rates was no longer gauged by the Treasury-bill rate but by the federal funds rate. At first, a range was set for the federal funds rate. The federal funds rate would be kept at the midpoint of the range so long as some monetary aggregate (mostly M_1, but sometimes M_2) was growing at the same rate as orthodox theory predicted for the long-period tendency of aggregate output. If the monetary aggregate was growing above its target rate, the federal funds rate would be permitted to rise toward the upper bound of its range, and vice versa (Melton, 1985, pp. 93–109). Eventually, the different measures of the supply of reserves and of the monetary aggregates were dropped, so that the Federal Reserve simply targets a precise value for the federal funds rate. Along with the different measures of the supply of reserves and of the monetary aggregates, all efforts to impose quantity restraints on the U.S. bank cartel were also dropped, in favor of letting the level of the federal funds rate affect the economy through changes in the exchange rate of the dollar.

Notes

1 Discount-rate increases are requested by the regional-bank presidents then accepted or rejected by a majority vote of the Board of Governors. Therefore, it takes four governors and one regional-bank president to initiate discount-rate increases. There were five governors and three regional-bank presidents who supported a discount-rate increase in March 1956. The five governors were C. Canby Balderston, William McChesney Martin Jr., Abbot Low Mills Jr., James Louis Robertson, and Charles Noah Shepardson (FOMC *Minutes*, 27 March 1956, pp. 18, 26–7 & 34–5). The three regional-bank presidents were Malcolm H. Bryan (Atlanta), Delos C. Johns (St. Louis), and Alfred H. Williams (Philadelphia) (FOMC *Minutes*, 17 April 1956, pp. 9, 14; FOMC *Minutes*, 9 May 1956, p. 14).

2 The two regional banks that increased their discount rates to 3 percent in April 1956 were the Federal Reserve Bank of Minneapolis and the Federal Reserve Bank of San Francisco (Board of Governors, 1971, Table 12.1).

3 There was also pressure from some non-New York regional-bank presidents to lower reserve requirements. Since lower reserve requirements enhance bank profits far more than they stimulate the economy, they could only be justified as part of a larger stabilization policy. Consequently, some non-New York regional-bank presidents argued for decreasing the discount rate in order to provide cover for reducing reserve requirements (see, for example, FOMC *Minutes*, 13 November 1956, p. 27; FOMC *Minutes*, 26 March 1957, pp. 28, 42; FOMC *Minutes*, 18 June 1957, pp. 22–3; FOMC *Minutes*, 7 May 1957, p. 22).

4 The four regional banks that increased their discount rates in August 1958 were the Federal Reserve Bank of Atlanta, the Federal Reserve Bank of Dallas, the Federal Reserve Bank of Kansas City, and the Federal Reserve Bank of San Francisco (Board of Governors, 1971, table 12.1).

5 The four regional banks that refused to increase their discount rates in October 1958 were the Federal Reserve Bank of Boston, the Federal Reserve Bank of Kansas City, the Federal Reserve Bank of New York, and the Federal Reserve Bank of San Francisco (Board of Governors, 1971, table 12.1).

6 The following eight non-New York regional-bank presidents also aligned themselves with the effort to strengthen capital against labor in the tri-annual rounds of wage negotiations in the automobile and steel industries in the late 1960s and early 1970s:

a   Karl R. Bopp of Philadelphia (FOMC *Minutes*, 25 November 1969, pp. 79–81);
b   W. Braddock Hickman of Cleveland (FOMC *Minutes*, 12 January 1965, p. 69; FOMC *Minutes*, 26 July 1966, p. 79; FOMC *Minutes*, 10 March 1970, p. 76);
c   George H. Clay of Kansas City (FOMC *Minutes*, 14 January 1969, p. 50; FOMC *Minutes*, 15 January 1970, pp. 67–8; FOMC *Minutes*, 10 February 1970, pp. 67–8);
d   Philip E. Coldwell of Dallas (FOMC *Minutes*, 10 February 1970, p. 80);
e   Aubrey N. Heflin of Richmond (FOMC *Minutes*, 15 January 1970, p. 80);
f   Darryl R. Francis of St. Louis (FOMC *Minutes*, 23 June 1970, pp. 23–4);
g   Monroe Kimbrel of Atlanta (FOMC *Minutes*, 20 October 1970, p. 51); and
h   Charles J. Scanlon of Chicago (FOMC *Minutes*, 18 July 1967, p. 75).

7 The prime rate is the interest rate at which the banks lent to their most creditworthy customers.

8 Regulation Q was the New Deal statute under which the Federal Reserve set maximum rates that banks could pay for deposits of different maturities.

9 As is shown below, the opposite was also true—namely, that the Federal Reserve could give firms an incentive to shift working capital from CDs to Treasury bills by increasing the Treasury-bill rate above the ceiling on large-denomination CDs. The manager of the Open Market Account (Stone) summed up as follows the situation that made this form of monetary restraint possible:

> Large banks were now adjusting their reserve deficiencies not through changes in their [Treasury] bill holdings but by changing their rates on time certificates of deposit by as little as 5 basis points.
>
> (Stone, FOMC *Minutes*, 28 January 1964, p. 45)

10 The new operating procedure had the support of the Federal Reserve Bank of New York:

> It is important that the banks exercise greater selectivity in loans. High cost of credit is not enough. Restricted availability is essential.
>
> (Treiber, FOMC *Minutes*, 15 July 1969, p. 43)

The following nine non-New York regional-bank presidents also supported the new operating procedure (Presidents Clay, Coldwell, Galusha, Hickman, and Patterson are quoted because their statements succinctly express both the opinion that the demand for credit was interest-rate inelastic and the opinion that holding down the Regulation Q ceilings on large-denomination CDs was the key to restricting credit availability, and thus fighting wage-push inflation):

a   President of the Federal Reserve Bank of Richmond, Robert P. Black (see, for example, FOMC *Minutes*, 1 April 1969, p. 77);

b   President of the Federal Reserve Bank of Kansas City, George H. Clay:

> The banks reported little resistance to increases [in interest rates]. Several reported almost complete lack of success in getting rid of customers by substantial rate hikes intended to discourage without direct turndown (Clay, FOMC *Minutes*, 22 March 1966, p. 63). ... pursuit of a restrictive monetary policy ... could have a salutary influence upon these ["labor contract"] negotiations.
>
> (Clay, FOMC *Minutes*, 25 November 1969, p. 69; see also FOMC *Minutes*, 1 April 1969, p. 80);

c   President of the Federal Reserve Bank of Dallas, Philip E. Coldwell:

> Interest rate increases had gone so far that the impact of further advances on the credit demands of businessmen or consumers appeared negligible. The only thing that avid borrowers understood was a firm "no, we have no funds for new loans." Thus availability of credit and attitudes of bankers were the keys to real restraint ... if bankers were not serious about making adjustments and merely wanted to sustain their overloaned positions, then a [discount] rate increase would just add to the fire of higher costs and might be a destabilizing influence.
>
> (Coldwell, FOMC *Minutes*, 24 June 1969, p. 60; see also FOMC *Minutes*, 17 December 1968, p. 82);

d   President of the Federal Reserve Bank of St. Louis, Darryl R. Francis (see, for example, FOMC *Minutes*, May 1966, pp. 48–50);

e   President of the Federal Reserve Bank of Minneapolis, Hugh D. Galusha Jr.:

> The Regulation Q ceilings represented the fixed jaw of the vice against which the [Federal Reserve] System had to exert its tightening action on banks and through them, on the business community. The availability of funds, not signals or rates, was the key consideration. If businessmen could obtain the funds, it would be very hard for them to postpone programmed expenditures in the current inflationary environment.
>
> (Galusha, FOMC *Minutes*, 17 December 1968, p. 79);

f   President of the Federal Reserve Bank of Cleveland, W. Braddock Hickman:

> His guess, which was consistent with the strongly held views of industrialists on the Cleveland Bank's Board of Directors, was that if the generous auto settlement was passed on to steel and other industries labor costs would rise faster in 1965 than productivity, and profits would be squeezed.
>
> (FOMC *Minutes*, 12 January 1965, p. 69);

> Recent experience had shown that the way to restrict the rate of growth of bank credit was to permit bill rates to press on Q ceilings. ... That pressure reduced the rate of growth of CD's outstanding and, in turn, of bank credit. ... The failure in late 1965 and early 1966 to validate the discount rate increase of December 1965 had held bill rates below the Q ceilings. That had prompted intermediation and had prompted an inflationary expansion of bank credit. To avoid a repetition of the earlier experience he would favor a higher

bill rate (FOMC *Minutes*, 19 April 1968, p. 9). ... The basic goal should be to prevent too rapid expansion of bank credit, by keeping the 91-day bill rate close to the relevant Q ceilings.

(FOMC *Minutes*, 30 April 1968, p. 72;
FOMC *Minutes*, 17 December 1968, p. 61);

g   President of the Federal Reserve Bank of Boston, Frank E. Morris (see, for example, FOMC *Minutes*, 1 April 1969, pp. 97–8; FOMC *Minutes*, 7 October 1969, p. 48);

h   President of the Federal Reserve Bank of Atlanta, Harold T. Patterson:

the [Open Market] Desk had allowed interest rates to go higher without trying to curtail the growth of bank credit. Since most people chose to pay a higher rate rather than do without the funds, that would not restrict credit very much. ... Banking figures ... gave little evidence of any slowdown in bank credit growth in response to more restrictive monetary policy ... the Committee had not been at all successful in restricting the growth of the reserve base, bank credit, and the money supply, even though it had moved toward large net borrowed reserve figures.

(FOMC *Minutes*, 11 January 1966, p. 70;
FOMC *Minutes*, 10 May 1966, pp. 51–3); and

i   President of the Federal Reserve Bank of San Francisco, Eliot J. Swan (see, for example, FOMC *Minutes*, 17 December 1968, p. 81; FOMC *Minutes*, 14 January 1969, p. 41).

11 The following seven non-New York regional-bank presidents also made statements arguing for sustaining tight monetary policy during the 1969–70 recession in order to weaken labor (Presidents Clay and Coldwell are quoted at length because they were particularly adamant in this regard):

a   Karl R. Bopp of Philadelphia (FOMC *Minutes*, 10 February 1970, pp. 53–4);
b   George H. Clay of Kansas City:

[Given] the heavy concentration of wage negotiations in the year ahead [particularly the tri-annual round of wage negotiations in the automobile industry] ... it was going to take restraining pressure for a considerable time if price inflation was to be corrected. Two quarters of no real economic growth followed by an economic upturn was unlikely to set the stage for price stability.

(Clay, FOMC *Minutes*, 16 December 1969, p. 50);

In fact, success in the battle against price inflation probably would require little or no overall economic growth over a full year or more.

(Clay, FOMC *Minutes*, 15 January 1970, pp. 72–3);

[The problem faced by the Federal Reserve System was] the institutional arrangements whereby wage patterns and the prices that flowed from them became established in negotiations between powerful labor unions and large business corporations.

(Clay, FOMC *Minutes*, 10 February 1970, pp. 67–8);

c   Philip E. Coldwell of Dallas:

The [Federal Open Market] Committee was ... at a crucial turning point; if it backed away, all its efforts and the costs already paid could prove to have been in vain.

(FOMC *Minutes*, 10 February 1970, pp. 76, 80);

d   Darryl R. Francis of St. Louis (FOMC *Minutes*, 23 June 1970, pp. 23–4);

e   Aubrey N. Heflin of Richmond (FOMC *Minutes*, 15 January 1970, p. 16; FOMC *Minutes*, 21 July 1970, p. 40);

f   Monroe Kimbrel of Atlanta (FOMC *Minutes*, 10 February 1970, p. 95; FOMC *Minutes*, 20 October 1970, p. 51); and

g   Frank E. Morris of Boston (10 February 1970, p. 81).

12   The federal funds rate is the interbank lending rate. In this section, I explain the level at which the federal funds rate was targeted by the Federal Reserve, not its actual level. The actual level of the federal funds rate will be whatever the major participants in the financial markets expect it to be (Keynes, 1936, pp. 203–4). Monetary policy is the principal determinant of expectations in financial markets and thus the major determinant of the federal funds rate. But there are other determinants. For example, the Federal Reserve targeted the federal funds rate at 4.25 percent in May 1971, but the widespread expectation that the dollar would be devalued caused the major market participants to push the federal funds rate to 4.41 percent. The Manager of the Federal Reserve's Open Market Account (Holmes) summed up this situation as follows:

> the super-cautious approach to reserve management by the major money center banks ar[ose] from uncertainty about the exchange crisis, rather than to any shortage of reserves. In fact, the [Federal Reserve] System vigorously resisted the high funds rate … the banking system had free reserves of over $200 million—a statistic not consistent for long with a federal funds rate averaging 4.41 per cent.
> (Holmes, FOMC *Minutes*, 11 May 1971, p. 36)

Nonetheless, I show in this section that the turning points and the direction of change of the actual federal funds rate reflect decisions of the monetary authorities.

13   Brunner (1975), Haberler (1976), and Mayer (1999) are representative of the Monetarist analyses. Lucas (1973), Barro and Gordon (1983), and Sargent (1999) are representative of the New Classical approach. Gordon (1975), Bruno and Sachs (1975), Sachs (1979), and Okun (1981) are representative of the New Keynesian analyses.

14   M_1 is defined as currency in circulation, traveler's checks, and demand deposits.

15   For similar statements by George H. Clay, President of the Federal Reserve Bank of Kansas City; Eliot J. Swan, President of the Federal Reserve Bank of San Francisco; Governor J. Dewey Daane; and Monroe Kimbrel, President of the Federal Reserve Bank of Atlanta respectively, see FOMC *Minutes*, 7 April 1970, pp. 40, 42, 49).

16   Most importantly, the Teamsters used wildcat strikes in most urban centers to pressure their leadership into demanding, and receiving, annual wage and benefit increases averaging 9 percent over a thirty-nine-month period (see, for example, FOMC *Minutes*, 21 July 1970, p. 40).

17   To fight the demand by the UAW for cost-of-living adjustments, the automakers decided to shut down for the annual model change-over in late-June and July, so that full production of 1971 model cars would be underway by late August. But the Federal Reserve believed that, in addition to inventories of new cars, the automakers needed the government's help in order to restrain the UAW (see, for example, FOMC *Minutes*, 7 April 1970, p. 43; FOMC *Minutes*, 15 September 1970, p. 11).

18   As initially proposed, the National Development Bank would have been authorized to raise $4 billion in order to subsidize mortgage payments for families with incomes between $8,000 and $12,000. The proposed bill also authorized banks to hold the obligations of the National Development Bank as reserves. See Pollin (1993) for a proposal on how to transform the Federal Reserve into a national development bank.

19   The Federal Reserve also controlled short-term interest rates in the 1920s and 1930s. But from the outbreak of World War II to March 1951, the Treasury determined short-term interest rates, after consulting with the Federal Reserve.

20 See Endnote 13 for representative monetary theorists writing from the Monetarist, New Classical, and New Keynesian perspectives. Boddy and Crotty (1975), Epstein (1987), and Epstein (1992) are representative of the radical political economic perspective underlying this section.
21 Technically speaking, short-period Phillips curves represent a trade-off between the inflation rate and the real growth rate. But because of the close negative correlation between the real growth rate and the unemployment rate, it is common to draw short-period Phillips curves as in Figure 4.1.
22 Monetarists and New Classical economists acknowledge that their analyses are marred to the degree that they do not incorporate the wage and price rigidities that are of central concern to the New Keynesians (see, for example, Haberler, 1976, p. 150; McCallum, 1977, 1979, 1980).
23 For similar statements by other members of the Federal Open Market Committee, see, for example, FOMC *Minutes*, 16 July 1974, p. 77; FOMC *Minutes*, 20 August 1974, pp. 57–8, 64, 67; FOMC *Minutes*, 10 September 1974, pp. 57–8, 70, 73, 84; FOMC *Minutes*, 15 October 1974, pp. 36–7, 67, 70; FOMC *Minutes*, 19 November 1974, pp. 47–9; FOMC *Minutes*, 20–1 January 1975, p. 97; and FOMC *Minutes*, 19 February 1975, p. 68.

Bibliography

Ackley, G. 1966. "The Contribution of Guidelines." In *Guidelines, Informal Controls, and the Market Place: Policy Choices in a Full Employment Economy.* G. P. Schultz and R. Z. Aliber (eds). Chicago, IL: University of Chicago Press, pp. 67–78.

Barro, Robert J. and David B. Gordon. 1983. "A Positive Theory of Monetary Policy in a Natural Rate Model." *Journal of Political Economy.* Vol. 91, pp. 586–610.

Board of Governors of the Federal Reserve System. 1971. *Banking and Monetary Statistics: 1941–70.*

Boddy, Raford and James Crotty. 1975. "Class Conflict and Macro-policy: The Political Business Cycle." *Review of Radical Political Economics*, Vol. 7, No. 1, pp. 1–19.

Brinkley, Alan. 1995. *The End of Reform: New Deal Liberalism in Recession and War.* New York: Alfred A. Knopf.

Brinkley, Alan. 1989. "The New Deal and the Idea of the State." In *The Rise and Fall of the New Deal Order, 1930–1980.* Steve Fraser and Gary Gerstle (eds). Princeton, NJ: Princeton University Press, pp. 85–121.

Brunner, Karl. 1975. "Comment: The Demand and Supply of Inflation." *Journal of Law and Economics*, Vol. 18, pp. 837–49.

Bruno, Michael and Jeffrey D. Sachs. 1975. *Economics of Worldwide Inflation.* Cambridge: Cambridge University Press.

CITIBASE

Council of Economic Advisors. 1962. *Annual Report.* Washington, DC: U.S. Government Printing Office.

Davis, Mike. 1986. *Prisoners of the American Dream: Politics and Economy in the History of the U.S. Working Class.* London: Verso Press.

Dornbusch, Rudiger and Stanley Fischer. 1994. *Macroeconomics.* Sixth edition. New York: McGraw Hill.

Dymski, Gary. 1990. "Money and Credit in Radical Political Economy: A Survey of Contemporary Perspectives." *Review of Radical Political Economics*, Vol. 22, Nos. 2 and 3, pp. 38–65.

Epstein, Gerald. 1992. "Political Economy and Comparative Central Banking." *Review of Radical Political Economics*, Vol. 24, No. 1, pp. 1–30.

Epstein, Gerald. 1987. "Federal Reserve Behavior and the Limits of Monetary Policy in the Current Economic Crisis." In *The Imperiled Economy: Macroeconomics from a Left Perspective*, R. Cherry (ed.). New York: Union for Radical Political Economics, pp. 247–55.

Epstein, Gerald and Juliet Schor. 1995. "The Federal Reserve Treasury Accord and the Construction of the Postwar Monetary Regime in the United States." *Social Concept*, Vol. 7, No. 1 (July), pp. 7–48.

Epstein, Gerald and Juliet Schor. 1990. "Corporate Profitability as a Determinant of Restrictive Monetary Policy: Estimates for the Postwar United States." In *The Political Economy of American Monetary Policy*, Thomas Mayer (ed.). New York: Cambridge University Press, pp. 51–63.

Epstein, Gerald and Juliet Schor. 1986. "The Political Economy of Central Banking." Harvard Institute for Economic Research. Discussion Paper No. 1281.

Federal Advisory Council. *Minutes, 1950–1975*. Washington, DC: Board of Governors of the Federal Reserve System.

Federal Open Market Committee. *Minutes, 1950–1975*. Washington, DC: Board of Governors of the Federal Reserve System.

Fellner, William J. 1980. "The Valid Core of Rationality Hypotheses in the Theory of Expectations." *Journal of Money, Credit and Banking*. Vol. 12, No. 4, pp. 763–87.

Fellner, William J. 1978. "Contemporary Economic Problems." Washington, DC: American Enterprise Institute, pp. 10–41.

Fraser, Steve. 1989. "The 'Labor Question'." In *The Rise and Fall of the New Deal Order, 1930–1980*. Steve Fraser and Gary Gerstle (eds). Princeton, NJ: Princeton University Press, pp. 55–84.

Friedman, Milton. 1962 [1968]. "Should There Be an Independent Monetary Authority?" In *Dollars and Deficits*. Milton Friedman (ed.). Englewood Cliffs, NJ: Prentice Hall, pp. 173–94.

Gerstle, Gary and Steve Fraser. 1989. "Introduction." In *The Rise and Fall of the New Deal Order, 1930–1980*. Steve Fraser and Gary Gerstle (eds). Princeton, NJ: Princeton University Press, pp. ix–xxv.

Goldfeld, Steven M. and Lester V. Chandler. 1985. *The Economics of Money and Banking*. Ninth edition. New York: Harper and Row.

Gordon, David, Thomas E. Weisskopf and Samuel Bowles. 1987. "Power, Accumulation and Crisis: The Rise and Demise of the Postwar Social Structure of Accumulation." In *The Imperiled Economy: Macroeconomics from a Left Perspective*. Robert Cherry (ed.). New York: Union for Radical Political Economics, pp. 43–57.

Gordon, Robert J. 1975. "The Demand and Supply of Inflation." *Journal of Law and Economics*. Vol. 18, pp. 807–36.

Haberler, Gottfried. 1976. "Some Currently Suggested Explanations and Cures for Inflation." In *Institutional Arrangements and the Inflation Problem*. Karl Brunner and Allan H. Meltzer (eds). Carnegie-Rochester Conference Series on Public Policy, Vol. 13. New York: North Holland, pp. 143–77.

Hofstadter, Richard. 1955. *The Age of Reform: From Bryan to F.D.R.* New York: Vintage Books.

Jackson, D., H. A. Turner and F. Wilkinson. 1972. *Do Trade Unions Cause Inflation? Two Studies: With a Theoretical Introduction and Policy Conclusion*. Cambridge: Cambridge University Press.

Kalecki, Michal. 1971. "Political Aspects of Full Employment." In *Selected Essays on the Dynamics of the Capitalist Economy: 1933–70*. Michal Kalecki (ed.). Cambridge: Cambridge University Press, pp. 138–45.

Katznelson, Ira. 2013. *The New Deal and the Origins of Our Time*. New York: W.W. Norton.

Katznelson, Ira. 1989. "Was the Great Society a Lost Opportunity?" *The Rise and Fall of the New Deal Order: 1930–1980*. Steve Fraser and Gary Gerstle (eds). Princeton, NJ: Princeton University Press, pp. 185–211.

Kettl, Donald F. 1986. *Leadership at the Fed*. New Haven, CT: Yale University Press.

Keynes, John Maynard. 1936 [1964]. *The General Theory of Employment, Interest, and Money*. New York: Harcourt, Brace Jovanovich.

Kotz, David M. 2015. *The Rise and Fall of Neoliberalism*. Cambridge, MA: Harvard University Press.

Lichenstein, Nelson. 1989. "From Corporatism to Collective Bargaining: Organized Labor and the Eclipse of Social Democracy in the Postwar Era." In *The Rise and Fall of the New Deal Order, 1930–1980*, Steve Fraser and Gary Gerstle (eds). Princeton, NJ: Princeton University Press, pp. 122–52.

Lombra, Raymond E. 1988. "Monetary Policy: Rhetoric Versus the Record." In *Political Business Cycles: The Political Economy of Money, Inflation, and Unemployment*. Thomas D. Willet (ed.). Durham, NC: Duke University Press, pp. 337–65.

Lombra, Raymond E. and Michael Moran. 1980. "Policy Advise and Policy Making at the Federal Reserve." In *Institutional Arrangements and the Inflation Problem*. Karl Brunner and Allan H. Meltzer (eds). Carnegie-Rochester Conference Series on Public Policy, Vol. 13. New York: North Holland, pp. 9–68.

Lucas, Robert. 1973. "Some International Evidence on Output-Inflation Tradeoffs." *American Economic Review*. Vol. 63, pp. 326–34.

Mayer, Thomas. 1999. *Monetary Policy and the Great Inflation in the United States*. Northamton, MA: Edward Elgar.

Mayer, Thomas. 1981. "Federal Reserve Monetary Policy in the 1973–5 Recession: A Case Study of Fed Behavior in a Quandary." In *Crises in the Economic and Financial Structure*. Paul Wachtel (ed.). Lexington, MA: Lexington Books.

McCallum, Bennet T. 1980. "Rational Expectations and Macroeconomic Stabilization Policy: An Overview." *Journal of Money, Credit, and Banking*. Vol. 12, pp. 716–46.

McCallum, Bennet T. "Monetarism, Rational Expectations, Oligopolistic Pricing, and the MPS Econometric Model." *Journal of Political Economy*. Vol. 87, pp. 57–73.

McCallum, Bennet T. 1977. "Price-level Stickiness and the Feasibility of Monetary Stabilization Policy with Rational Expectations." *Journal of Political Economy*. Vol. 85, pp. 627–34.

Melton, William C. 1985. *Inside the Fed: Making Monetary Policy*. Homewood, IL: Dow Jones Irwin.

Minsky, Hyman P. 1986 [2008]. *Stabilizing an Unstable Economy*. New York: McGraw Hill.

New York Times, 1950–75.

Okun, Arthur M. 1981. *Prices and Quantities: A Macroeconomic Analysis*. Washington, DC: Brookings Institution.

Panico, Carlo. 1988. *Interest and Profit in the Theories of Value and Distribution*. New York: St. Martins Press.

Pivetti, Massimo. 1985. "On the Monetary Explanation of Distribution." *Political Economy —Studies in the Surplus Approach*, Vol. 1 No. 2, pp. 73–103.

Pollin, Robert. 1993. "Public Credit Allocation through the Federal Reserve: Why It is Needed; How it Should be Done." In *Transforming the U.S. Financial System: Equity and Efficiency for the 21st Century*. Gary A. Dymski, Gerald Epstein and Robert Pollin (eds). Economic Policy Institute. Armonk, NY: M.E. Sharpe, pp. 321–54.

Ross, A. M. 1966. "Guideline Policy—Where We Are and How We Got There." In *Guidelines, Informal Controls, and the Market Place: Policy Choices in a Full Employment Economy.* G. P. Schultz and R. Z. Aliber (eds). Chicago: University of Chicago Press, pp. 97–141.

Sachs, Jeffrey. 1979. "Wages, Profits and Macroeconomic Adjustments." *Brookings Papers on Economic Activity.* Vol. 2, pp. 269–319.

Sargent, Thomas J. 1999. *Conquest of American Inflation.* Princeton, NJ: Princeton University Press.

Schor, Juliet B. 1987. "Class Struggle and the Cost of Job Loss." In *The Imperiled Economy: Macroeconomics from a Left Perspective.* Robert Cherry (ed.). New York: Union for Radical Political Economics, pp. 171–82.

Schor, Juliet B. 1985. "Wage Flexibility, Social Welfare Expenditures, and Monetary Restrictiveness." In *Money and Macro Policy.* Marc Jarsulic (ed.). Boston: Kluwer-Nijhoff Publishing, pp. 135–54.

Shultz, G. P. and R. A. Aliber. 1966. "Introduction." In *Guidelines, Informal Controls, and the Market Place: Policy Choices in a Full Employment Economy.* G. P. Schultz and R. Z. Aliber (eds). Chicago: University of Chicago Press, pp. 1–14.

Solow, Robert M. 1966. "The Case Against the Guideposts." In *Guidelines, Informal Controls, and the Market Place: Policy Choices in a Full Employment Economy.* G. P. Schultz and R. Z. Aliber (eds). Chicago: University of Chicago Press, pp. 41–54.

Steinberg, Bruce and the Crisis Reader Editorial Collective 1978. *U.S. Capitalism in Crisis.* New York: The Union For Radical Political Economists.

Strauss, George. 1962. "The Shifting Power Balance in the Plant." *Industrial Relations,* Vol. 1, No. 3, pp. 65–96.

Weir, Margaret and Theda Skocpol. 1985. "State Structures and the Possibilities for 'Keynesian' Responses to the Great Depression in Sweden, Britain and the United States." In *Bringing the State Back In.* Peter B. Evans, Dietrich Rueschemeyer and Theda Skocpol (eds). Cambridge: Cambridge University Press.

Willet, Thomas D. 1988. *Political Business Cycles: The Political Economy of Money, Inflation, and Unemployment.* Durham, NC: Duke University Press.

Wolfson, Martin H. 1986 [1994]. *Financial Crises: Understanding the Postwar U.S. Experience.* Armonk, NY: M.E. Sharpe.

Woolley, John T. 1984. *Monetary Politics: The Federal Reserve and the Politics of Monetary Policy.* New York: Cambridge University Press.

5 The End of the Golden Age of Relatively Stable Capitalist Development

Since 1966, the U.S. economy has been characterized by both financial crises and financial instability. This simultaneous emergence of financial crises and financial instability has prompted many monetary theorists to argue that financial crises are symptoms of financial instability.[1] From this perspective, financial crises are caused by increasing debt burdens. The purpose of this chapter is to argue instead that financial crises are caused by class and intra-class conflict, with the class conflict taking the form of the movement toward social democracy and the intra-class conflict at issue here being between the large regional banks and the large New York banks.

The 1966 financial crisis is particularly significant from the perspective of the financial-instability hypothesis because it divides the postwar Golden Age of U.S. capitalism from the current Neoliberal Era of recurrent financial crises. My purpose in this chapter is to affirm the significance of the 1966 financial crisis as the dividing line between two eras in the history of capitalism, but not the characterization of these two eras in terms of increasing debt burdens. Instead of contrasting the current Neoliberal Era with a postwar Golden Age of financial stability, I argue that it is best understood by contrasting it with a social-democratic era launched by the New Deal in the U.S. The issue underlying the 1966 financial crisis is thus seen not as increasing debt burdens, but as the extension of the New Deal financial reforms of 1933–5 with an incomes policy and capital controls by the Kennedy and Johnson administrations. In this chapter, after showing that increasing debt burdens do not account for the 1966 financial crisis, I explain it in terms of the interaction between the Federal Reserve's implacable opposition to the movement toward social democracy and its role as the manager of the U.S. bank cartel.

In Section 5.1, I show how the 1966 financial crisis, the first major financial crisis of the postwar period, is explained as an indication that the financial system had become unstable. The purpose of this chapter, however, is to argue that financial instability is an important problem, but is not the cause of financial crises. In Section 5.2, I thus show that the 1966 financial crisis is not adequately explained in terms of financial instability.

In Sections 5.3 and 5.4, I argue that financial crises are caused by class and intra-class conflict rather than financial instability. In Section 5.3, I show that, in the 1960s, there was intra-class conflict between the large New York banks and the large regional banks over monetary policy. In Section 5.4, I place this intra-class conflict over monetary policy within the context of a conflict between capital and labor over the distribution of income, and thus over the best way to control inflation. This, I argue, provides a more satisfactory explanation of the 1966 financial crisis. In Section 5.5, I provide a summary and conclusions.

Section 5.1 The Financial Instability Hypothesis

Financial crises occur when relatively large groups of people panic in a financial market, disposing of assets in order to meet payment obligations, or in response to the threat of a financial institution becoming insolvent, or to the threat of an asset-market collapse (Dickens and O'Hara, 1999). The 1966 financial crisis began on 17 August, when large groups of people panicked at the threat of an asset-market collapse. The crisis came down to the fact that many bond dealers, unwilling to hold inventories of bonds, stopped quoting bid prices for bonds on a routine basis. On 29 August, bond dealers began to build inventories of bonds again. On 30 August, when this fact became widely known, the bond market rallied and the 1966 financial crisis ended.

In contrast with the above, financial instability is caused by the fact that households and firms take on debt-payment commitments during economic expansions that they do not have adequate incomes to service during periods of slow growth.[2] When looked at as a problem of financial instability, financial crises arise either the moment significant numbers of creditors realize that the build-up of debt burdens is unsustainable and modify their behavior accordingly (see, for example, Guttentag and Herring, 1984) or the moment when tight monetary policy forces creditors to curtail their investments abruptly (see, for example, Wojnilower, 1980). Financial-instability theorists conclude that central banks must intervene as lenders of last resort in order to prevent financial crises from devolving into debt-deflations.[3]

For Martin H. Wolfson (1986, chapter 4), the foremost theorist of financial crises in terms of the problem of financial instability (also see Minsky 1982; 1986, pp. 3–10), the 1966 financial crisis was an example of tight monetary policy forcing creditors (e.g. the banks) to curtail abruptly their investments. Wolfson surveys the build-up of debt by non-financial corporations during the economic expansion of the mid 1960s. He then points out that banks obtained the funds they needed to make new loans by issuing large-denomination negotiable time deposits. In July 1966, the banks bid the secondary-market yields on time deposits above the interest-rate ceilings that the Federal Reserve maintained on the yields banks could offer on new time deposits. Maturing time deposits could not be rolled over at interest rates held by administrative fiat below market interest rates. Wolfson argues that the 1966 financial crisis thus occurred in late August because participants in the financial markets panicked at the threat that banks would have to sell bonds in order to replace funds lost as time deposits matured (also see Wojnilower, 1980, p. 287).

In order to prevent the 1966 financial crisis from devolving into a debt-deflation, Wolfson (1986, p. 50) concludes that the Federal Reserve abandoned its tight monetary policy at the 23 August 1966 meeting of the Federal Open Market Committee. Since the financial markets remained jittery even after the Federal Reserve had eased monetary policy, Wolfson argues further that, on 1 September, the Federal Reserve sent a letter to the banks assuring them of access to the discount window for all the funds they wanted. According to Wolfson, this letter calmed the financial markets and brought the financial crisis to an end.

Section 5.2 Critique of the Financial Instability Hypothesis

The major problem with these efforts to understand the 1966 financial crisis as a consequence of financial instability is that the crisis is reduced to a panicked response by financial-market participants to the prospect of banks selling bonds because maturing time deposits could not be rolled over. This interpretation is a problem simply because there was no prospect that banks would have to sell off their bond portfolios.

In July 1966, as Wolfson and other financial-instability theorists emphasize, banks bid the secondary-market yields on time deposits above the interest-rate ceilings they could offer on new time deposits. However, for the banking system as a whole, outstanding time deposits increased by $680 million in August and $949 million in September.[4] Banks may choose to sell bonds under such circumstances, but there was no danger that they would be *forced* to sell bonds.

There was a run-off of $193 million in time deposits at the large New York banks in August, followed by a $511 million decrease in time deposits at the large New York banks in September. However, this $704 million run-off of time deposits was offset by $686 million that the large (mostly New York) banks borrowed from their foreign branches in the Eurodollar market during the August–September period.[5] Moreover, the large New York banks could have obtained all the funds they wanted in the Eurodollar market. Again, there was no danger that they would be forced to sell bonds.

Perhaps most damaging to the hypothesis that the 1966 financial crisis was a panicked response to the prospect of banks selling bonds because maturing time deposits could not be rolled over is the fact that in February 1966 there was a $410 million run-off of time deposits at large New York banks that was not offset by bank borrowings of Eurodollars. Why would a run-off of domestic time deposits that was offset by a build-up of time deposits in the Eurodollar market cause a financial crisis in August 1966, when a run-off of domestic time deposits that was not offset by a build-up of Eurodollar deposits failed to cause a financial crisis in February 1966?

Moreover, on 19 August 1966, there was no danger of a forced sell-off of bank-bond portfolios. This was explicitly stated in a front-page article in the *New York Times*. It should be difficult to argue that financial-market participants caused a financial crisis because they were ignorant of readily available facts.

Wolfson and other financial-instability theorists compound their difficulties when they attribute the end of the 1966 financial crisis to an easing of monetary policy at the 23 August meeting of the Federal Open Market Committee, an easing of monetary policy that was allegedly reinforced by a letter to the banks on 1 September. The problem here is that the Federal Open Market Committee did not ease monetary policy until its meeting on 4 October. At its meeting on 23 August, the central question of concern for the Federal Open Market Committee was whether the next step in implementing monetary restraint should be an increase in the discount rate, an increase in reserve requirements, or stricter criteria for member banks' access to the discount window (see, for example, FOMC *Minutes*, 23 August 1966, pp. 7, 53). The Federal Open Market Committee decided to increase monetary restraint by means of an increase in reserve requirements and stricter criteria for member banks' access to the discount window. This fact was clearly stated in the *New York Times* on 29 August (pp. 41, 43).

What is more, the letter from the Federal Reserve to the banks on 1 September was irrelevant to the 1966 financial crisis. The crisis began on 17 August when bond dealers, unwilling to hold inventories of bonds, stopped quoting bid prices for bonds on a routine basis. On 29 August, bond dealers began to build inventories of bonds again. On 30 August, when this fact became widely known, the bond market rallied and the 1966 financial crisis was over. Monetary policy was still tight and the letter from the Federal Reserve to the banks had not yet been written.

In short, Wolfson and other financial-instability theorists cannot explain why the 1966 financial crisis began on 17 August nor why it ended on 30 August.

Section 5.3 The Intra-class Conflict Underlying the 1966 Financial Crisis

Contributing to the 1966 financial crisis was a shift by the large New York banks in the early 1960s from asset management to liability management. The banks financed the Second World War by borrowing funds from the Federal Reserve in order to purchase government securities at premium prices (see, for example, Eccles 1951, pp. 360–6). During the late 1940s and 1950s, banks could sell the government securities accumulated during the Second World War whenever they wanted to make new loans. 'Asset management' denotes this change in the composition of the banks' assets—from portfolios heavily weighted toward government securities to portfolios heavily weighted toward commercial loans.

Banks must hold government securities as collateral against any government revenues placed on deposit with them, including deposits by State and local governments. By the early 1960s, large New York banks had reduced their holdings of government securities to the minimum needed to meet pledging requirements against government deposits. In order to make additional loans, large New York banks had to resort to 'liability management': that is, they had to issue new liabilities whenever they wanted to raise funds to make new loans. The first type of new liability that the large New York banks came up with was large-denomination negotiable time deposits (see, for example, Moore, 1988, p. 27; Goodhart, 1989, pp. 30–2).[6]

Negotiable time deposits were first introduced, in February 1961, by First National City Bank (now Citibank). By July 1963, Citibank and other large New York banks bid the interest rates on time deposits up to their interest-rate ceilings. In July 1963—and when the large New York banks bid the secondary-market yields on time deposits up to their interest-rate ceilings for a second time, in November 1964—an expansionary open-market policy was providing a large reservoir of liquid funds that the large New York banks could tap into by simply notching up the return they offered on new time deposits (see, for example, Goodhart, 1989, pp. 30–2). Consequently, the large regional banks acquiesced to requests by the large New York banks for the Federal Reserve Board to increase the interest-rate ceilings on time deposits.

The situation was different in December 1965, the third time the large New York banks bid the interest rates on time deposits up to their ceilings. By December 1965, liquid funds had been drained from the banking system by a contractionary open-market policy that the Federal Reserve had begun in February 1965. Given the illiquidity created by the contractionary open-market policy, when the large New York banks tried to obtain additional funds by offering higher and higher interest rates on time deposits, they were effectively trying to bid away the deposits of the large regional banks. With the large New York banks aggressively bidding for funds in the CD market and the large regional banks protecting their deposit bases by adjusting "rates upward in line with rates in New York,"[7] it took less than three months in the winter of 1965–6 to once again bid the interest rates on time deposits up to their ceilings. Archie K. Davis, President of the American Bankers Association and Chairperson of the largest bank in the South, the Wachovia Bank and Trust Company, called the combination of contractionary open-market policy and large New York banks bidding for time deposits "highly destructive and undesirable competition" (*New York Times*, 1 February 1966, p. 49).

In spring 1966, the large New York banks attempted to placate the large regional banks. They reduced their demand for funds in the market for time deposits by telling their clients to draw on lines of credit with the large regional banks. But the large New York banks miscalculated the effect on their regional rivals of what was ostensibly a conciliatory gesture. As Edward A. Wayne, President of the Federal Reserve Bank of Richmond, put it at the 22 March 1966 meeting of the Federal Open Market Committee:

> Banks in his District thought the New York banks had acted imprudently, and they were strongly critical of the New York banks for suggesting, when they ran short of funds, that their customers draw on credit lines outside of New York and thus relieve the pressure on them. The hope had been expressed to him that the [Federal Reserve] System would not raise Regulation Q ceilings again because banks could not be relied on to exercise prudence in setting time deposit rates.
>
> (Wayne, FOMC *Minutes*, 22 March 1966, p. 61)

Regulation Q was the statute under which the Federal Reserve Board administered interest-rate ceilings on time deposits. The other regional-bank presidents expressed similar sentiments at the 22 March 1966 meeting of the Federal Open Market Committee. For example, Watrous H. Irons, President of the Federal Reserve Bank of Dallas, said that

> like Mr. Wayne he had heard from a few banks some rather sharp and sever criticisms of the New York banks—not only for suggesting to customers that they 'go west' for accommodations, but also for working up the rates on [time deposits] ... some ... bankers ... had commented that they hoped there would be no further revisions of Regulation Q.
>
> (Irons, FOMC *Minutes*, 22 March 1966, p. 77)[8]

In spring 1966, the Federal Reserve thus found itself unable to implement a tight monetary policy on terms acceptable to both the large regional banks and the large New York banks. That is, whereas the large New York banks wanted a contractionary open-market policy only so long as the interest-rate ceilings on time deposits were raised when they bid market interest rates on time deposits up to those ceilings, the large regional banks wanted a contractionary open-market policy only so long as the interest rate ceilings were not raised.

In Chapter 3, I provide evidence for the disproportionate influence of the large banks on U.S. monetary policy. In the next section, I show that, because of this disproportionate influence, the inability of the Federal Reserve to implement a tight monetary policy on terms acceptable to both the large New York banks and the large regional banks generated a shock to the financial system. In the context of the class conflict then coming to a head, this shock devolved into the 1966 financial crisis.

Section 5.4 The 1966 Financial Crisis

As I explain in Chapter 2, the Federal Reserve exists because it can enforce the U.S. bank cartel's quality-control standards and thus put pressure on bank profit margins in the face of the free-rider problem, without having an incentive to use clearinghouse enforcement mechanisms to increase its own market share (also see Goodhart, 1988).[9] But how can the Federal Reserve then be expected to turn around and undermine bank profit margins in order to control the stock of money?

The Federal Reserve's discount-rate policy in the late 1960s, shown in Figure 5.1, illustrates its dilemma of having to preserve bank profit margins and undermine them at one and the same time.

In Figure 5.1, the discount rate is plotted against the banks' profit margin, or the spread between the prime rate and the yield on large-denomination three-month CDs.[10] Until 1969, each time the banks pushed bid prices to equality with ask prices, they increased the latter. And except in 1966 and 1969, the Federal Reserve's role as bank-cartel manager is evident, with increases in the prime rate being sustained by increases in the discount rate (see, for example, Epstein, 1990).

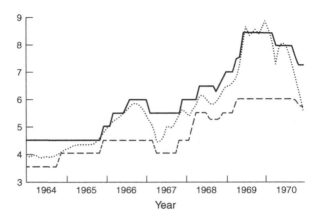

Figure 5.1 Prime rate (–), market yield on three-month CDs (. . .), and the discount rate (——), 1964–70.

The reasons for the Federal Reserve's failure to act as bank-cartel manager in 1966 are the topic of this section. The reasons for its failure in 1969 are explained in Chapter 6.

In December 1965, as shown in Figure 5.1, the banks had been locked into a 4.5 percent prime rate since before their introduction of negotiable CDs in 1961. For the first time, then, the banks had bid the yield on what had become their principal source of funds to the prime rate. And, as manager of the bank cartel, the Federal Reserve responded by increasing the discount rate because, as Federal Reserve Board Chair William McChesney Martin Jr. put it, the banks "had let themselves become bound into the prime rate in a ridiculous way" (FOMC *Minutes*, 23 November 1965, p. 86; also see Epstein, 1987, p. 248). Of course, this is an understatement, since the 4.5 percent prime rate was the linchpin of the New Deal's low-interest-rate rule. As we will see below, raising it undermined the Johnson administration's incomes policy. On the other hand, we will also see that, by not acting as cartel manager in 1966 and raising the discount rate, but increasing reserve requirements instead,[11] the Federal Reserve allowed the Administration to revive its incomes policy.

Bankers know more about credit conditions than borrowers do. As I explain in Chapter 2, banks thus have an incentive to take advantage of this information asymmetry, exaggerate the tightness of credit-market conditions, and thereby justify a higher prime rate. Insofar as discount-rate increases are justified as necessary for anti-inflationary purposes, borrowers can prevent bankers from taking advantage of them by insisting that the banks link prime-rate increases to increases in the discount rate (also see, for example, Goodhart, 1989, pp. 17–18).

That is to say, the Federal Reserve can use discount-rate increases to preserve bank profit margins, as it did by Martin's own account in December 1965, only to the degree that it is plausible to argue that the Federal Reserve is *not* using the discount rate to preserve bank profit margins. This fact explains the paradox of an institution that exists to preserve bank profit margins turning around and undermining them in order to control the stock of money. In order to sustain credibility with borrowers, who are trying to use discount-rate policy to overcome the information asymmetry in credit markets, the Federal Reserve must at times subordinate its role as bank-cartel manager to its role of inflation fighter.[12]

For example, with the tri-annual rounds of wage negotiations in the automobile and steel industries in 1964–5, there were inflationary pressures in December 1965. However, the Johnson administration was implementing an effective incomes policy to deal with them. By December 1965, in the same way that President Kennedy had contained the inflationary pressures of the tri-annual rounds of wage negotiations by confronting the steel industry in April 1962, forcing U.S. Steel to rescind an announced price increase, President Johnson had forced the aluminum and copper industries to rescind announced price increases. Consequently, to justify a higher discount rate and thus a higher prime rate, Martin was forced to argue that there was quite a difference

> between interest rates, steel, aluminum and copper prices. But without going into the wisdom, or lack of wisdom ... on the part of the Administration in rolling back aluminum or copper prices ... if one was going to roll back those prices because of a fear of inflation, one also ought, at the same time, to permit adjustment of interest rates to restrain inflation. The two things were compatible—not incompatible—as operating techniques.
>
> (Martin, FOMC *Minutes*, 23 November 1965, p. 85)

Martin was wrong. Since non-financial corporations can use higher borrowing costs to justify higher prices, an incomes policy can only work if the Federal Reserve holds the line on interest rates. The Democratic appointees to the Federal Reserve Board understood this. For example, Sherman J. Maisel responded to Martin by arguing that:

> he [Maisel] still hoped that incomes policy, as opposed to monetary policy, would continue to be used at this point. In his judgment the Administration had properly been using incomes policy. If a change were made now to monetary policy, that would amount to giving up. It would amount to saying that the [Federal Reserve] System did not favor the present way of handling national policy and, therefore, was going to use monetary policy. ... It should be clear that he felt that not changing interest rates was very definitely a part of the economics of full employment.
>
> (Maisel, FOMC *Minutes*, 23 November 1965, p. 85)

Underlying the debate between Martin and Maisel was not so much the question of whether to use an incomes policy or monetary policy to combat inflationary pressures. Exercising monetary restraint by raising reserve requirements and restricting the banks' access to the discount window to control the stock of money are compatible with, and probably essential to, a successful incomes policy. Rather, the underlying confrontation was between an incomes policy and the interests of the U.S. bank cartel. In other words, if the Johnson administration could not stop the large New York banks from preserving their profit margins by raising the prime rate, then it could not justify trying to stop other businesses from preserving their profit margins by raising the prices of their products. In the wake of the December 1965 discount-rate increase, the Administration thus accepted in silence a rash of price increases in chemicals, paper, cigarettes, and metals. In an effort to coax the Federal Reserve into lowering interest rates, the Administration also tightened fiscal policy. On 13 January 1966, President Johnson called for a tax increase—what Martin ostensibly wanted in order to lower interest rates (see, for example, *New York Times*, 16 March 1966, pp. 57, 66). And in testimony before the Joint Economic Committee of Congress on 1 February 1966, Gardner Ackley, Chair of the Council of Economic Advisors, expressed Administration acceptance of the Federal Reserve's high-interest-rate policy (U.S. Congress, 1 February 1966a, p. 17).

These conciliatory gestures were in vain. On 15 March 1966, barely two weeks after the new taxes President Johnson had called for became law (excise taxes on automobiles and phone services were passed, as well as provisions for more rapid collection of corporate taxes and increased withholding taxes on personal incomes), Martin told reporters at the closing banquet of the Eighth International Savings Congress that more tax increases would be necessary before he would consider lowering interest rates. On 12 May, his words were repeated verbatim by J. Dewey Daane, a Martin loyalist on the Federal Reserve Board, in a speech to the Investment Bankers Association (*New York Times*, 13 May 1966, p. 57).

However, between Martin's off-the-cuff remarks to reporters and Daane's speech, the conflict between the large New York banks and the large regional banks over interest-rate-ceiling policy broke out (on 22 March), creating an opening for the Administration to try to revive its incomes policy. In a speech to the Association of Reserve City Bankers on 5 April, Treasury Secretary Henry H. Fowler proposed that the Federal Reserve exercise monetary restraint without raising interest rates, presumably by raising reserve requirements and restricting bank access to the discount window instead (*New York Times*, 6 April 1966, p. 55). On 9 May, this presumption was confirmed by Frederick L. Deming, Under Secretary of Treasury for Monetary Affairs, in a speech to a joint meeting of the American Society of Business Writers and a National Mortgage Conference of the American Bankers Association. Deming explained how such monetary restraint could work through limitations on the "overly aggressive behavior on the part of some banks in competing for time deposits" (*New York Times*, 10 May 1966, p. 66).

Of all Administration officials, Deming was the most influential within the Federal Reserve System. He had resigned from the Federal Open Market Committee in order to become Under Secretary of Treasury. Indeed, it was at the next meeting of the Federal Open Market Committee, the day after Deming's speech, that the Democratic appointees to the Federal Reserve Board—Arthur F. Brimmer, Sherman J. Maisel, and George Mitchell, with the acquiescence of the non-New York regional-bank presidents, resolved to use reserve requirements to pursue the objectives specified by Fowler and Deming: monetary restraint through raising reserve requirements and restricting access to the discount window rather than raising interest rates (see, for example, FOMC *Minutes*, 10 May 1966, p. 79, *passim*).

The first step was the new reserve-requirement policy. As can be seen in Figure 5.1, with the large New York banks aggressively bidding for funds in the CD market and the large regional banks protecting their deposit bases by adjusting "rates upward in line with rates in New York," bank profit margins were reduced to zero twice more in the first half of 1966. However, unlike in December 1965, the Federal Reserve responded, not by increasing the discount rate because the banks "had let themselves become bound into the prime rate in a ridiculous way," but by increasing reserve requirements on CDs because, as Arthur F. Brimmer, who moved from the Commerce Department to the Federal Reserve Board in February 1966, put it:

> it was important ... to let the market—and especially the larger banks— know that the [Federal Open Market] Committee did not subscribe to a pattern of activity in which those banks competed actively for funds to relend to their costumers.
>
> (Brimmer, FOMC *Minutes*, 28 June 1966, p. 75)

With the Federal Reserve thus falling into line, the Johnson administration turned to Congress for support in reviving its incomes policy, where opposition to high interest rates was never in doubt. For example, William Proxmire, Democrat from Wisconsin and Chair of the Senate Banking Committee, reacted to the December 1965 discount-rate increase by telling reporters it was imperative

> to determine what action must be taken to prevent this creation of Congress from endangering the nation's prosperity and from doing so in defiance of the President of the United States.
>
> (*New York Times*, 7 December 1965, p. 74)

Wright Patman, Democrat from Texas and Chair of the House Banking and Currency Committee, was no less adamant in his reaction to the December 1965 discount-rate increase. He told reporters that:

> Congress should move immediately ... to put an end to Mr. Martin's power to thumb his nose at the President, the Congress and the American people. Once again we are seeing the folly of allowing a handful of banker-dominated members of the Federal Reserve dictate the economic future of the country.
>
> (*New York Times*, 7 December 1965, p. 74)

Consequently, on 11 May, there was widespread elation on Capitol Hill when John E. Horne, Chair of the Federal Home Loan Bank Board, endorsed legislation to bar commercial banks from issuing small-denomination time deposits (*New York Times*, 12 May 1966, p. 65; *New York Times*, 17 May 1966, p. 69). Then, on 19 May, Treasury Secretary Fowler expressed sympathy to the House Banking and Currency Committee for legislation that would prevent commercial banks from paying more than 5 percent on small-denomination time deposits (U.S. Congress, 19 May 1966b, p. 136).[13]

Martin bent under the pressure, telling the American Bankers Association, on 25 May, that he understood the President's reluctance to advocate further tax increases "until he knows where we are going in Vietnam" (*New York Times*, 26 May 1966, p. 1). However, the large New York banks were more recalcitrant. In direct rebuttal of Martin, on 26 May, David Rockefeller, Chair of Chase Manhattan Bank and the most influential voice on Wall Street, went before the annual meeting of the American Iron and Steel Institute, which adamantly opposed tax increases, to insist that tax increases were necessary (*New York Times*, 27 May 1966, p. 61).

Rockefeller's intervention backfired. For it prompted a "high official in the Johnson administration" to telephone H. Erich Heinemann, a leading correspondent on monetary and financial affairs, to say that, as Heinemann reported it, "the legislation [to prevent commercial banks from paying more than 5 percent on small-denomination time deposits] was considered a 'priority measure' . . . 'We hope to get a meeting of minds in the next day or two'" (*New York Times*, 31 May 1966, p. 59).

To derail the momentum toward legislated interest-rate ceilings, on 8 June, in testimony before the House Banking and Currency Committee, Martin was compelled to ask for the discretionary authority to pursue the reserve-requirement policy outlined by Brimmer, Maisel, and Mitchell on 10 May (U.S. Congress, 8 June 1966c, p. 483). The result was a $400 million increase in reserve requirements on large-denomination time deposits, effective 26 June, which was criticized by the Johnson administration and Congress as too little too late (*New York Times*, 26 June 1966, p. 69; *New York Times*, 29 June 1966, p. 61). The Johnson administration thus renewed its call for mandatory interest-rate ceilings because of "the apparent unwillingness of the Federal Reserve Board to exercise this power" when granted on a discretionary basis (*New York Times*, 13 June 1966, pp. 1, 48).

On 26 June, as can be seen in Figure 5.1, the large New York banks had once again bid the market yield on large-denomination time deposits to equality with the prime rate and restored their profit margins by increasing the latter to 5.5 percent. Wall Street wanted the Federal Reserve to do the same thing it did in December 1965 and support the large New York banks with a discount-rate increase. When the Federal Reserve increased reserve requirements instead, signaling that there would be no more interest-rate increases, the Administration was finally in a position to revive its incomes policy, which it did with a vengeance on 12 July, when it forced American Climax Incorporated to rescind a 5 percent increase in the price of molybdenum (*New York Times*, 14 July 1966, p. 1).[14]

Nonetheless, the increase in reserve requirements failed to slow the large New York bank lending to corporations (see, for example, *New York Times*, 26 June 1966, p. 69; *New York Times*, 29 June 1966, p. 1). Consequently, in tandem with the reactivation of its incomes policy on 12 July, the Johnson administration also pressed ahead with its call for legislation prescribing interest-rate ceilings (*New York Times*, 13 June 1966, pp. 1, 48). In response, on 15 July, the Federal Reserve reduced interest-rate ceilings to 4 percent on 'multiple maturity time deposits', i.e. on automatically renewable time deposits that were payable only after written notice of withdrawal. Singling out 'multiple maturity deposits' for a lower interest-rate ceiling was first suggested by Federal Home Loan Bank Board Chair Horne as a way to stop the large New York banks from financing their rapidly expanding loan portfolios without adversely affecting other banks and non-bank financial institutions (*New York Times*, 29 June 1966, p. 66). But the idea had too many loopholes to work (see, for example, *New York Times*, 16 July 1966, p. 21). Therefore, on 25 July, by which time it was clear that the Federal Reserve had again failed to slowdown the rate of growth of lending by the large New York banks (*New York Times*, 16 July 1966, p. 21; *New York Times*, 29 June 1966, p. 66), legislation cleared the House Banking and Currency Committee that would impose interest-rate ceilings on different types of deposits then give the Federal Reserve authority to raise them, but only with the approval of the President (*New York Times*, 26 July 1966, p. 43).

The concerted assault on their funding operations prompted the large New York banks to discover that they could avoid monetary restraint by borrowing Eurodollars. This new source of funds had enormous implications for the future of the financial system, which is the topic of Chapter 6. What is important to note here is that the borrowing of Eurodollars by the large New York banks provided them with a way to meet the demands of their customers for new loans without antagonizing the large regional banks. By July 1966, by shifting the bulk of their funding operations from the domestic negotiable CD market to the Eurodollar market, the large New York banks ameliorated their conflict with the large regional banks sufficiently to gear up the American Bankers Association, as well as other bank lobbies, to stop the interest-rate ceiling legislation. These lobbying efforts prompted the Johnson administration to back off somewhat in its lobbying for the legislation (see, for example, *New York Times*, 23 July 1966, p. 35; *New York Times*, 26 July 1966, p. 41; *New York Times*, 28 July 1966, p. 43).

However, on 2 August 1966, Inland Steel Company jumped the gun, when it concluded from the Administration's retreat on the interest-rate ceiling legislation that the Administration would also retreat from its incomes policy and acquiesce to an increase in the price of steel by 2.1 percent. On 4 August, by which time the rest of the steel industry had matched Inland Steel's price increase, the Administration launched a campaign to force the steel industry to rescind the price increases. All eyes then turned to the Federal Reserve to see if it would once again sustain Wall Street's demand for inflation, as it had done in December 1965 by raising the discount rate. Robert V. Roosa, former Vice-President of the Federal Reserve Bank of New York and Under Secretary of Treasury in the Kennedy and early Johnson administrations, summed up best this paradoxical situation of Wall Street demanding inflation as "the critical phase in the confrontation between the new inflation and the New Economics" (*New York Times*, 1 September 1966, p. 49). Clearly, Wall Street preferred the new inflation to the New Economics of sustaining full employment with price stability by means of an incomes policy, including monetary restraint imposed by raising reserve requirements and, as we will see below, by restricting the banks' access to the discount window.

In the wake of the increase in reserve requirements on 26 June, the Federal Reserve did nothing as the steel industry and the Johnson administration confronted each other, which was interpreted on Wall Street as support for the Administration. On 16 August, in exasperation at the Federal Reserve's support for the New Economics, the large New York banks took matters into their own hands and raised the prime rate to 6 percent, its highest level since 1929. Since the higher borrowing costs for the steel industry justified the higher prices for its output, in one stroke the struggle over the country's anti-inflation policy was reduced to a confrontation between the Administration and the large New York banks. That is to say, the large New York banks thus relieved the pressure on the steel industry by prompting the Administration to redirect its fire toward them. For example, Treasury Secretary Fowler responded to the 16 August prime-rate increase by issuing the following statement:

> Raising the price of money should not be the sole means of determining who gets credit. When demand exceeds a bank's resources, credit expansion can and should be restrained by banker's saying 'no' to borrowers on criteria other than that of who is willing to pay the highest rate.
>
> (Fowler, *New York Times*, 17 August 1966, pp. 1, 58)

To prevent the first major financial crisis of the postwar period, all the Federal Reserve had to do was signal its support for the large New York banks and the new inflation by defying Secretary Fowler and increasing the discount rate. The question that transfixed Wall Street, the question that made participants in the bond markets reluctant to quote bid prices, was whether or not the Federal Reserve would relieve the pressure on the large New York banks—after all, that is what Federal Reserve independence means. If Wall Street wants higher prices, including a higher price for money (interest rates), despite the Administration's efforts to hold them down, then the Federal Reserve is supposed to have the autonomy to take Wall Street's side against the Government. As Lawrence Goodwyn (1978, p. 267) puts it, the establishment of the Federal Reserve System was supposed to remove "the bankers from the harsh glare of public view. Popular attention thenceforth was to focus upon 'the Fed,' and not upon the actions of the New York commercial bankers."

However, the Federal Reserve's independence from the government is tantamount to its dependence on the U.S. bank cartel, and the split of the latter over interest-rate-ceiling policy ended up meaning that, on 17 August 1966, the Federal Reserve precipitated the 1966 financial crisis by siding with the Administration. In direct response to Fowler's statement, it increased reserve requirements from 5 percent to 6 percent on time deposits of $5 million or more (see, for example, *New York Times*, 18 August 1966, p. 1).

It was this increase in reserve requirements that caused Wall Street to panic. In particular, it panicked at the fact that, by leaving the large New York banks without a rationale for charging the highest lending rate since 1929, the Federal Reserve provided the impetus for the legislation which cleared the House Banking and Currency Committee on 25 July to become law. This legislation imposed temporary interest-rate ceilings on different types of deposits then gave the Federal Reserve authority to raise them, but only with the approval of the President. The heated words of Fowler, on 16 August, made this legislation appear imperative, and it was assured of passage when, on 1 September, the National League of Insured Savings Associations, one of the most powerful lobbies in Congress, reversed its longstanding opposition to governmental authority to fix interest rates (*New York Times*, 2 September 1966, p. 41).

On 28 August, the crisis reached its nadir, when the bond market seized up completely in response to a statement by former Democratic President Harry S. Truman saying that either interest rates had to be lowered or irreparable harm would be done to the economy (see, for example, *New York Times*, 29 August 1966, p. 1). This was Truman's first intervention in a public debate since leaving office in 1953 and, on Wall Street, it seemed unimaginable that Truman would issue such a statement without being personally asked to do so by the President. As H. Erich Heinemann reported in the *New York Times* (30 August 1966, pp. 1, 53), Truman's statement thus seemed to "have been inspired by the Johnson Administration as the opening shot in an all-out political attack on the independence of the Federal Reserve System." After all, it was Truman who had agreed to the March 1951 Accord which gave the Federal Reserve independence from the Treasury Department in the wake of the New Deal financial reforms which had curtailed it.

The 1966 financial crisis ended on 29 August 1966 when President Johnson issued a statement rebutting these rumors. In response to this statement, Wall Street breathed a collective sigh of relief, bond-market participants began bidding for bonds again, and the 1966 financial came to an end (see, for example, *New York Times*, 30 August 1966, p. 53).

Section 5.5 Summary and Conclusions

The current Neoliberal Era of free-market economies was preceded by a Golden Age of government-managed economies. In this chapter, I have identified as a key moment in the transition from the Golden Age to the Neoliberal Era the thirteen days in August 1966 when the bond market revolted against government management of the U.S. economy.

Both orthodox and Post Keynesian economists have glossed over the historical significance of the bond-market revolt. As we saw in Chapter 4, orthodox economists—from New Classicals and Monetarists on the right to New Keynesians on the left—identify the Golden Age with Keynesian demand management, or fiscal and monetary policies designed to stabilize economies at full employment with price stability. In contrast, I identified the Golden Age with the social-democratic reforms of the New Deal, as extended by the Kennedy and Johnson administrations.

Post Keynesians accept the orthodox identification of the Golden Age with Keynesian demand management, with the caveat that rising debt burdens created a fragile financial environment that is increasingly susceptible to shocks. 1966 marks a trend change in the uniform, or average, rate of profit, from a postwar rise to a tendency to fall (see, for example, Dumenil and Levy, 2004, p. 24; Kotz, 2015, p. 88). For this reason, Wolfson's (1986) argument for increasing financial instability is the most compelling one. He argues that the falling rate of profit caused debt burdens, taken on under more auspicious circumstances for profit-making, to become unsustainable in August 1966.

As we saw in Chapter 4, the tightening of monetary policy in 1965–6 was not more extreme than in the late 1950s. Nonetheless, for financial-instability theorists, the transition from a stable financial system to a fragile one turned the tight monetary policy of 1965–6 into the shock that precipitated the 1966 financial crisis. Banks bid the market yields on time deposits above the interest-rate ceilings that the Federal Reserve maintained on new time deposits. Maturing time deposits could not be rolled over at interest rates held by administrative fiat below market interest rates. Bond-market participants allegedly panicked on 17 August at the threat that banks would have to sell bonds in order to replace funds lost as time deposits matured. To prevent the 1966 financial crisis from devolving into a debt-deflation, Wolfson (1986, p. 50) concludes that the Federal Reserve abandoned its tight monetary policy at the 23 August 1966 meeting of the Federal Open Market Committee. Since the bond market remained jittery even after the Federal Reserve had eased monetary policy, Wolfson argues further that, on 1 September, the Federal Reserve sent a letter to the banks assuring them of access to the discount window for all the funds they wanted. According to Wolfson, this letter calmed the bond market and brought the financial crisis to an end.

There are five major reasons to question Wolfson's application of Minsky's financial instability hypothesis to the 1966 financial crisis. First, even though secondary-market yields on time deposits were above their interest-rate ceilings, in both August and September time deposits for the banking system as a whole increased. Banks may *choose* to sell bonds under such circumstances but there was no danger that tight monetary policy would *force* them to sell bonds.

Second, even though there was a run-off of large-denomination time deposits at the large New York banks in August, this run-off of domestic time deposits was offset by the funds large New York banks obtained by issuing new time deposits in the Eurodollar market. Moreover, the large New York banks could have obtained all the funds they wanted in the Eurodollar market. Again, there was no danger that tight monetary policy would force the banks to sell bonds.

Third, in February 1966 there was a run-off of domestic time deposits at the large New York banks that was not offset by bank borrowings of Eurodollars. Why would a run-off of domestic time deposits that was offset by a build-up of time deposits in the Eurodollar market cause a financial crisis in August 1966 when a run-off of domestic time deposits that was not offset by a build-up of Eurodollar deposits did not cause a financial crisis in February 1966?

Fourth, the Federal Reserve did not ease monetary policy until 4 October 1966. Contrary to Wolfson's interpretation of the 1 September letter from the Federal Reserve Board to member banks as assuring them of access to the discount window for all the funds they wanted and thus calming the bond market, the letter confirmed the rumors, which spread after the 23 August meeting of the Federal Open Market Committee, that the discount window as well as reserve requirements would be used to support the Administration's incomes policy. In a front-page commentary in the *New York Times* on 19 August, H. Erich Heinemann summed up as follows the Federal Reserve's intentions with regard to discount-window policy:

The [Federal Reserve] Board's aim, apparently, is to slow, if not halt, the expansion of total bank loans. From all appearances, the Federal Reserve does not intend at present to increase the maximum rate commercial banks are allowed to pay on fixed-maturity time deposits. ... Because interest rates on other alternative forms of money market instruments have already risen well over the ... time deposit ceiling, the expectation—indeed the hope—is that the failure to increase the rate will lead to a marked reduction in the total of negotiable time certificates of deposit now outstanding at the major banks ... in effect the [Federal] Reserve was telling the banks not to feel shy about borrowing at the Federal Reserve discount window if the need arises. As had been traditional at the Federal Reserve, these loans will continue to be for temporary periods only. However, "temporary" is a flexible term, and banks that "cooperate" with the Federal Reserve authorities in reducing their loans could expect to receive more liberal accommodation (presumably to keep their loans outstanding for longer periods of time) than those that do not. This would be a considerable shift in the "tone" of the way the regional Federal Reserve discount window is administered. For the first time, the discount officers at the 12 regional Federal Reserve Banks would be using their credit-granting power to achieve a specific aim of monetary policy, namely a reduction of bank lending. ... "They had better be careful they do not push too far" a New York banker said last night in a telephone interview.
(Heinemann, *New York Times*, 19 August 1966, pp. 1, 47)

Two days before the 1 September letter confirmed the more activist discount-window policy, Edwin L. Dale wrote in the *New York Times* that:

the new device involves the use of Federal Reserve lending through the "discount window" as a lever to induce individual banks to change the composition of their assets. This approach, it was suggested by banking observers, will probably involve a number of direct confrontations between the presidents of the 12 Regional Reserve Banks and the presidents of individual commercial banks. ... "We will not, of course, tell a bank not to make a specific loan," says one Federal Reserve official. "But we will look at its total portfolio." It is entirely possible that the program will see an increase in the already-high total of Federal Reserve loans to member banks. But if it works as intended, bank loans, particularly to business, will be reduced.

(Dale, *New York Times*, 29 August 1966, pp. 41, 43)

In short, how could an easing of monetary policy end the crisis if no such easing occurred?

Finally, Wolfson explains the 1966 financial crisis as a cyclical phenomenon. As such, he is in accord with Charles Kindleberger (1978), who also sees himself as applying Minsky's financial instability hypothesis and, as I explain in Chapter 1, defines the "art of central banking" as the ability to exercise monetary control during periods of calm between financial crises despite the fact that the Federal Reserve must intervene, and financial-market participants know it must intervene, as lender of last resort when financial crises do occur. Indeed, Wolfson adds nothing to Carron's (1982, p. 418; also see Wojnilower, 1980) thesis "that monetary policy has been controlled so as to force the economy through a financial crunch into the early stages of a crisis. But that is as far as the Federal Reserve seems willing to go." But this is not Minsky's thesis about the 1966 financial crisis, which is that it marks the transition from the postwar Golden Age of relative financial stability to the current Neoliberal Era of chronic financial instability (see, for example, Minsky, 1981, p. 199).

My critique of Minsky's financial instability hypothesis embraces his interpretation of the 1966 financial crisis as marking the structural transformation of the economy, from the Golden Age to the Neoliberal Era. It is just that I identify different persistent and systematic forces at work: not increasing debt burdens but class and intra-class conflict over the distribution of income. The problem underlying the 1966 financial crisis was not caused by households and firms taking on more debt-payment commitments during economic expansions than they had adequate incomes to service during economic downturns, but by the large New York banks' adamant refusal to accept an incomes policy.

In other words, the large New York banks—Wall Street, if you wish—is the key protagonist in U.S. capitalism. Wall Street quite simply could no longer abide by the fixed-interest-rate structure at the heart of the New Deal. Their shift from asset management to liability management eroded this structure, insofar as their bid prices were concerned, but the movement toward social democracy could still be sustained so long as their ask prices—the prime rate—could be held in place, for the key to the movement toward social democracy in 1966 was implementing an incomes policy to contain the inflationary pressures unleashed by the Treaty of Detroit. And non-financial corporations can use increases in the prime rate to justify increasing the prices of their output.

In short, the future of social democracy in the U.S. was reduced, in August 1966, to a question of what the Federal Reserve would do. Since February 1965, it had been conducting a contractionary open-market policy. To sustain the movement toward social democracy, in the form of the Administration's incomes policy, the Federal Reserve needed to complement the incomes policy with reserve requirements on large-denomination time deposits and restrictions on the U.S. bank cartel's access to the discount window. On the other hand, the Federal Reserve could undermine the movement toward social democracy by complementing its contractionary open-market policy with increases in the discount rate, or a high-interest-rate policy, since the banks' ask prices would rise in tandem.

Bond-market participants panicked when, by increasing reserve requirements on 17 August 1966, the Federal Reserve reaffirmed its preference for an incomes policy at the very moment when the large New York banks had taken the lead in the struggle for a high-interest-rate policy. Therefore, to end the crisis, all the Federal Reserve had to do was reverse itself and signal its resolve to pursue a high-interest-rate policy by increasing the discount rate. To end a financial crisis by tightening monetary policy in this way is incomprehensible from the perspective of the problem of financial instability. Yet it is precisely what Alfred Hayes, President of the Federal Reserve Bank of New York, argued for at the 23 August 1966 meeting of the Federal Open Market Committee (FOMC *Minutes*, 23 August 1966, p. 53).

The Federal Reserve did not increase the discount rate in August 1966. This was not because it was easing monetary policy, as Wolfson argues. Rather, as Governor Arthur F. Brimmer reiterated for Hayes's benefit, on 23 August, the Federal Reserve did not increase the discount rate because: 1) since late June it had substituted a high-reserve-requirement policy for a high-interest-rate policy in order to force the large banks to reduce the rate of growth of the stock of money; 2) since the large banks were currently using Eurodollars to thwart the Federal Reserve's objective of controlling the stock of money, the next policy move should be to put reserve requirements on those borrowings; and 3) once the high-reserve-requirement policy began to take effect, the large banks would be forced to the discount window. Therefore, it was important to make clear that discount-window borrowings would themselves be contingent on the banks doing their part to reduce the rate of growth of their new loans, and thus of the stock of money, which the banks create in the process of granting new loans (FOMC *Minutes*, 23 August 1966, p. 7, *passim*).

At the 23 August meeting of the Federal Open Market Committee, Hayes spoke for the large New York banks, Brimmer spoke for the Johnson administration, and their audience was the large regional banks, represented by the non-New York regional-bank presidents. The implications of Hayes's demand for a discount-rate increase had already been demonstrated by the increase in the discount rate in December 1965. In both cases, Hayes wanted a discount-rate increase to provide cover for an increase in the prime rate by the large New York banks. In December 1965, the discount-rate increase temporarily halted the movement toward social democracy, as the Administration was forced to accept a rash of price increases. If the Administration could not stop the large New York banks from preserving their profit margins by raising the prime rate, then it could not justify trying to stop other businesses from preserving their profit margins by raising the prices of their products.

Similarly, the implications of Brimmer's demand for higher reserve requirements and an activist discount-window policy had already been demonstrated in
June 1966, when the large New York banks had also bid the yield on large-
denomination time deposits to equality with the prime rate and, once again, tried
to preserve their profit margins by increasing the latter. But this time the Federal
Reserve did not increase the discount rate because it was no longer able to
implement a high-interest-rate policy on terms acceptable to both the large
regional banks and the large New York banks. That is to say, the large New York
banks wanted a contractionary open-market policy only so long as the interest-rate
ceilings on time deposits were raised when market yields on time deposits
breached them. However, the large regional banks wanted a contractionary open-
market policy only so long as the interest-rate ceilings were not raised.

The conflict between the large New York banks and the large regional banks
over the proper terms for a high-interest-rate policy ended up prompting the
Federal Reserve, in late June 1966, to opt for exercising monetary restraint by
increasing reserve requirements rather than the discount rate—precisely the
monetary policy needed for an incomes policy to work. Consequently, the intra-
class conflict allowed the Administration to revive its strategy of maintaining full
employment with price stability, in early July, by reviving its incomes policy.

In June 1966, after their conflict with the large regional banks took the form of
an increase in reserve requirements, the large New York banks responded to the
criticisms of their liability management by shifting their demand for new funds
from the domestic money market to the more expensive Eurodollar market.
I show in Chapter 6 that this shift provided the basis for a reconciliation between
the large New York banks and the large regional banks in May 1967. The large
New York banks agreed to accept a contractionary open-market policy without
increases in the interest-rate ceilings on domestic time deposits as long as the
Federal Reserve guaranteed them unhindered access to the Eurodollar market.

However, Wall Street jumped the gun, in July 1966, when it concluded that the
large New York banks and the large regional banks had resolved their differences
over monetary policy just because they had joined forces to fight legislation
setting mandatory interest-rate ceilings on small-denomination time deposits.
On 17 August, Wall Street realized its error, and panicked, after the Federal
Reserve once again increased reserve requirements rather than using a discount-
rate increase to confirm a prime-rate increase by the large New York banks.

In short, if the Federal Reserve had increased the discount rate on 17 August,
rather than reserve requirements, then the 1966 financial crisis would not have
occurred. Therefore, it was not, as financial-instability theorists argue, because of
tight monetary policy that the financial crisis occurred. On the contrary, the
1966 financial crisis occurred because monetary policy was not tight enough for
Wall Street.

Nor did the crisis end because monetary policy was eased, as financial-instability
theorists argue. It ended because the President assured Wall Street that he would not
let the Administration's strategy for sustaining full employment with price stability
through an incomes policy impinge upon the Federal Reserve's independence.

In other words, the 1966 financial crisis came to an end when the President held out the prospect of higher interest rates in the future.

Of course, there was a fundamental contradiction between sustaining full employment with price stability and the prospect of higher interest rates in the future. As we will see in Chapter 6, it was the resolution of this contradiction in favor of higher interest rates that caused the structural transformation from the Golden Age to the Neoliberal Era.

Notes

1 See Martin H. Wolfson (1986) for an exposition (and attempted synthesis) of the extant theories of financial crises. Wolfson makes clear how current theories of financial crises are subordinated to (conflated with?) theories of financial instability.
2 See Hyman Minsky (1982) for the most widely accepted version of the financial instability hypothesis, whereby psychological factors cause firms to overextend themselves. Martin H. Wolfson (1986) substitutes a falling rate of profit for psychological factors to explain why firms overextend themselves. Robert Pollin (1987) augments Minsky's account with the argument that declining real incomes have caused households to overextend themselves as well.
3 See, for example, Andrew S. Carron (1982: 418) who concludes a survey of financial crises in the postwar period as follows:

> It appears that monetary policy has been controlled so as to force the economy through a financial crunch into the early stages of a crisis. But that is as far as the Federal Reserve seems willing to go.

4 Data on outstanding time deposits at all banks are from *Citibase*. The other data referred to in this chapter, on outstanding time deposits at the large New York banks, on interest rates, and interest-rate ceilings, are from the *Federal Reserve Bulletin*, various issues.
5 Chase Manhattan Bank, First National City Bank, and Manufacturers Hanover Trust Company accounted for most of the borrowing of Eurodollars by U.S. banks in the late 1960s (Kelly, 1976, p. 98). If Bank of America, Bankers Trust Company, and Morgan Guaranty Trust are added to this list, or at a maximum if Chemical Bank, Continental Illinois, First Chicago Bank, Marine Midland Bank, and the First National Bank of Boston are also added, then practically all U.S. bank Eurodollar borrowings in the late 1960s are probably accounted for (Kelly 1976, pp. 15, 147).
6 There was nothing new about large-denomination time deposits in the early 1960s. What was new was that the large-denomination time deposits were 'negotiable'. That is to say, the banks developed a secondary market where these time deposits could be easily sold prior to maturity, thereby making them a viable alternative to Treasury bills for corporate-finance officers seeking a return on idle working capital. As we will see in Section 5.4, the large New York banks issued small-denomination time deposits, too.
7 As George H. Clay, Harold T. Patterson, and Elliot J. Swan, Presidents of the Federal Reserve Banks of Kansas City, Atlanta and San Francisco respectively, said of the banks in their Districts at the 22 March 1966 meeting of the Federal Open Market Committee (FOMC *Minutes*, 22 March 1966, pp. 43, 62, 74).
8 For similar statements by other regional-bank presidents, see FOMC *Minutes*, 22 March 1966, pp. 43, 61–2, 74, 77.
9 Establishing this point is the reason why Goodhart wrote *The Evolution of Central Banks* (1988).

10 Since other bank costs are fixed, and thus decline per unit of output as output increases, they reinfore the logic of this analysis.
11 Tobin (1989, pp. 260–1) calls attention to the importance of reserve requirements for controlling the stock of money by reviving the idea of 100-percent reserves against demand deposits (i.e. checking accounts). That it would undermine bank profits is the principal critique made of Tobin's 100-percent-reserve-requirements proposal (see, for example, Goodhart, 1988, p. 88).
12 The need for the Federal Reserve to inject randomness into the relationship between the prime rate and the discount rate is analogous to the need for sellers in markets characterized by information asymmetries to incorporate white noise into prices. As Gould and Verrecchia (1985) point out, when buyers know sellers are more informed than they are, they tend to see a higher price as signifying a higher future value and thus increase demand, i.e. the information asymmetry gives sellers an incentive to charge a higher price. But to the degree that sellers act on this incentive, prices no longer reflect their superior knowledge of future value, i.e. randomness enters into prices. Analogously, it is only because of their apparent randomness that discount-rate increases do not cause a hemorrhaging of demand for bank credit.
13 Whereas the large New York banks bid for large-denomination time deposits at the expense of the large regional banks, they bid for small-denomination time deposits at the expense of the small commercial banks, mutual savings banks, credit unions, and Savings and Loan Associations. It was the latter which had the most influence in Congress.
14 Molybdenum is an alloy used with iron in the production of high-precision machine tools. It was in explanation of the Federal Reserve Board's decision to increase reserve requirements rather than the discount rate on 26 June that Brimmer told the Federal Open Market Committee, as noted above, that "it was important ... to let the market— and especially the larger banks—know that the Committee did not subscribe to a pattern of activity in which those banks competed for funds to relend to their customers" (FOMC *Minutes*, 28 June 1966, p. 75).

Bibliography

Bulletin, Federal Reserve Bank of New York, various issues.
Carron, Andrew S. 1982. "Financial Crises: Recent Experiences in US and International Markets." *Brookings Papers on Economic Activity*. Vol. 2, pp. 395–422.
CITIBASE.
Dickens, Edwin and Phillip A. O'Hara. 1999. "Financial Crises." In *The Encyclopedia of Political Economy*. Phillip A. O'Hara (ed.). New York: Routledge, pp. 347–9.
Dumenil, Gerard and Dominique Levy. 2004. *Capital Resurgent: Roots of the Neoliberal Revolution*. Cambridge, MA: Harvard University Press.
Eccles, Marriner S. 1951. *Beckoning Frontiers: Public and Personal Reflections*. Sidney Hyman (ed.). New York: Alfred A. Knopf.
Epstein, Gerald. 1990. "Prime Rates, Federal Reserve Signaling, and Financial Instability." *Journal of Post Keynesian Economics*, Vol. 12, No. 1, pp. 618–35.
Epstein, Gerald. 1987. "Federal Reserve Behavior and the Limits of Monetary Policy in the Current Economic Crisis." In *The Imperiled Economy: Macroeconomics from a Left Perspective*, Robert Cherry (ed.). New York: Union for Radical Political Economics, pp. 247–55.
Federal Open Market Committee. 1965–7. *Minutes*.
Goodhart, Charles. 1989. *Money, Information and Uncertainty*. Second edition. Cambridge, MA: MIT Press.

Goodhart, Charles. 1988. *The Evolution of Central Banks*. Cambridge, MA: MIT Press.

Goodwyn, Lawrence. 1978. *The Populist Movement: A Short History of the Agrarian Revolt in America*. New York: Oxford University Press.

Gould, J. P. and R. E. Verrecchia. 1985. "The Information Content of Specialist Pricing." *Journal of Political Economy*. Vol. 93, No. 1, pp. 66–83.

Guttentag, Jack and R. Herring. 1984. "Credit Rationing and Financial Disorder." *Journal of Finance*. Vol. 34, No. 5 (December), pp. 1359–82.

Kelly, Janet. 1976. *Bankers and Borders: The Case of American Banks in Britain*. Cambridge, MA: Ballinger.

Kindleberger, Charles P. 1978 [2005]. *Manias, Panics, and Crashes: A History of Financial Crises*. New York: Wiley.

Kotz, David M. 2015. *The Rise and Fall of Neoliberalism*. Cambridge, MA: Harvard University Press.

Minsky, Hyman P. 1986 [2008]. *Stabilizing an Unstable Economy*. Armonk, NY: M. E. Sharpe.

Minsky, Hyman P. 1982. "The Financial Instability Hypothesis: A Restatement." In *Can "It" Happen Again? Essays on Instability and Finance*. Armonk, NY: M. E. Sharpe, pp. 90–116.

Minsky, Hyman P. 1981. "James Tobin's Asset Accumulation and Economic Activity: A Review Article." *Eastern Economic Journal*, Vol. 7, pp. 199–209.

Moore, Basil J. 1988. *Horizontalists and Verticalists: The Macroeconomics of Credit Money*. New York: Cambridge University Press.

New York Times. 1966.

Pollin, Robert. 1987. "Structural Change and Increasing Fragility in the U.S. Financial System." In *The Imperiled Economy: Macroeconomics from a Left Perspective*. Book One. New York: The Union for Radical Political Economics, pp. 145–58.

Tobin, James. 1989. "Financial Innovation and Deregulation in Perspective." In *Policies for Prosperity*. Cambridge, MA: MIT Press.

U.S. Congress. 1966a. Hearings on the "January 1966 Economic Report of the President." Part 1, Before the Joint Economic Committee. 89th Congress, 2nd Session, 1 February 1966.

U.S. Congress. 1966b. Hearings on the "Certificates of Deposit: Effects on Bank Competition, Savings, Money Supply, and Home Buying." Before the House Banking and Currency Committee. 89th Congress, 2nd Session, 19 May 1966.

U.S. Congress. 1966c. Hearings on the "Bill to Prohibit Banks from Issuing Negotiable Interest-Bearing or Discounted Notes, Certificates of Deposit, or Evidences of Indebtedness." Before the House Banking and Currency Committee. 89th Congress, 2nd Session, 8 June 1966.

Wojnilower, Albert M. 1980. "The Central Role of Credit Crunches in Recent Financial History." *Brookings Papers on Economic Activity*, Vol. 2, pp. 277–325.

Wolfson, Martin H. 1986 [1994]. *Financial Crises: Understanding the Postwar U.S. Experience*. Armonk, NY: M.E. Sharpe.

6   The Eurodollar Market and Flexible Exchange Rates

The Linchpins of the Current Neoliberal Era of Global Financial Capitalism

In August 1971, the U.S. stopped offering to sell gold for $35 an ounce. It thus ended the system of fixed exchange rates that had governed international monetary relations since the Second World War, and ushered in the current Neoliberal Era of free international capital mobility and flexible exchange rates.[1] This monetary-regime change underlies the current wave of global financialization, the driving imperative of which is multinational corporations trying to hedge the risk that speculative flows of capital in and out of different currencies will cause unpredictable fluctuations of exchange rates.[2]

The postwar system of fixed exchange rates broke down because, since the late 1950s, most international trade has been conducted in dollars. Consequently, as international trade grows, the U.S. must provide more and more dollars by running balance-of-payments deficits (Triffin, 1961). By August 1971, there were quite simply more dollars sloshing around in the world trading system than there was gold to be exchanged for them at $35 an ounce.

Nonetheless, in the 1960s alternative bases for an international monetary system of fixed exchange rates and regulated capital flows were both possible and under active consideration in official circles. The most promising alternatives—such as proposals for Special Drawing Rights issued by the International Monetary Fund— were conceived as mechanisms to channel the funds accumulated by countries with balance-of-payments surpluses to countries with balance-of-payments deficits (see, for example, Solomon, 1982). The need for such state-controlled mechanisms was justified on the grounds that markets could not handle the job without putting deflationary pressure on the world economy. That is to say, surplus countries were under no pressure to reinvest the funds they accumulated while deficit countries were under market pressure to attract investments by reducing wages and prices (see, for example, Block, 1977, chapters 3, 5; Helleiner, 1994).

The purpose of this chapter is to show that the growth of the Eurodollar market— the market for dollars on deposit at banks that are not subject to regulation or control by any monetary authority—undermined the rationale for, and thus the momentum toward, international monetary reform. I situate the failure of the movement toward international monetary reform in the context of the end of the larger movement toward social democracy in the U.S., of which it was an essential component. If we ignore the interlude of monetary ease before the 1968 presidential election, from

May 1968 to February 1970 the Federal Reserve conducted a tight monetary policy. As I show in Chapter 4, the Federal Reserve's goal was to weaken labor by precipitating then sustaining a recession. I show that this tight monetary policy failed to achieve its goal because of U.S. bank borrowings of Eurodollars for the purpose of financing their domestic lending operations.

Of course, the Federal Reserve was not ignorant of this fact. I thus explain the two reasons why the Federal Reserve chose to pursue an ineffective tight monetary policy. First, the U.S. bank cartel would only accept tight monetary policy if they could borrow Eurodollars. That is to say, the bank cartel wants a tight monetary policy that only restrains the lending operations of banks and non-bank financial institutions that are not members of the cartel. Second, the combination of a tight monetary policy and the bank cartel's borrowings of Eurodollars provided an *ad hoc* means of financing the U.S. war in Vietnam.

My central point in this chapter is that this combination of tight monetary policy and U.S. bank Eurodollar borrowings caused the extraordinary growth of the Eurodollar market itself in such a way that the postwar international order of fixed exchange rates could no longer be sustained. Once the fixed-exchange-rate regime collapsed, it became possible for the Federal Reserve to shift from monetary restraint in the form of quantity restraints on the banks to monetary restraint in the form of high interest rates, thereby ending the conditions for the movement toward social democracy and ushering in the current Neoliberal Era, which has no place for a strong and organized labor movement aligned with the interests of the unemployed.

In Section 6.1, I show that, as late as 1965, the Eurodollar market was of little international consequence beyond the confines of the former British Empire.

In Section 6.2, I show how the large New York banks discovered the borrowing of Eurodollars to finance their domestic lending operations as a means to resolve their intra-class conflict with the large regional banks over interest-rate-ceiling policy, which was a key factor, as I explain in Chapter 5, in causing the 1966 financial crisis. Once the institutional alliance between the large New York banks and the large regional banks was restored in May 1967, it was only a matter of time before the U.S. bank cartel emerged as an implacable force blocking progressive economic reforms. Instead, the Federal Reserve's control of short-term interest rates became the be-all and end-all of interventionist government policies.

In Section 6.3, however, I explain why, given the united front of the U.S. bank cartel, it became impossible for the Federal Reserve to impose quantity restraints on the economy, including the form of monetary restraint required to make an incomes policy effective—namely, reserve requirements and limits on the banks' access to Federal Reserve loans.

In Sections 6.4 and 6.5, I turn my attention to the breakdown of the international monetary order of fixed exchange rates, another essential component of progressive efforts to control inflation, and thus to build and sustain the movement toward social democracy. In Section 6.4, I explain how U.S. bank Eurodollar borrowings transmitted the inflationary pressures unleashed by the Treaty of Detroit to the rest of the world and, in the process, exerted unbearable pressures on the fixed-exchange-rate regime. All of a sudden, the central issue in international monetary affairs was no longer the question of how deficit countries were going to get funds without having to first deflate their wages and prices. Instead, the question became how they were going to protect themselves from being whipsawed by funds flowing at lightning speed from the Eurodollar market into their currencies, then out again.

In Section 6.5, I explain the apparent paradox that it was the easing of U.S. monetary policy from February 1970 to February 1972 (Chapter 4) that precipitated the replacement of the fixed-exchange-rate regime with a flexible-exchange-rate regime.

In Section 6.6, I provide a summary and conclusions.

Section 6.1 The Origins of the Eurodollar Market

The growth of the Eurodollar market was precipitated by the last gasp of the British Empire in the late 1950s. During the Second World War, the U.S. forced the U.K. to eliminate the colonial trading system that favored U.K. manufacturers, but U.K. banks maintained control of the financing of the neo-colonial trading system that replaced it (Gardner, 1980; Strange 1971). Until 1957, the financing of this trading system—accounting for about 40 percent of all international trade—took the form of loans of the U.K. pound sterling (Johnston, 1982, p. 33). But, in 1957, the U.K. government, after seizing the Suez Canal from Egypt with the assistance of France and Israel, only to be ordered by the U.S. to give it back, was forced to limit the amount of sterling loans that U.K. banks provided to the former colonies. Without the inflow of capital which would have come from control of the Suez Canal, the U. K. banking system could no longer supply an outflow of capital to finance the trade of the former colonies. Nonetheless, U.K. banks did not concede defeat and give up their international financial business. Instead, they started bidding for dollar deposits to lend to their clients in the former colonies. Even though there is no data available prior to 1964, the data presented in Table 6.1 suggest that between 48.6 percent and 68.6 percent of the net size of the Eurodollar market can be accounted for by U.K. banks replacing an international financial business based on sterling with one based on dollars.[3]

Two factors explain the ability of U.K. banks to substitute dollars for sterling in their international financial operations. First, with cumulative U.S. balance-of-payments deficits of $33.8 billion by the end of 1965, there were plenty of dollars sloshing around for U.K. banks to bid for. Second, with a bank cartel in the U.S. maintaining a monopoly price for dollar loans in the early 1960s, there was ample opportunity for U.K. banks to build a profitable dollar-based business and still entice clients with loans priced below the monopoly price.

To speak more precisely, the monopoly price for dollar loans in the early 1960s was a 4.5 percent lending rate (i.e. the U. S. prime rate) plus a requirement that borrowers maintain compensating balances of 10 percent to 20 percent of loans. The cost of borrowing dollars from the U. S. bank cartel thus ranged from

Table 6.1 Net size of the Eurodollar market and the U.K. share of it ($ millions and percent)

Year	(1) Net size	(2) U.K. share	(3) (2) as % of (1)
1964*	9,000	4,379	48.6
1965	11,500	5,300	46.1
1966	14,500	7,636	52.7
1967	17,500	9,691	55.4
1968	25,000	15,370	61.5
1969	37,500	25,747	68.6
1970	46,000	31,406	68.3
1971	54,000	36,928	68.4

Sources: Bank For international Settlements, *Annual Report*, various issues; Bank of England, *Quarterly Report*, various issues.
*The first year for which data are available.

0.045/1 − 0.1 to 0.045/1 − 0.2, or from 5 percent and 5.6 percent. During the same period, the interest rate on Eurodollar deposits averaged 4.1 percent. Therefore, U.K. banks had ample room to bid for Eurodollar deposits then lend them at profitable margins while still underpricing loans offered by the U.S. bank cartel. As a reflection of this fact, by the end of 1965 U.K. banks had attracted $5.3 billion of Eurodollar deposits, an amount equal to 15.7 percent of the $33.8 billion sloshing around in the world economy as a result of U. S. balance-of-payments deficits.[4]

Section 6.2 The U.S. Bank Cartel and the Eurodollar Market

In the late 1960s, U.K. banks continued to whittle away around the edges of the U.S. bank cartel. Nonetheless, from 1966 on, the growing use of Eurodollars by U.K. banks to finance their foreign lending operations was complemented by the growing use of Eurodollars by the U.S. bank cartel to finance its domestic lending operations. Two factors explain why the U.S. bank cartel turned to the Eurodollar market for funds. First, the U. S. invasion of Vietnam in July 1965 increased its balance-of-payments deficits dramatically. Second, the cartel wanted to push the interest rate on dollar loans higher still. Table 6.2 illustrates how these two factors interacted to produce U.S. bank Eurodollar borrowings.

First, note in column 1 that, between the collaring of the U.K. in 1957 and the sending of an occupation army to Vietnam in 1965, U.S. overseas military expenditures and foreign aid to support client states totaled $42.7 billion, an annual average expenditure of $5.34 billion. The costs of empire thus accounted for 126.4 percent of the $33.8 billion sloshing around in the world economy by 1965 on account of U.S. balance-of-payments deficits. Contemporary observers in official U.S. circles concluded from this fact that there were underlying strengths in the U.S. balance of payments, such as trade surpluses until 1970, which were

Table 6.2 Financing the costs of empire ($ millions and percent)

Year	(1) Overseas military and aid expenditures	(2) U.S. bank Eurodollar borrowings	(3) (2) as % of (1) in Table 6.1
1966	6,300	2,685	18.5
1967	7,300	3,655	20.9
1968	7,000	6,016	24.1
1969	6,900	12,118	32.3
1970	7,200	10,949	23.8
1971	7,300	3,300	6.1

Sources: U.S. White House, *International Economic Report*, March 1973; *Federal Reserve Bulletin*, various issues.
Note: Annual averages: 1958–65: 5,340; 1966–71: 7,000.

offsetting some of the costs of empire. However, these observers felt that more needed to be done, such as more burden-sharing with client states, and capital controls, like the Interest-Rate Equalization Tax imposed in July 1963, and the Voluntary Foreign Credit Restraint Program, implemented in January 1965 (see, for example, Hawley, 1987).

As can be seen in column 1 of Table 6.2, the balance of payments deteriorated dramatically in the wake of the U. S. invasion of Vietnam in July 1965, with the average annual costs of empire rising by 76 percent, to $7 billion. It was impractical to expect client states to share the costs of an unpopular war. Moreover, the U.S. bank cartel revolted at the prospect of the government extending the controls on private capital outflows by enough to offset the adverse effect on the balance of payments of the growing costs of empire. In particular, as I show in Chapter 5, in February 1965 the large New York banks demanded a contractionary open-market policy as a *quid pro quo* for submitting to the Voluntary Foreign Credit Restraint Program and, most importantly, in August 1966 they raised lending rates (e.g. the prime rate), despite the opposition of the U.S. monetary authorities, both at the Treasury Department and the Federal Reserve.

The Democratic appointees to the Federal Reserve Board and the U.S. monetary authorities at the Treasury Department opposed the large New York banks' August 1966 increase of the prime rate on the grounds that the higher lending rates were tantamount to higher costs of working capital, which non-financial corporations could use to justify higher prices. The higher lending rates, according to the U.S. monetary authorities, would then precipitate a wage-price spiral as unions pointed to the higher prices to justify higher wages. Consequently, as I show in Chapter 5, to foreclose a wage-price spiral, the U.S. monetary authorities responded to the large New York banks' raising of lending rates in August 1966 by raising reserve requirements on domestic time deposits and by placing restrictions on the banks' access to loans from the Federal Reserve System.[5]

The confrontation between the large New York banks and the U.S. monetary authorities had a twofold effect. First, as I explain in Chapter 5, it created an opening for the passage, in September 1966, of mandatory-interest-rate-ceiling legislation. New Deal legislation had imposed interest-rate ceilings, but given the Federal Reserve discretionary authority under Regulation Q to raise them. The legislation passed in September 1966 took this discretionary authority away, making changes in the interest-rate ceilings on how much banks could pay for small-denomination time deposits subject to presidential approval. However, this threat to the Federal Reserve's independence expired in September 1967. The Federal Reserve thus felt compelled to ease monetary policy in order to ensure that the legislation would not be renewed.

Consequently, the contractionary open-market policy begun in February 1965 was abandoned in October 1966. By April 1967, interest rates had fallen sufficiently to make a reduction in the discount rate seem imperative, and the U.S. bank cartel looked to the Federal Reserve for price leadership in determining how far interest rates would come down. For example, Hugh G. Galusha, Jr., President of the Federal Reserve Bank of Minneapolis, expressed as follows the considerations behind the April 1967 reduction in the discount rate:

> He [Galusha] had to report concern among city bankers about their being, as they put it, returned to the circumstances of November 1965 and before.[6] In those areas, like the Twin Cities, where the competition for consumer CDs [certificates of deposit] was intense among all financial institutions, the first move might be severely penalized. The move yesterday by a New York bank to lower the rate paid on consumer-type CDs might be infectious but he was afraid it might be something less than contagious. The President of one of the District's large banks had argued that the [Federal Reserve] Board would have to change Regulation Q to correct the increasing imbalance between bank lending and borrowing rates. He found it distasteful even to contemplate the Board taking on the task of assuring a profitable spread between those rates. But, at the same time, he did believe that District banks were going through agonies in getting their consumer deposit rates down and, in that connection, a half-point reduction in the discount rate would be quite helpful.
> (Galusha, FOMC *Minutes*, 4 April 1967, p. 58)

Once the April 1967 reduction in the discount rate eliminated the tension between the large regional banks and the large New York banks over how far interest rates would come down, it took the bank cartel less than a month to agree on terms for a return to a high-interest-rate policy. These terms were presented to the Federal Reserve Board for approval at its May meeting with the Federal Advisory Council (FAC).

Governor George Mitchell opened the May 1967 meeting of the FAC with the Federal Reserve Board by asking why, with only $19 billion of $370 billion in total deposits outstanding in the form of CDs, the bankers were so concerned with the interest-rate ceilings on them (FAC *Minutes*, 16–17 May 1967, p. 23).

In response, the bankers pointed out that only a few banks issued CDs and those banks, which happened to be the largest ones represented on the FAC, were heavily dependent on them (FAC *Minutes*, 16–17 May 1967, p. 23). But the bankers quickly added that they no longer opposed interest-rate ceilings on CDs. They said they were prepared to drop their longstanding opposition to them because the September 1966 mandatory-interest-rate-ceiling legislation "raised questions of whether it was politically feasible to remove the rate ceilings at this juncture" (FAC *Minutes*, 16–17 May 1967, p. 25). While the bankers were correct in their assessment of the political situation, since the same situation had prevailed for months it does not account for the dramatic reversal, in May 1967, of their longstanding opposition to the interest-rate ceilings.

What accounts for the bankers' change of heart became clear with the next turn in the discussion. Immediately after saying that they no longer demanded a suspension of the interest-rate ceilings on CDs, the bankers added that they "were taking steps to assure themselves of funds" "in the Eurodollar market" and sought assurances from the Federal Reserve Board that it would not interfere (FAC *Minutes*, 16–17 May 1967, p. 32). In other words, the temporary interest-rate-ceiling legislation pressed home to the U.S. bank cartel the need for unity. As explained in Chapter 5, it had split, in March 1966, over how best to implement a high-interest-rate policy, with the large New York banks demanding a contractionary open-market policy only so long as the interest-rate ceilings on CDs were raised along with market interest rates, and the large regional banks demanding a contractionary open-market policy only so long as the interest-rate ceilings were not raised. In May 1967, for the sake of cartel unity, the large New York banks ceded the point to the large regional banks, but only on condition that the Federal Reserve Board guaranteed them unrestricted access to the Eurodollar market.

In Section 6.4, I explain why the Democratic appointees to the Federal Reserve Board agreed to the terms demanded by the U.S. bank cartel for renewed monetary restraint (see, for example, FAC *Minutes*, 16–17 May 1967, p. 32). But first, in the next section, I show that it was completely ineffective in combatting the Great Inflation unleashed by the Treaty of Detroit.

Section 6.3 The Endogeneity of the U.S. Money Supply

If we ignore an interlude of monetary ease before the November 1968 presidential election, from May 1968 to February 1970, the Federal Reserve sold Treasury bills in the open market to push short-term interest rates above the interest-rate ceilings on domestic CDs.[7] The resulting run-off of CDs was supposed to compel the banking system to reduce the rate of growth of bank credit, and thus the money supply, "to an annual rate of 5 percent" by forcing the banks to adopt "more selective" lending policies (FOMC *Minutes*, 13 April 1966, p. 63; FOMC *Minutes*, 23 August 1966, pp. 68, 99–100). Therefore, the best measure of the degree of monetary restraint the Federal Reserve attempted to impose in the late 1960s is the market yield on CDs minus the interest-rate ceilings on them, which I have constructed into the variable *MR*.

The purpose of this section is to explain why this tight monetary policy failed in its purpose which, as I show in Chapter 4, was to weaken labor by precipitating then sustaining a recession. I argue that, in a world in which the U.S. bank cartel has unrestricted access to the Eurodollar market, the Federal Reserve cannot control the U.S. money supply. The money supply is instead endogenously determined by the demand for it.

More precisely, given the terms on which bank-cartel unity was obtained in May 1967, we would expect U.S. bank Eurodollar borrowings for the purpose of financing domestic lending operations ($EUROD$) to be a positive function of MR:

$$EUROD = +f(MR) \tag{6.1}$$

However, Equation 6.1 is too mechanistic: it assumes that U.S. bank Eurodollar borrowings were a response to tight monetary policy. This ignores their political dimension. My thesis in this section is that the bank cartel's decision to build up their Eurodollar borrowings was not so much a response to, as it was a condition for, the tight monetary policy from May 1968 to February 1970. If I am correct, then a dummy variable representing the cartel's decision in May 1967 to support a contractionary open-market policy, without increases in the interest-rate ceilings on CDs, so long as its access to the Eurodollar market was unrestricted, should be a statistically significant determinant of U.S bank Eurodollar borrowings.

To test this hypothesis, I begin by specifying the determinants of U.S bank Eurodollar borrowings as follows:[8]

$$EUROD_t = a + b_1 i_{cd,t} + b_2 i_{ff,t} + b_3 i_{pr,t} - b_4 i_{ed,t} + e_t \tag{6.2}$$

where i_{cd} is the market yield on CDs; i_{ff} is the federal funds rate (the Federal Reserve's control variable), i_{pr} is the prime rate (the banks' lending rate to their best customers), and i_{ed} is the interest rate on Eurodollar deposits.

In Equation 6.2, U.S. bank Eurodollar borrowings as a source of funds for the bank cartel's domestic lending operations are thus specified as follows: 1) a negative function of their own yield (i_{ed}); 2) a positive function of the market yield on CDs (i_{cd}) and of the federal funds rate (i_{ff}), or of the rates of return on the primary alternative sources of funds; and 3) a positive function of the prime rate (i_{pr}), or the rate of return on relending the Eurodollars.

In addition to the measure of monetary restraint formalized in Equation 6.1, the cost of setting up operations in the Eurodollar market must be taken into account before estimating Equation 6.2. That is to say, because the costs in both time and money were so high, by the end of the 1960s, no more than eleven U.S. banks accounted for most Eurodollar borrowings.[9] However, once a bank decided to set up operations in the Eurodollar market and the initial expenses were absorbed, the benefits from using Eurodollars would increase cumulatively, i.e. U.S. bank Eurodollar borrowings are a lagged function of themselves:[10]

$$EUROD_t = +f(EUROD_{t-1}) \tag{6.3}$$

Moreover, U.S. bank Eurodollar borrowings were not so much a function of the prime rate, or the rate of return on loans, as they were a function of the degree of pressure banks were under from their clients to provide loans. Since changes in the prime rate are headline news, they tend to respond sluggishly to changes in the degree of this pressure. The yield on commercial paper (i_{cmp}) is a better reflection of it because it reflects the willingness of U.S. corporations to obtain loans at comparable rates.[11]

By taking into account Equations 6.1 and 6.3 and substituting i_{cmp} for i_{pr}, Equation 6.2 becomes:

$$EUROD_t = b_1 + b_2 EUROD_{t-1} + b_2 i_{cmp,t} + b_4 MR_t + e_t \qquad (6.4)$$

Since interest rates move in tandem, to avoid multicollinearity the federal funds rate and the interest rate on Eurodollar deposits have been dropped from Equation 6.4. But these two variables have been dropped for theoretical reasons, too. As my analysis of Equation 6.1 makes clear, U.S. bank Eurodollar borrowings were an alternative to issuing CDs, not to obtaining funds in the federal funds market. And the bankers on the Federal Advisory Council said in May 1967 that they "were taking steps to assure themselves of funds [in the Eurodollar market] *even though the rates may not be especially attractive*" (FAC *Minutes*, 16–17 May 1967, p. 32; my emphasis).

I estimated Equation 6.4 for the period from January 1964, when data is first available, to May 1970, when the Federal Reserve took advantage of the financial crisis, the second major one in the postwar period, to permanently eliminate the interest-rate ceilings on CDs. The variables have the right sign and are statistically significant with an adjusted R^2 of 99.5 percent and a Durban h statistic of 1.18. Since at a 5 percent level the critical value of the normal distribution is 1.645, we cannot reject the null hypothesis of no serial correlation, i.e. ordinary least squares estimation can be used. The relevant results are in Table 6.3.[12]

Table 6.3 shows the results of estimating Equation 6.4 with the following two dummy variables:

$$D_1 = \begin{cases} 0, t \le \text{May 1967} \\ 1, t > \text{May 1967} \end{cases}$$

$$D_2 = \begin{cases} 0, t < \text{September 1969} \\ 1, t \ge \text{September 1969} \end{cases}$$

Table 6.3 Results from estimating the May 1967 U.S. bank cartel reunification (D_1) with the Sept. 1969 imposition of reserve requirements (D_2)

Parameter	Coefficient	t-Statistic
D_1	431	3.3
D_2	−966	5.2

D_1 represents the bank cartel's decision, in May 1967, to accept a contractionary open-market policy without timely increases in the interest-rate ceilings on CDs so long as no restrictions (e.g. reserve requirements) were placed on their borrowing of Eurodollars. And D_2 represents the imposition of such reserve requirements. I analyze the reasons for the imposition of reserve requirements on U.S. bank Eurodollar borrowings in Section 6.4. For our purposes in this section, we need only note that both dummy variables are highly significant. While the bank cartel's decision in May 1967 caused a $431 million monthly increase, the September 1969 imposition of reserve requirements caused a $966 million monthly decrease in U.S. bank Eurodollar borrowings.

Tables 6.4, 6.5, and 6.6 illustrate why, until the run-off of U.S. bank Eurodollar deposits from September 1969, the Federal Reserve's tight monetary policy was ineffective. In Table 6.4, I show how a Eurodollar deposit is created. In Table 6.5, I extend the analysis to the case where the Eurodollar deposit is used as a basis for a loan to U.S. banks (i.e. it is used for U.S. bank Eurodollar borrowings). Then, in Table 6.6, I compare the effects of the Eurodollar borrowings with the effects of changes in the monetary base in order to show that, no matter how many Treasury bills the Federal Reserve sold in the open market or how high it pushed short-term interest rates above the interest-rate ceilings on domestic CDs in the late 1960s, it was not restricting the rate of growth of either bank credit or the money supply.

The set of T-accounts in Table 6.4 represents the creation of a Eurodollar deposit.

As represented Table 6.4's set of T-accounts, a Eurodollar deposit has been created by a holder of domestic demand deposits—a resident wealthholder (WH)—drawing a check on them for $1 million in order to make a $1 million deposit at a foreign bank (FB). The foreign bank then deposits the $1 million at its U.S. correspondent bank (USCB). Since the demand deposits at the U.S. correspondent

Table 6.4 Creation of a Eurodollar deposit

Resident wealthholder (WH) (in millions of dollars)

Assets:	Liabilities:
Demand deposits at USCB −1	
Demand deposits at FB +1	

Foreign banks (FB) (in millions of dollars)

Assets:	Liabilities:
Demand deposits at USCB +1	+1 WH's demand deposits

U.S. correspondent banks (USCB) (in millions of dollars)

Assets:	Liabilities:
	+1 FB's demand deposits
	−1 WH's demand deposits

Table 6.5 U.S. bank borrowing of Eurodollars

Foreign banks (FB) (in millions of dollars)

Assets: Liabilities:
  Demand deposits as USCB −1
  Loans to USFB +1

Foreign branches of U.S. banks (USFB) (in millions of dollars)

Assets: Liabilities:
  Bank deposits at HO +1   +1 FB's loan

Home offices of foreign branches (HO) (in millions of dollars)

Assets: Liabilities:
                                                  +1 US FB's bank deposits

U.S. correspondent banks

Assets: Liabilities:
                                                  −1 FB's demand deposits

---

Table 6.6 The mitigation of tight U.S. monetary policy by U.S. bank Eurodollar borrowings

	1965	*1966*	*1967*	*1968*	*1969*
1. M (in millions of dollars)	1535	2685	3660	6294	12,066
2. ΔM (in millions of dollars)	413	1150	975	2634	5772
3. R_d (percentage)	0.165	0.165	0.165	0.170	0.175
4. R_e	−	−	−	−	−
5. Z (days)	90	90	90	90	90
6. $\Delta M (R_d - R_e) + M(R_d)/Z$	71	195	168	460	1034
7. ΔH (in millions of dollars)	2408	2664	2629	3669	3505
8. line 6 as % of line 7	3	7	6	13	29

banks do not change, these transactions do not change the monetary base of the U.S. However, as is shown in Table 6.5, if U.S. banks borrow the Eurodollars, they will be able to make more loans out of a given monetary base.

In the set of T-accounts in Table 6.4, the foreign banks are in a position to make a $1 million loan. When the loan is to U.S. banks, it is represented in Table 6.5. In this set of T-accounts, a $1 million demand deposit at the U.S. correspondent banks of foreign banks is replaced by a $1 million within-bank deposit at the home offices of the foreign branches (or subsidiaries) of U.S. banks operating in the Eurodollar market. Since reserve requirements are less for within-bank deposits than they are for demand deposits, the borrowing of Eurodollars by U.S. banks will increase the amount of free reserves for a given monetary base by

$$\Delta M(R_d - R_e)$$

where ΔM is the change in the borrowing of Eurodollars by U.S. banks , R_d is the reserve requirements on domestic demand deposits, and R_e is the reserve requirements on within-bank deposits (or Eurodollar borrowings by U.S. banks for the purpose of financing domestic lending operations).

For example, if there were no reserve requirements on within-bank deposits but reserve requirements of 17.5 percent on domestic demand deposits, then the $1 million borrowed by U.S. banks, as represented in the two sets of T-accounts in Tables 6.4 and 6.5, would have increased by $175,000 for the given monetary base the free reserves at the disposal of the U.S. banking system.

The formula ΔM $(R_d - R_e)$ represents the principal means by which U.S. bank Eurodollar borrowings prevented the Federal Reserve's tight monetary policy in the late 1960s from putting pressure on the banks to adopt more selective lending policies, and thus slow down the rate of growth of their outstanding loans. As I show below, until August 1969 what is called the "Eurodollar float" also undermined the Federal Reserve's tight monetary policy.

The Eurodollar float resulted from a combination of the accounting treatment of "Cash Items in Process of Collection" and the fact that interbank checks took one day to clear. Cash Items in Process of Collection, including checks that have not cleared, are deducted from gross demand deposits before required reserves are calculated so that reserve requirements are not imposed on demand deposits before the deposits are actually available to be withdrawn. The relevance of this accounting practice is that the foreign branches (or subsidiaries) of U.S. banks borrowed Eurodollars for their home offices by requesting that the lenders order their U.S. correspondent banks to send checks to the home offices of the U.S. branches borrowing the funds. For twenty-four hours after receiving the checks, the home offices recorded the checks as Cash Items in Process of Collection and thereby reduced gross demand deposits subject to reserves.

No matter the maturity of a Eurodollar deposit, if it was borrowed by U.S. banks then it generated a one-day "Eurodollar float" equal to $M(R_d)$. If Z denotes the average maturity of the claims on the foreign branches (or subsidiaries) of U.S. banks operating in the Eurodollar market (note that Z does not denote the average maturity of within-bank deposits), then the smaller Z, the greater the Eurodollar float. The effect of the Eurodollar float on the required reserves of U.S. banks was thus equal to $M(R_d)/Z$.

By combining the Eurodollar float with the lack of reserve requirements on within-bank deposits until September 1969, I obtain the following formula for the degree to which U.S. bank Eurodollar borrowings increased the velocity of money in the U.S. in the late 1960s, thereby undermining the Federal Reserve's efforts to exercise monetary control:

$$\Delta M(R_d) + M(R_d)/Z$$

Table 6.6 gives the values of each variable in this formula, combines them, and then shows to what percentage of the adjusted monetary base they were equal.[13]

Line 6 of Table 6.6 represents by how much U.S. bank Eurodollar borrowings in the late 1960s increased the free reserves, for a given monetary base, at the disposal of the U.S. banking system. In line 8 the significance of the numbers in line 6 is emphasized by expressing them as a percentage of changes in the adjusted monetary base.

For example, in 1969, the reserves freed by the borrowing of Eurodollars by U.S. banks were equal to 29 percent of the change in the monetary base during that year. It follows that no matter how much it used contractionary open-market operations to restrict the supply of bank reserves, the Federal Reserve was not restricting the rate of growth of either bank credit or the volume of bank deposits that the banks create in the process of extending bank credit, i.e. what it was ostensibly trying to do. All it was doing was increasing the velocity of money.

Section 6.4 The End of the Movement toward Social Democracy in the U.S.

As I explain in Chapter 5, to sustain the movement toward social democracy in the late 1960s, and in particular to sustain the fixed-interest-rate structure in the face of the inflationary pressures unleashed by the Treaty of Detroit, the Federal Reserve needed to combine a contractionary open-market policy with reserve requirements on the U.S. bank cartel's sources of funds, which appears to be the monetary policy put in place in September 1969. Unfortunately, by this time the movement toward social democracy had already floundered because of the U.S. war in Vietnam, which caused a sharp right turn of the monetary policymaking elites within the Democratic Party. In particular, as I show in this section, the Democratic appointees to the Federal Reserve Board accepted the terms for restored bank-cartel unity in the late 1960s because they became mesmerized with U.S. bank Eurodollar borrowings as an *ad hoc* means of financing the war in Vietnam.

As shown in column 1 of Table 6.2., U.S. overseas military expenditures and foreign aid to support client states are debits to the U.S. balance of payments. And U.S. bank Eurodollar borrowings to finance domestic lending operations, shown in column 2, are credits to the U.S. balance of payments. We thus see, in column 3, that the large New York banks' discovery of the Eurodollar market as a way to escape monetary restraint in 1966 offset 18.5 percent of the adverse effects of the costs of the war in Vietnam on the U.S. balance of payments. After May 1967, as the U.S. bank cartel financed more and more lending at higher and higher rates by borrowing Eurodollars, it also financed an ever growing percentage of the costs of empire, culminating at 32.3 percent of them in 1969.

As a result, the Democratic appointees to the Federal Reserve Board embraced a "tight" monetary policy that included what Federal Reserve Board Chair William McChesney Martin Jr. called "the safety valve offered by the Eurodollar market" (FOMC *Minutes*, 4 March 1969, p. 104). As I showed in Section 6.3, this policy was ineffective in counteracting the inflationary pressures unleashed by the Treaty of Detroit. Rather than dousing the upward pressures on the price level, the "tight" monetary policy only increased the velocity of money. Nonetheless, as Democratic Governor Arthur Brimmer put it:

> The Administration had decided, under the present circumstances, with the Vietnam War a major source of drag on the balance of payments, and in view of the political opposition that would be encountered in an attempt to adopt other balance of payments measures such as taxes on direct investments, to look for means of financing the deficit. He [Brimmer] thought it appropriate, if one accepted the Administration's position that the principal source of the deficit was short-term, to look for means, on an *ad hoc* basis, to finance the deficit.
> (Brimmer, FOMC *Minutes*, 16 July 1967, pp. 66–7)

Democratic Governor George Mitchell, who had been the principal advocate within the Federal Reserve System of extending the movement toward social democracy by means of an incomes policy and capital controls, became so enamored of a "tight" monetary policy that included the safety valve of U.S. bank Eurodollar borrowings as an *ad hoc* means of financing the war that, in April 1968, he proposed lowering the interest-rate ceilings on domestic CDs to force the banks to borrow even more Eurodollars (FOMC *Minutes*, 2 April 1968, p. 25). More realistically, Mitchell

> favored retaining the present ceiling on large CD's partly for balance of payments reasons. It would be desirable to influence banks with access to the Euro-dollar market to seek funds in that market on as large a scale as possible.
> (Mitchell, FOMC *Minutes*, 5 March 1968, p. 96)

Federal Reserve Bank of New York President Alfred Hayes, who, in August 1966, had practically single-handedly beat back an effort by the Democratic appointees to the Federal Reserve Board to extend social democracy by means of reserve requirements of U.S. bank Eurodollar borrowings (Chapter 5; and, for example, FOMC *Minutes*, 23 August 1966, p. 53), was sanguine in his assessment of this turn of events, simply noting that

> I [Hayes] have recently sensed a feeling of satisfaction in some Government quarters whenever these [Eurodollar] borrowings rose further and thereby added, for the moment, to our official payments surplus.
> (Hayes, FOMC *Minutes*, 25 November 1969, pp. 51–2)

The problem was that this *ad hoc* means of financing the war not only fueled the inflationary pressures unleashed by the Treaty of Detroit by increasing the velocity of money, it also transmitted them to the world economy. I will now show that the West German central bank (the Bundesbank) felt compelled to step in and stop the U.S. monetary authorities from committing this egregious error, thereby confronting the U.S. bank cartel with the same choice it faced in August 1966 between inflation and a tight monetary policy that would impinge upon its domestic lending operations. And, just as in August 1966, the bank cartel opted for the former.

The causal mechanism that transmitted the inflationary pressures in the U.S. to the world economy was the toppling of the fixed-exchange-rate structure. That the combination of "tight" U.S. monetary policy and U.S. bank Eurodollar borrowings would undermine the fixed-exchange-rate structure was already evident in autumn 1966 when the relatively small amount of U.S. bank Eurodollar borrowings at that time exerted "a strong pull on funds ... held in sterling" (Coombs,[14] FOMC *Minutes*, 22 November 1966, p. 5) and thereby threatened the value of the dollar because:

> In the event of a [British] devaluation ... the French might move quickly to parallel the British action. The Scandinavians and others might also move. So there could be a crumbling of the parity system around the world. Talk of an increase in the price of gold and a new set of parities would generate a drive against the dollar.
>
> (Coombs, FOMC *Minutes*, 23 August 1966, p. 25)

The desire to not roil the political situation in the wake of the passage of temporary mandatory interest-rate ceilings in September 1966 prompted the Federal Reserve to ease monetary policy, and thus obviate the need for the Eurodollars the large New York banks had already obtained. But after their May 1967 agreement with the large regional banks on the new terms for a "tight" monetary policy, the following statements illustrate how quickly renewed U.S. bank Eurodollar borrowings put pressure on the value of sterling (and thus the dollar):

> He [Coombs] had been getting some mild complaints from Bank of England officials regarding the occasionally strong bidding for Euro-dollar money by United States banks, which tended to put some pressure on sterling ... he hoped such bidding would not reach the intensity of last summer [i.e., the summer of 1966) since, in view of the fragile British problem, that could easily trigger another major crisis in sterling from which no recovery might be possible.
>
> (Coombs, FOMC *Minutes*, 18 July 1967, p. 16)

> [Because of continued] interest arbitrage flows out of sterling to the Euro-dollar market ... all of the British reserve losses had been attributed to a run-off of maturing forward contracts which could not be renewed because the foreign investors could reinvest more profitably in the Euro-dollar market than in London. ... Under these circumstances, if the New York banks continued to draw funds from that market at the July–August [1967] rate they would be putting pressure on sterling ... during September the British had suffered a further sizeable reserve loss of $345 million, mainly owing to a continuing drain of short-term funds from London to the Euro-dollar market ... the

activity of the New York banks in the Euro-dollar market might very well hold the key as to whether sterling would survive through year-end.

(Coombs, FOMC *Minutes*, 3 October 1967, pp. 4–8)

At first, the West German central bank (the Bundesbank) relieved the pressure on sterling by reducing interest rates in West Germany and providing forward cover at sufficiently attractive rates to induce recycling of dollars from West Germany to the Eurodollar market (see, for example, FOMC *Minutes,* 18 July 1967, pp. 20–2; FOMC *Minutes*, 12 December 1967, p. 7). However, after these efforts failed to prevent sterling from being devalued in November 1967, the Bundesbank reduced the rate at which it provided forward cover (see, for example, FOMC *Minutes*, 27 November 1967, pp. 48–9; FOMC *Minutes*, 9 January 1968, pp. 17–18).

The policymakers at the Bundesbank believed that the U.S. approach to the *ad hoc* financing of the U.S. war in Vietnam was covering up fundamental problems in the international position of the U.S. Table 6.7 illustrates their concern.

Column 1 of Table 6.7 shows that, between 1966 and 1969, the U.S. balance of payments was always in deficit. Column 2 then shows persistent surpluses in the balance of payments, once overseas military expenditures and aid to client states are netted out—evidence for the argument popular in U.S. official circles that there was underlying strength in the country's international position. Column 3 vitiates this evidence. Once U.S. bank Eurodollar borrowings as well as the costs of empire are netted out, the U.S. balance of payments deficit balloons to just over $1 billion in 1967, $616 million in 1968, and an incredible $11.318 billion in 1969. As a result of this evidence of fundamental weakness in the international position of the U.S., the West German authorities felt compelled to demand changes in the way the U.S. was financing its empire, particularly its war in Vietnam.

By March 1968, the reduced rate at which the Bundesbank provided forward cover had halted the recycling of dollars from West Germany to the Eurodollar

Table 6.7 An underlying deterioration of the balance of payments ($ millions and percent)

Year	(1)	(2)	(3)
	Net liquidity in the balance of payments	*(2) in the absence of (1) in Table 6.2*	*(2) in the absence of (2) in Table 6.2*
1966	−2,200	4,100	1,415
1967	−4,700	2,600	−1,055
1968	−1,600	5,400	−616
1969	−6,100	800	−11,318
1970	−4,700	2,500	−8,449
1971	−22,700	−15,400	−18,700

Sources: (1) U.S. White House, *International Economic Report*, March 1973; *Federal Reserve Bulletin*, various issues.

market, bringing the pressure on the gold price of the dollar to breaking point. The Bundesbank then agreed to salvage the fixed-exchange-rate structure by means of the expedient of a two-tier gold market[15] on the condition that the U.S. would meet the following conditions (see, for example, FOMC *Minutes*, 2 April 1968, pp. 23–4, 90; FOMC *Minutes*, 19 April 1968, p. 2; FOMC *Minutes*, 14 March 1968, pp. 4, 7–8, 21; FOMC *Minutes*, 28 May 1968, pp. 23, 27–8):

a   Increase the interest-rate ceiling on large-denomination CDs (under Regulation Q) in order to take away the incentive for U.S. banks to borrow Eurodollars;

b   impose a 10 percent income-tax surcharge in order to reduce the need for tight monetary policy;

c   remove the 25 percent gold-cover requirement backing Federal Reserve notes so that U.S. gold reserves would be available for purchase by the Bundesbank;

d   hold the rate of increase of U.S. bank Eurodollar borrowings down to $200 million a month; and

e   facilitate "multilateral surveillance" of U.S. macroeconomic policies by imposing a common maturity date on credits the U.S. government received from the European central banks in order to defend the dollar price of gold.

A majority of the Board of Governors (Brimmer, Maisel, Mitchell, and Robertson) opposed this deal with West Germany (see, for example, FOMC *Minutes*, 17 December 1968, pp. 20, 23). The basis for their opposition is illustrated by the following statement by Mitchell:

> The world was moving into a situation of fundamental disequilibrium in international monetary relationships. Under present circumstances—which in his [Mitchell's] judgment involved the beginning of the demonetization of gold, brought about in an unexpected way—it was no longer possible to apply the rules of the game that had been followed in the 1960s. In the current crisis situation and with new international monetary relationships developing, he [Mitchell] thought the United States should protect its credit resources. The British had mortgaged too much of their assets in defending the pound, and while the situations were not closely comparable, he [Mitchell] would not want to see the United States follow a similar course in defending the dollar. . . . He [Mitchell] thought that under the circumstances the other central banks should be prepared to hold uncovered dollars until the situation had calmed down somewhat.
>
> (Mitchell, FOMC *Minutes*, 14 March 1968, pp. 9–10)

The views of the majority of the Board of Governors were ignored during the intra-governmental negotiations which led to the two-tier gold market, which were conducted by Coombs, Daane, Hayes, Martin, and representatives of the Treasury Department. However, their views could not be ignored once the immediate crisis was over. In December 1968, Brimmer, Maisel, Mitchell, and Robertson thus led the Federal Reserve back to its three-pronged "tight" monetary policy of open-market sales of Treasury bills, holding down the interest-rate ceilings on domestic CDs and encouraging U.S. bank Eurodollar borrowings (see, for example, FOMC *Minutes*, 18 June 1968, pp. 78–9; FOMC *Minutes*, 29 October 1968, p. 53; FOMC *Minutes*, 26 November 1968, pp. 56–8; FOMC *Minutes*, 17 December 1968, p. 3).

Consequently, by spring 1969, there was renewed pressure on the value of the pound sterling. A member of the international-finance staff at the Federal Reserve Bank of New York (Hersey) summarized this situation for the Federal Open Market Committee as follows:

> This year's large inflow [of Eurodollars] had been made possible by the flight from sterling—which has been pulled into dollars rather than marks or Swiss francs by the much higher interest rates on dollar deposits—and has been accompanied by a heavy drain on U.K. reserves.
>
> (Hersey, FOMC *Minutes*, 28 May 1969, p. 55)

Instead of demanding the gold the U.S. made available in March 1968 by removing the 25 percent gold-cover requirement backing Federal Reserve notes, the Bundesbank responded to this renewed pressure on sterling by reverting to its policy of providing forward cover to anyone willing to exchange D-marks for dollars cheaply enough to recycle dollars to the Eurodollar market (see, for example, FOMC *Minutes*, 10 September 1968, p. 4; FOMC *Minutes*, 8 October 1968, p. 4; FOMC *Minutes*, 26 November 1968, pp. 13, 41; FOMC *Minutes*, 17 December 1968, pp. 14–16, 20, 26–7; FOMC *Minutes*, 14 January 1969, p. 5; FOMC *Minutes*, 4 February 1969, p. 10).

The other continental European central banks were less sanguine. U.S. bank Eurodollar borrowings put pressure mostly on the pound sterling because it was the weakest major currency. But the Eurodollar borrowings also drained foreign exchange reserves from the other major European countries and Canada (see, for example, FOMC *Minutes*, 5 March 1968, p. 100). For this reason, after France took the lead by requiring its residents to repatriate all funds from the Eurodollar market in February 1969 (see, for example, FOMC *Minutes*, 4 March 1969, pp. 19, 27), *ad hoc* arrangements to stop the leakage of funds into the Eurodollar market began to proliferate throughout Europe. Coombs summarized the resulting situation as follows:

> Over the past few months there had been a great many protests from the European central banks to the effect that Regulation Q, together with the absence of reserve requirements on bank takings from the Euro-dollar market, had been artificially intensifying the impact of United States credit policy on the Euro-dollar market. ... The European central banks now seemed to be taking defensive action but in an independent, uncoordinated way. ... In the last few weeks, the Netherlands Bank had instructed Dutch commercial banks to repatriate funds from the Euro-dollar market and strengthen their liquidity positions, the Bank of Italy had called on Italian

banks to bring back $800 million by the end of June, and the Swiss National Bank had refused to give swaps to its commercial banks at the end of March in order to induce a repatriation of funds from aboard and an injection of new liquidity into the Swiss banking system.

(Coombs, FOMC *Minutes*, 1 April 1969, pp. 7–8)

To force the Bundesbank to harden its position toward the U.S., in late April 1969 the West German government announced that the D-mark might have to be revalued. Over the next two weeks, $4.6 billion flowed into West Germany. On 11 May, in exchange for an announcement by the West German government that the D-mark should not be revalued after all, the Bundesbank agreed to the following revisions of its policy (see, for example, FOMC *Minutes*, 27 May 1969, pp. 5–6, 21–2; FOMC *Minutes*, 24 June 1969, p. 8):

a   forward cover would be offered for recycling only $3.5 billion of the $4.6 billion inflow to the Eurodollar market; and
b   the Federal Reserve would be compelled to abandon monetary restraint by means of a request for $2.3 billion in Treasury bills, $1 billion of which would have to be obtained in the open market.

Belgium followed suit by requiring its residents to repatriate funds from the Eurodollar market (see, for example, FOMC *Minutes*, 24 June 1969, pp. 6–7).

The Federal Reserve responded to these revisions of the Bundesbank's policy by offering to put reserve requirements on U.S. bank Eurodollar borrowings if the Bundesbank would move $1.7 billion from the Treasury-bill market to the Eurodollar market (see, for example, FOMC *Minutes*, 27 May 1969, p. 39; FOMC *Minutes*, 24 June 1969, pp. 30, 52–4). Coombs explained the reasons for the Federal Reserve's accommodation of the Bundesbank as follows:

European central banks had now become so concerned over the speculative threat to their currency parities that any new threat might lead them to take drastic restrictive action on the credit side in order to protect their reserve positions. At some point, strains on both the Euro-dollar and national credit markets in Europe might produce a few spectacular bankruptcies here and there, and cast a shadow over credit risks throughout the European financial market. In that situation, it would not take much to frighten the Swiss banks, for example, into heavy repatriation of short-term funds from the Euro-dollar market. In general ... the situation could be moving toward the incipient stage of a self-defeating scramble for liquidity, both official and private. ... Any holdback of needed funds on the part of central banks or other sources of funds could precipitate a sudden break in the parity structure.

(Coombs, FOMC *Minutes*, 27 May 1969, pp. 7–9)

The reserve requirements on U.S. bank Eurodollar borrowings became effective in September 1969, and the Bundesbank responded by allowing the D-mark to float.

Throughout the floating period,the Bundesbank kept a firm floor just below current market quotations by stepping in with over $1 billion in purchases for its own account. When the D-mark was 9.25 percent above par it then announced the "market-determined" rate to be the new parity (see, for example, FOMC *Minutes*, 7 October 1969, p. 41; FOMC *Minutes*, 28 October 1969, pp. 4–9).

As it became clear that their access to the Eurodollar market was going to be restricted with reserve requirements, the U.S. bank cartel tried to develop the commercial-paper market as an alternative source of funds (see, for example, FOMC *Minutes*, 12 August 1969, p. 23). However, for reasons I explain in Chapter 4, the Federal Reserve responded on 29 October 1969 by announcing its intention, effective 2 December,

> to apply Regulation Q to funds received by member banks from the issuance of commercial paper or similar obligations by bank holding companies or collateral affiliates.
>
> > (Martin, FOMC *Minutes*, 25 November 1969, p. 5)

> the [Federal Reserve] Board's proposed ruling with respect to commercial paper was generally regarded—particularly by those banks with paper outstanding—as an indication of the [Federal Reserve] System's intention to pursue a policy of relentless pressure on the banking system.
>
> > (Holmes, FOMC *Minutes*, 25 November 1969, p. 32)

In Chapter 4, I explain how the U.S. bank cartel responded to this "relentless pressure" by demanding an easing of U.S. monetary policy (i.e. an expansionary open-market policy to supply their liquidity needs), which occurred in February 1970. In the next section, I explain the effects that ensued for the international monetary system.

Section 6.5 The Denouement

The Bundesbank was the principal source of the Eurodollars that the U.S. bank cartel borrowed in the late 1960s. West Germany ran persistent trade surpluses with the U.S., which led to the accumulation of dollar reserves by the West German central bank. The U.S. companies that imported goods from West Germany were financed by the U.S. bank cartel. The Eurodollar market thus constituted a recycling machine. At one end was the Bundesbank keeping interest rates low and offering forward cover to anyone willing to exchange D-marks for dollars, thereby pumping their dollar reserves into the Eurodollar market. At the other end was the U.S. bank cartel borrowing dollars in the Eurodollar market to finance trade credits for the purchase of West German goods, as well as for other domestic purposes. A limited stock of dollars, supplied by the U.S. balance of-payments deficit, was thus showing up as an endless upward spiral of West German dollar reserves on the sources side and U.S. bank borrowings on the uses side of the Eurodollar market.

Moreover, the spiral of West German dollar reserves and U.S. bank Eurodollar borrowings was feeding the wage-price spiral which had, as anticipated, been unleashed in the U.S. by the higher lending rates charged by the U.S. bank cartel. As I explain in Chapter 5, U.S. corporations were able to use their higher borrowing costs as justification for charging higher prices for their output. And the organized labor movement in the U.S. was able to use the higher prices for output to justify demands for higher wages.

On the grounds that it needed to prevent the Eurodollar market from potentially recycling inflation as well as dollars, the West German central bank persuaded its U.S. counterpart in 1969 to impose reserve requirements on U.S. bank Eurodollar borrowings. (As I explained in Section 6.4, the Bundesbank prevailed on the Federal Reserve by threatening to sell its vast holdings of U.S. Treasury bills if reserve requirements were not imposed on U.S. bank Eurodollar borrowings.)

As shown in Table 6.3, the reserve requirements imposed, in September 1969, on U.S. bank Eurodollar borrowings for domestic lending operations caused a $966 million monthly decrease in them. However, the repatriation of Eurodollars by the U.S. bank cartel did not stop the growth of the Eurodollar market (or the wage-price spiral). This is because the return of dollars from the U.S. bank cartel, by providing a source of funds, liberated the Eurodollar market from its moorings in West Germany's official dollar reserves. The unwinding of U.S. bank Eurodollar borrowings in 1970–1 thus institutionalized a vast pool of short-term capital, outside the control of any monetary authority, which was ready and able to move with lightning speed in and out of different currencies.

That this would be the result of the February 1970 easing of U.S. monetary policy did not come as a surprise to the Federal Open Market Committee. As early as April 1969, Hayes reported to his colleagues on the Committee that:

> From a longer-run point of view it is a bit unnerving to contemplate the effects on our official settlements balance of any future turn to easier money in this country and a consequent heavy reversal of the inflows of funds from foreign branches [of U.S. banks operating in the Eurodollar market].
>
> (Hayes, FOMC *Minutes*, 29 April 1969, p. 42)

Reinforcing Hayes' point, in May and July 1969 the staff member at the Federal Reserve Bank of New York responsible for international finance (Hersey) informed the Federal Open Market Committee that:

> When our interest rates fall, it may become hard to hold the [international monetary] system together.
>
> (Hersey, FOMC *Minutes*, 27 May 1969, p. 35)

> the further the buildup of Euro-dollar debt goes, the greater the chances become later on, when the U.S. banks can find cheaper sources of time money at home, they will repay much of this foreign debt in a rush. Their foreign branches would let deposits run off and would also expand lending,

and the result of the whole process, with the underlying United States payments deficit still large, might be to pump a flood of unwanted dollars into foreign reserve holders' hands in a relatively brief period, and possibly generate cumulative speculative reactions.

(Hersey, FOMC *Minutes*, 15 July 1969, p. 40)

The current Neoliberal Era of global financialization, based on the Eurodollar market, was foreshadowed by the November 1967 sterling devaluation and the May 1971 D-mark revaluation. U.K. corporations could use the Eurodollar market to speculate against the pound sterling by instructing U.K. banks to transform sterling deposits into dollar deposits during the interval between U.K. corporations receiving incomes denominated in sterling and using them to meet payment commitments also denominated in sterling. Consequently, it is not surprising that "all of the British reserve losses" that forced the November 1967 sterling devaluation can be accounted for by such deposit transfers (Coombs, FOMC *Minutes*, 3 October 1967, pp. 4–8).

Similarly, between the partial revaluation of the D-mark at the time of the imposition of reserve requirements on U.S. bank Eurodollar borrowings in September 1969 and the decision to let the market determine the value of the D-mark in May 1971, the Eurodollar market was a major source of the short-term dollars that were sold in order to purchase D-marks. Again, this result was fully anticipated by Hayes at the time of the partial revaluation of the D-mark in November 1969:

Those who attended the latest Basle meeting[16] heard many worried comments not only on the prospect of sharply higher central bank holdings of dollars whenever our credit policies are eased, but also on ... the alleged dilemma in which this placed various countries of choosing between being tied to a depreciating dollar and being forced to revalue. Clearly we face another major international payments crisis within the next year or two unless we do make significant progress against inflation.

(Hayes, FOMC *Minutes*, 25 November 1969, pp. 51–2)

When the Federal Reserve decided to ease monetary policy in February 1970, another staff member at the Federal Reserve Bank of New York (Solomon)[17] responsible for international finance summarized the likely unraveling of the international monetary system for the Federal Open Market Committee as follows:

What could happen is that the United States interest rates might decline while rates within European counties remain high. This could lead to a repayment of Euro-dollar borrowings by United States banks. As the foreign holders of Euro-dollar deposits reconvert into their own currencies, there would be a sizeable increase in dollar reserves of European central banks and an increase in domestic liquidity that the European central banks might find it difficult to offset. ... Euro-dollar flows have financed an underlying United States deficit and kept the dollar strong. As this protection disappears the underlying deficit will re-emerge and there is no great confidence that this problem is on the way to a lasting solution.

(Solomon, FOMC *Minutes*, 10 February 1970, p. 18)

The Bundesbank gave way to the speculators in May 1971. Given the length of the period from the partial revaluation of the D-mark in November 1969 to its complete revaluation in May 1971, traditional methods of speculation, such as U.S. multinational corporations delaying the repatriation of profits made abroad, and accelerating the payment of debts owed abroad, were probably more important than the Eurodollar market as a source of the short-term dollars that were sold to buy D-marks. Nonetheless, the new gnomes of finance inhabiting the Eurodollar market are evident in the fact that, in 1970 and the first quarter of 1971, the claims of banks operating in the Eurodollar market on foreign banks, official institutions, foreign non-banks, and "others" increased by $13.9 billion. After evaluating the evidence for these dollars being used in alternative ways, Kane (1983, pp. 55, 58, 159, 165) concludes that most of them were borrowed from the Euro-banks in order to exchange them for D-marks.

The U.S. hoped that the May 1971 D-mark revaluation would suffice to resolve the pressures on the international monetary system. But as the Bundesbank pointed out in fall 1969, and all the more emphatically in spring 1971, nothing short of the U.S. imposing wage and price controls and allowing the dollar to float downwards would staunch the speculative flows of dollars into D-marks through the Eurodollar market (see, for example, FOMC *Minutes*, 25 November 1969, pp. 27–8; FOMC *Minutes*, 6 April 1971, p. 56).

Monetary policymakers in the U.S. would not listen until the mesmerizing speculative frenzy in the first two weeks of August 1971, when the country lost $6 billion of reserves. No monthly data is available on the Eurodollar market *per se*, much less weekly data. But there is monthly data on the branches that the U.S. bank cartel operates in the Eurodollar market. Reflecting the withdrawal of Eurodollar deposits by foreign banks, official institutions, foreign non-banks, and "others" from these branches, so that they could be exchanged for U.S. reserves, the liabilities of the overseas branches of U.S. banks fell by $1,289 million in July, only to increase again by $1,152 million in August. This quick turnaround leaves no doubt about the speculative nature of the initial withdrawals.

It is impossible to overestimate the importance of convention in financial markets. As Keynes famously said, it is better for the reputation of financiers to lose money conventionally than to make money by unconventional methods. Therefore, it does not stretch credulity to assume that all Euro-banks were acting in much the same way as the branches of U.S. banks operating in the Eurodollar market. On the additional, and unrealistically conservative, assumption that the overseas branches of U.S. banks accounted for the whole of the Eurodollar market, except the 68.4 percent shown in column 3 of Table 6.1 accounted for by U.K. banks, then the amount of Eurodollar deposits used for the assault on U.S. reserves in the first two weeks of August would be $4,079 million, accounting for

68 percent of the total U.S. reserve losses of $6 billion, forcing the Nixon administration on 15 August, simultaneously with the announcement of wage and price controls, which it detested and made no effort to enforce, to sever the dollar's link to gold at a fixed exchange rate. The funds used to force the Administration's hand, augmented with speculative profits, would then have returned to the Eurodollar market to standby, waiting for the next opportunity to profit from short-term speculation. The current Neoliberal Era of free international capital mobility and flexible exchange rates thus opened most inauspiciously.

Section 6.6 Summary and Conclusions

The most important monetary event during the Federal Reserve's first one hundred years was the replacement of fixed exchange rates, based on the gold-exchange standard, with flexible exchange rates. In this chapter, I have explained how flexible exchange rates became necessary to accommodate the Federal Reserve's relentless efforts to undermine the movement toward social democracy in the U.S. The thesis presented here is that the Federal Reserve is an institutionalized alliance of the large New York banks and the large regional banks. When these two groups of banks are united, they constitute an unassailable force in the class conflict between workers and capitalists over the distribution of income. Since the New Deal, the class conflict has taken the form of a movement toward social democracy. The replacement of fixed exchange rates with flexible exchange rates was necessary to unite the large New York banks and the large regional banks. As a result, the movement toward social democracy was decimated.

The industrial proletariat organized itself into a cohesive political force for the first time with labor insurgencies that began in 1933. At the peak of its strength, from the sit-down strikes in Detroit in 1936–7 to the national strikes in the immediate postwar period, the industrial proletariat sought some form of democratic national economic planning to redress mass unemployment. However, the need for national economic planning was called into question in 1938 and again in 1948–9, when the Government used stabilization policies to pull the economy out of recessions. Consequently, in 1950, the UAW was lulled into accepting the Treaty of Detroit, whereby it accepted managerial control of investment decisions and of the labor process in exchange for a promise by General Motors to negotiate three-year contracts tying wages (including benefits) to labor productivity and the cost of living.

The Federal Reserve was given independence in 1951 as part of the Government's putative efforts to create institutions to pull the economy out of recessions. Except for a couple of years in the early 1950s, the Federal Reserve never took its mandate seriously. Instead, it turned its attention to breaking the movement toward social democracy by raising short-term interest rates during the tri-annual rounds of wage negotiations. The Federal Reserve hoped the higher interest rates would precipitate, or at least exacerbate, recessions. Rising unemployment would then weaken labor's ability to obtain real-wage increases equal to the increases in labor productivity.

The problem was that, to the degree that the Federal Reserve is independent of the Government it is dependent on the large banks. Therefore, the Federal Reserve had to devise a high-interest-rate policy on terms acceptable to the large banks, whose primary concern is that the Federal Reserve acts as lender of last resort whenever their liquidity positions come under pressure. Since the early 1960s, the large New York banks have secured their liquidity positions by offering whatever yield is required to attract buyers of their large-denomination CDs. During the period of the Government's incomes policy in the early 1960s, when monetary policy was easy, the large New York banks issued their CDs in the domestic market. But after tight monetary policy supplanted the incomes policy in the late 1960s and drained the domestic market of liquidity, when the large banks offered ever higher yields on the CDs they issued, they were in effect attempting to attract liquidity away from the large regional banks, in what Archie K. Davis, President of the American Bankers Association and Chair of Wachovia Bank, the largest bank in the South, called "highly destructive and undesirable competition" (*New York Times*, 1 February 1966, p. 49).

In spring 1966, the large New York banks attempted to placate the large regional banks. Rather than increasing loans, and thus increasing their need to issue CDs, they told their customers to draw on lines of credit with the large regional banks. But the large New York banks miscalculated the effect on their regional rivals of what was ostensibly a conciliatory gesture. For example, Edward A. Wayne, President of the Federal Reserve Bank of Richmond, said the

> [b]anks in his District thought the New York banks had acted imprudently, and they were strongly critical of the New York banks for suggesting, when they ran short of funds, that their customers draw on credit lines outside of New York and thus relieve pressure on them.
>
> (FOMC *Minutes*, 22 March 1966, p. 61)

And Watrous H. Irons, President of the Federal Reserve Bank of Dallas, said that

> like Mr. Wayne he had heard from a few banks some rather sharp and severe criticism of the New York banks—not only for suggesting to customers that they 'go west' for accommodations, but also for working up rates on [CDs].
>
> (FOMC *Minutes*, 22 March 1966, p. 77)

To accommodate the large regional banks, and at the same time secure their liquidity positions despite the Federal Reserve's tight monetary policy, the large New York banks turned to the Eurodollar market, a market for dollar deposits outside the purview of the U.S. monetary authority. The Eurodollar market was established by U.K. banks in the late 1950s and early 1960s as a way to maintain their role in international finance despite the relative decline of the U.K. economy and, consequently, of the U.K. currency, the pound sterling. But in the late 1960s, the large New York banks supplanted U.K. banks as the principal source of demand for Eurodollar deposits by issuing new CDs there rather than in the domestic market. As William McChesney Martin Jr., Chair of the Federal Reserve Board, summed up the situation that emerged in the late 1960s, the Federal

Reserve could only try to use a high interest-rate policy to engineer, or at least exacerbate, recessions "because of the safety valve offered by the Eurodollar market" (FOMC *Minutes*, 4 March 1969, p. 104).

However, the borrowing of Eurodollars by the large New York banks was incompatible with fixed exchange rates. In the first instance, this was because, when they issued CDs at ever higher yields in the Eurodollar market, the large New York banks drew funds away from U.K. banks. And, according to Charles Coombs, the Federal Reserve's Manager of Foreign Exchange Operations, this "strong pull of funds ... held in sterling" threatened the fixed exchange-rate structure because

> [i]n the event of a devaluation of sterling ... the French might move quickly to parallel the British action. The Scandinavians and others might also move. So there could be a crumbling of the parity system around the world. Talk of an increase in the price of gold and a new set of parities would generate a drive against the dollar.
>
> (FOMC *Minutes*, 22 November 1966, p. 5;
> FOMC *Minutes*, 23 August 1966, p. 25)

The following summer, after saying he "had been getting some mild complaints from Bank of England officials regarding the occasionally strong bidding for Euro-dollar money by United States banks, which tended to put some pressure on sterling[,]" Coombs said "he hoped such bidding would not reach the intensity of last summer since, in view of the fragile U.K. problem, that could easily trigger another major crisis in sterling from which no recovery might be possible" (FOMC *Minutes*, 18 July 1967, p. 16). And later in 1967 he indicated that, because of continued

> interest arbitrage flows out of sterling to the Euro-dollar market ... all of the British reserve losses had been attributed to a run-off of maturing forward contracts which could not be renewed because the foreign investors could reinvest more profitably in the Euro-dollar market than in London. ... [T]he activity of the New York banks in the Euro-dollar market might very well hold the key as to whether sterling would survive through year-end.
>
> (FOMC *Minutes*, 3 October 1967, pp. 4–8)

As Coombs predicted, in November 1967 the U.K. was forced to devalue, unleashing speculation against the dollar. In March 1968, this speculation was temporarily halted by introducing a two-tier gold market, which allowed for a market-determined price of gold for private investors while maintaining a fixed rate of exchange between the dollar and gold for central banks.

Nothing could be done to salvage the fixed-exchange-rate regime, however, once the problem became not the bidding by large New York banks for Eurodollars to finance their domestic lending operations but the unwinding of those Eurodollar borrowings when the funds were no longer needed, as occurred during the 1970–1 easing of U.S. monetary policy. By 1971, the large New York banks had paid back the principal on almost all the CDs they had issued in the Eurodollar market, upon their maturity, and thus created a vast pool of short-term capital outside the control of any monetary authority, in desperate search of investment opportunities. The investment opportunity of choice was speculation against the dollar, forcing the Nixon administration to sever the dollar's link to gold at a fixed exchange rate, thereby ushering in the current era of free international capital mobility and flexible exchange rates.

Notes

1 The postwar monetary system was a 'gold-exchange standard', meaning that only the dollar was exchangeable for gold at a fixed price, while all other currencies were exchangeable for the dollar at a fixed price. Therefore, ending the exchangeability of gold for $35 an ounce in August 1971 removed the central pillar of the postwar international monetary regime. Nonetheless, there is controversy about when the postwar monetary regime ended. On the one hand, Fred L. Block (1977, pp. 199, 203) argues that it ended in 1973 on the grounds that the U.S.'s decision to eliminate a fixed gold price in 1971 set-off a flurry of diplomatic efforts to restore it, and it was only after these efforts failed, in 1973, that the postwar regime broke down. On the other hand, David P. Calleo and Benjamin M. Rowland (1973, p. 284) argue that the postwar monetary regime ended in 1968, when the leading European central banks, led by the German central bank, agreed to stop selling dollars for gold. However, it is from August 1971 that uncertainty about future exchange rates became endemic. Consequently, it is from August 1971 that the imperative emerged for multinational corporations to hedge against unexpected changes in exchange rates. See any mainstream textbook in international finance (e.g., Madura, 2003) for an explanation of exchange-rate risk as the principal problem in international finance today.
2 The late twentieth century marked the fourth wave of global financialization. The first wave was based in Italy in the late fourteenth and early fifteenth centuries. The second wave was based in the Netherlands in the sixteenth and seventeenth centuries. The third wave was based in England in the late nineteenth and early twentieth centuries. The fourth wave in the late twentieth and early twenty-first centuries was unique in being based, not in some country's regulated banking system, but in an unregulated and stateless banking system (i.e. the Eurodollar market). For a comparative study of all four waves see Giovanni Arrighi (1994).
3 See R. B. Johnston (1982, pp. 9–34) for a comprehensive survey of factors underlying the origins of the Eurodollar market (e.g. the desire of the Soviet Union to keep the dollars it earned from the export of oil and other raw materials beyond the reach of the U.S. monetary authorities). The data in Table 6.1 support the hypothesis that the growth of the dollar-based business of U.K. banks was the most significant factor.
4 The data used in this chapter on the U.S. balance-of-payments deficit come from the *International Economic Report of the President*, U.S. White House, March 1973, pp. 82, 86, as quoted in Gowa (1983, p. 42). The data on U.K. banks and the Eurodollar market come from the Bank of England *Quarterly Bulletin*, various issues, and the *Annual Report* of the Bank for International Settlements, various issues, respectively, as quoted in Kane (1983, pp. 2–3, 155–7). Finally, the data below on U.S. bank Eurodollar borrowings and the assets and liabilities of the overseas branches of U.S. banks come from the *Federal Reserve Bulletin*, various issues, some of which is also quoted in Kane (1983, pp. 159, 164–5).
5 See Chapter 4 for a formal analysis of the inflationary pressures in the U.S. in the late 1960s, and Chapter 5 for a description of the wage and price controls which were

designed to contain them. The increased reserve requirements and restrictions on U.S. bank access to loans from the Federal Reserve were necessary complements to the wage and price controls. See Lance Taylor (1991, chapter 4) for a more general analysis of the conditions under which higher short-term interest rates will cause inflation, in contrast to the widely accepted view that higher interest rates are always and everywhere a means to combat inflation.

6 In December 1965, the Federal Reserve had signaled the high-interest-rate policy, begun more subtly with a contractionary open-market policy in February 1965, by increasing the discount rate. The April 1967 discount-rate decrease reversed the December 1965 discount-rate increase. See Chapter 5 for an analysis of the circumstances surrounding the latter, and why it was so controversial.

7 The tight monetary policy did not begin until May 1968 for two reasons. First, the Federal Reserve had to wait a decent interval after the expiration of the legislated interest-rate ceilings on small-denomination time deposits in September 1967 not to provoke Congress. Second, the Federal Reserve had to wait for the bank cartel to institutionalize mechanisms to assure itself of funds in the Eurodollar market. In Chapter 4, I explain the reasons why the Federal Reserve abandoned the tight monetary policy in February 1970.

8 The supply-side factors that Stanley W. Black (1971, pp. 84–5) suggests adding to this equation proved to be statistically insignificant.

9 Chase Manhattan Bank, First National City Bank, and Manufacturers Hanover Trust Company accounted for most of the borrowing of Eurodollars by U.S. banks in the late 1960s (Kelly 1976, p. 98). If Bank of America, Bankers Trust Company, and Morgan Guaranty Trust are added to this list, or, at a maximum, if Chemical Bank, Continental Illinois, First Chicago Bank, Marine Midland Bank, and the First National Bank of Boston are also added, then practically all U.S. bank Eurodollar borrowings in the late 1960s are probably accounted for (Kelly 1976, pp. 15, 147).

10 The specification of a more sophisticated lag structure did not improve on the assumption that U.S. bank Eurodollar borrowings are a positive function of themselves lagged one period.

11 I use the yield on 4–6 month commercial paper for this variable, as reported in the *Federal Reserve Bulletin*, various issues. The other interest-rate variables are also taken from the *Federal Reserve Bulletin*, various issues.

12 The estimated equation is as follows (with *t*-statistics in parenthesis):

$$EUROD_t = -1175 + 0.85\,EUROD_{t-1} + 318\,i_{cmp,t}$$
$$(3.36) \qquad (19.91) \qquad\qquad (3.75)$$
$$+\,461MR_t + 431\,D_1 - 966\,D_2$$
$$(4.52) \qquad (3.28) \qquad (5.18)$$
$$R^2 = 0.995 \qquad\qquad\qquad D.H. = 1.18$$

13 The *Federal Reserve Bulletin* reports weekly data on the gross liabilities of U.S. banks to their foreign branches. I used the average of these liabilities as reported at the end of each month for U.S. bank borrowings of Eurodollars (M). I also took reserve requirements on domestic demand deposits and within-bank deposits from the *Federal Reserve Bulletin*. Following Jeffrey P. Owens (1974), the average maturity of the claims on the foreign branches (or subsidiaries) of U.S. banks (Z) was set equal to ninety days. The adjusted monetary base was taken from *Citibase*.

14 Statements reported in this section explaining the international repercussions of U.S. monetary policy are by the manager of the Federal Reserve's foreign-exchange operations (Coombs), the manager of the Open Market Desk (Holmes), the President of the Federal Reserve Bank of Minneapolis (Bruce K. Maclaury), and the staff members at the Federal Reserve Bank of New York responsible for international finance (Hersey

and Solomon). Also see Coomb's (1976) memoir for a fascinating anecdote about how technocrats come to see their small fiefdoms as the most important things in the world. Coombs fits the material covered in this chapter into a theoretical framework implying that all developments were "good" insofar as they contributed to sustaining the fixed-exchange rate of the dollar at $35 an ounce of gold, and "bad" insofar as they worked against that goal.

15 The two-tier gold market meant allowing a market-determined price of gold for private investors but maintaining the $35-an-ounce price for central banks.

16 Most of the negotiations between the central banks of the advanced capitalist countries take place at their regular meetings at the Bank for International Settlements in Basel, Switzerland.

17 Robert Solomon wrote an excellent book on the international monetary negotiations in the late 1960s, entitled *The International Monetary System, 1945–1981* (1982). Solomon hoped to reform the international monetary system in such a way that it would channel the funds accumulated by countries with balance-of-payments surpluses to countries with balance-of-payments deficits—which is the exact opposite direction from how speculators channel funds. His book is thus permeated with the miasma of missed opportunities as speculators seized the initiative while government officials lost themselves in mindless disputes over technicalities.

Bibliography

Arrighi, Giovanni. 1994. *The Long Twentieth Century: Money, Power, and the Origins of Our Times*. New York: Verso.

Black, Stanley W. 1971. "An Econometric Study of Eurodollar Borrowing by New York Banks and the Rate of Interest on Eurodollars," *Journal of Finance*, Vol. 26 (March).

Block, Fred L. 1977. *The Origins of International Economic Disorder: A Study of US International Monetary Policy from World War II to the Present*. Berkeley: University of California Press.

Calleo, David P. and Benjamin M. Rowland. 1973. *America and the World Political Economy: Atlantic Dreams and National Realities*. Bloomington, IN: Indiana University Press.

Coombs, Charles. 1976. *The Arena of International Finance*. New York: Wiley.

Federal Advisory Council. 1967. *Minutes*. Washington, DC: Board of Governors of the Federal Reserve System.

Federal Open Market Committee. 1966–1971. *Minutes*. New York: Federal Reserve Bank of New York.

Federal Reserve Bulletin. New York: Federal Reserve Bank of New York. Various issues.

Gardner, Richard. 1980. *Sterling–Dollar Diplomacy in Current Perspective: The Origins and Prospects for Our Current International Economic Order*. New York: Colombia University Press.

Gowa, Joanna. 1983. *Closing the Gold Window: Domestic Politics and the End of the Bretton Woods System*. Ithaca, NY: Cornell University Press.

Hawley, James. 1987. *Dollars and Borders*. Armonk, NY: M.E. Sharpe.

Helleiner, Eric. 1994. *States and the Reemergence of Global Finance: From Bretton Woods to the 1990s*. Cornell, NY: Cornell University Press.

Johnston, R. B. 1982. *The Economics of the Euro-market: History, Theory and Policy*. New York: St. Martin's Press.

Kane, Daniel R. 1983. *The Eurodollar Market and the Years of Crisis*. New York: St. Martin's Press.

Kelly, Janet. 1976. *Bankers and Borders: The Case of American Banks in Britain.* Cambridge, MA: Ballinger.

Madura, Jeff. 2003. *International Financial Management.* Seventh edition. Thomson, GA: South-Western.

New York Times. 1966.

Owens, Jeffrey P. 1974. *Growth of the Eurodollar Market.* Bangor Occasional Papers in Economics. No. 4. University of Wales Press.

Solomon, Robert. 1982. *The International Monetary System, 1945–1981.* New York: Harper & Row.

Strange, Susan. 1971. *Sterling and British Policy.* London: Oxford University Press.

Taylor, Lance. 1991. *Income Distribution, Inflation and Growth: Lectures on Structuralist Macroeconomic Theory.* Cambridge, MA: MIT Press.

Triffin, Robert. 1961. *Gold and the Dollar Crisis.* New Haven, CT: Yale University Press.

7 Summary and Conclusions

The moral of this book is that the experiment with an independent central bank in the U.S. has had disastrous consequences. There would be less poverty, better jobs, and greater social justice if, instead, the Federal Reserve was compelled to adhere to fixed-interest-rate rules.

We need a central bank to act as lender of last resort to the banking system since private-sector profit-maximizing banks cannot be relied upon to perform this necessary function. The temptation of forcing competitors into bankruptcy then purchasing their assets (i.e. loans) at fire-sale prices is a far more attractive option for them.

However, when establishing the Federal Reserve as a lender of last resort in 1913, it was an egregious error to also give it authority to exercise monetary control. Justified as necessary to stabilize the economy on a non-inflationary growth path, we have seen that the Federal Reserve has used this authority instead to engage in class warfare, against the populist movement prior to the New Deal then against the movement toward social democracy.

The Federal Reserve's shift from implacable opposition to populism to equally implacable opposition to social democracy reflects the transition of the U.S. from a predominantly agrarian to a modern industrial economy. The populist movement was the struggle for social justice by the majority of the U.S. people when they were mostly farmers. Its original target was the crop lien system in the South, which was established during Reconstruction and was characterized by "furnishing merchants" who lent farmers all the necessities of life between harvests in exchange for, first, a commitment to plant only cotton and, second, first claim on the proceeds from the sale of the cotton. Each year, the farmers discovered that the proceeds from the sale of the cotton fell short of what they owed the furnishing merchants. It could not have been otherwise, for the furnishing merchants charged exorbitant interest rates, usually over 100 percent and sometimes over 200 percent: high enough, at any rate, to ensure that the value of the farmers' crops was lower than their bills to the furnishing merchants.

In the effort to break out of the crop lien system, Southern farmers set up purchasing and marketing cooperatives that eventually spread to the Midwest and West. However, the cooperative movement floundered on the fact that the large regional banks would not finance their purchases. The cooperatives produced tokens and script for exchanges among members, but they were of no use in obtaining the farm implements and other commodities that the farmers did not produce themselves. The large regional banks would only lend to the furnishing merchants to finance such purchases.

What began as a cooperative movement to break out of the crop lien system was thus transformed into a political movement, organized around a subtreasuries plan for a central bank, the purpose of which was to break the stranglehold of the large regional banks on the money supply in the South, Midwest, and West. The subtreasuries were to be government-run warehouses and grain elevators in every county with significant agricultural production. But they were also to be central banks since, in exchange for crops put in storage, the subtreasuries would be empowered to issue bank notes, only now the bank notes would be receipts for cotton and grain put on deposit at the subtreasuries rather than for gold put on deposit at a bank.

In the face of the populist threat to their control of a money supply based on gold, the large regional banks in the South, Midwest, and West aligned themselves with the demand of the large New York banks (Wall Street) for a central bank that would both maintain the gold standard and act as lender of last resort. However, to gain this support of the large regional banks, the large New York banks had to agree to a decentralized central bank, with twelve equally powerful regional reserve banks created to give equal power to the bankers in each region of the country: three in the East (Boston, Philadelphia, and New York), three in the South (Atlanta, Dallas, and Richmond), three in the Midwest (Chicago, Cleveland, and Minneapolis), and three in the West (Kansas City, San Francisco, and St. Louis). The banks in each of the twelve Federal Reserve districts elect six of the nine members of the board of directors of the regional reserve bank in their district, thereby ensuring their control of them. The large regional banks and the large New York banks thus assured themselves of both a lender of last resort and a means to exercise monetary control over those who are too weak politically to keep themselves from being rationed out of credit markets: in the first instance, the farmers who supported the populist movement; subsequently, the workers and their middle-class allies who supported the social-democratic movement. We now live in a world in which the monetary-policymaking elites assume that it is inevitable that the economy will grow more slowly than it did in the 1950s and 1960s, and that the basic health of the economy depends upon the basic health of its corporations and banks. Under such circumstances, working people have to do with less than their predecessors. The Federal Reserve—and the propaganda that justifies its role in stabilizing the economy on a non-inflationary growth path—is the bulwark assuring that the majority of the U.S. people do with less so that big business can have more.

This state of affairs is not inevitable. It was broken between the New Deal reforms of 1933–5 and the Treasury–Federal Reserve Accord of 1951, when the government forced the Federal Reserve to abide by fixed-interest-rate rules. This break occurred because of labor insurgencies that began in 1933, when the industrial proletariat organized itself into a cohesive political force, launching a social-democratic movement that gathered momentum through sit-down strikes in Detroit in 1936–7 and a series of national strikes in the immediate postwar period.

The labor insurgencies were defeated after the Republicans won the 1946 Congressional elections and passed the Taft–Hartley Act of 1947. The Republicans then won the Presidency in 1952 and 1956, and President Eisenhower used the bank-to-work provisions of the Taft–Hartley Act to break a strike by the United Steel Workers in 1959.

There was a reprieve for the social-democratic movement under the Kennedy and Johnson administrations, which opted for an incomes policy rather than the back-to-work provisions of the Taft–Hartley Act to cope with organized labor's use of the strike weapon to demand real-wage increases tied to labor productivity. But this reprieve came to an end in August 1966, when the large New York banks insisted on protecting their profit margins by increasing the interest rate on bank loans (the prime rate). A fixed prime rate was the linchpin of the fixed-interest-rate rules that made the social-democratic movement possible. The Federal Reserve could have, and still can, sustain the movement toward social democracy by imposing reserve requirements on the U.S. bank cartel's sources of funds. But instead, initially out of a perceived need to use the bank cartel's borrowings of Eurodollars to finance the U.S. war in Vietnam, the Democratic appointees to the Federal Reserve Board have embraced high-interest-rate policies without reserve requirements on the cartel's sources of funds.

The initial result of this Faustian bargain was the Great Inflation of 1966–79, when the consumer price index rose by 130 percent. For corporations could use their higher borrowing costs (a higher prime rate) to justify charging higher prices for their output. After all, if the large banks could protect their profit margins by increasing the price of their output (money), then why couldn't non-financial corporations protect their profit margins by increasing the price of their output? The organized labor movement was thus reduced to rearguard actions, demanding wage increases to protect the incomes of their members from the higher prices.

This state of affairs was incompatible with fixed exchange rates, and the transition to a flexible-exchange-rate regime in August 1971 gave the majority of the monetary policymakers within the Federal Reserve System a mechanism through which to achieve its long-cherished goal of using high interest rates to weaken labor by precipitating then sustaining recessions, without jeopardizing the liquidity of the U.S. bank cartel. When the Federal Reserve kept interest rates high during the recessions of 1974–5 and 1980–2, it attracted short-term capital inflows into the country, putting upward pressure on the value of the dollar. Particularly in 1980–2, the overvalued dollar undermined the ability of U.S. automobile and steel manufacturers to compete in international markets at the same time that their domestic market was flooded with foreign imports. Massive layoffs and a weakening of labor ensued, bringing to an end the tri-annual rounds of wage negotiations where the UAW, followed by the United Steel Workers and other unions, demanded real-wage increases tied to increases in labor productivity. Instead, a two-tier wage structure was introduced, where new workers received much lower wages than older workers.

At the height of its strength in the mid 1950s, over 35 percent of the industrial proletariat was unionized. By the late 1980s, less than 17 percent was, and the decline has continued, redistributing income from wages to profits. Consequently, the Great Inflation has been replaced by the deflationary pressure of chronically insufficient aggregate demand. Nonetheless, the Federal Reserve remains poised to raise interest rates at the first sign of inflationary pressures, or even of inflationary expectations, like old generals always on the lookout for a chance to re-fight the last war.

Appendix

Table A.1 Index of the monetary-policy preference of the Federal Advisory Council, 1951–88

Date	Excerpt	Index
13 May 1951	... the Council does not believe that reserve requirements should be increased, or that the rediscount rate should be raised in the period immediately ahead. Open market operations should be continued on a basis that will supply the minimum reserves needed for business and for Treasury financing, and maintain a reasonably stable market for government obligations at or around present levels (p. 6).	0
16 Sept. 1951	[Because the Treasury needs $2.5-$3 billion in new money] it will be necessary for the Federal Reserve System to pump more reserves into the banking system, and that process is inflationary. If more reserves are not put into the banking system, then there is the possibility that interest rates will rise ... There is a question of whether it is better to allow short-term interest rates to rise or to pump in reserves (p. 2).	−½
18 Nov. 1951	Open market operations are being satisfactorily handled (p. 5).	0
17 Feb. 1952	The Council believes that the Open Market Committee has followed proper policy (p. 6).	0
18 May 1952	... continue ... the present rediscount rate and ... open market policy of keeping money reasonably tight (p. 2).	0
5 Oct. 1952	... the Council suggest[s] that the present open market policy be continued (p. 4).	0
16 Nov. 1952	[The Council repeated its statement of 5 October (p. 3).]	0
15 Feb. 1953	... the Council approves recent credit policies of the System (p. 5).	0
19 May 1953	... the Council believes that the recent increase in the rediscount rate from $1^3/_4$ per cent to 2 per cent was justified ... The Council believes that no increases should be made in present reserve requirements.	+½

Date	Excerpt	Index
	... If conditions in the next few months should make tighter money desirable, the Council suggests the use of open market operations for that purpose. ... some relief should now be given the money market ... Favorable consideration should also be given to an early reduction in Central Reserve City reserve requirements ... In the event of a business downturn, the System should ease the money market considerably (pp. 3–4).	
13–15 May 1953	... Federal Reserve policy in recent months has been good (p. 4).	0
17 Nov. 1953	The danger of disturbing the economy by making money unduly and artificially cheap is at present fully as great as the danger of restricting business by too high interest rates, and a consequent reduction in the use of credit. The Council believes the Board in its Open Market operations should be as ready to sell short-term securities if bank loans are repaid in volume and money rates are disorderly on the downward side, as to purchase securities if the level of interest rates and any difficulty of obtaining credit should threaten to accelerate the business decline (p. 2).	0
14 Feb. 1954	... the System has been buying on balance rather than selling in connection with its Open Market operations ... the Open Market Committee should have sold securities ... there is no excuse for a bill rate of .90 ... The operations since the latter part of January seem to the Council to have been poorly timed and to have produced undesirable results. At a time when loans were still decreasing, the Council feels the Board's policy should have been to continue to sell bills to an amount approximately offsetting the decline in loans. The Board's action in the early part of January seemed to accord with this view. Later, the Open Market Committee began buying bills again, despite the continuing decline in loans, with the result that the bill rate went below one per cent, which the Council believes represents undesirably cheap money (pp. 6–7).	−1
16 May 1954	... money was too cheap ... a bill rate below one per cent is too low ... open market operations could have been conducted so that the bill rate would not have fallen as low as it has recently (p. 7).	−½
19 Sept. 1954	... the Board's credit policies have been sound and open market operations have been extremely well conducted (p. 4).	0

(*Continued*)

Table A.1 Continued

Date	Excerpt	Index
14 Nov. 1954	. . . the bill rate has been sloppy . . . a bill rate of 1.05 to 1.25 percent would be better than .85 percent to .88 percent . . . Open market operations should be conducted to bring the bill rate up to a figure of 1.10 percent to 1.25 percent (pp. 3–4).	−½
13 Feb. 1955	. . . the Council is in accord with the policies of the System (p. 7).	0
17 May 1955	. . . it may become necessary to consider raising the rediscount rate (p. 3).	−½
18 Sept. 1955	. . . System credit policies have been generally good as some brake on the business boom is necessary (p. 5).	0
13 Nov. 1955	The Council does not believe that present policies should be changed (p. 4).	0
19 Feb. 1956	[The Council repeated its statement of 13 November] (see p. 10).	0
20 May 1956	The members of the Council approve the credit policies presently being pursued by the Board (p. 19).	0
16 Sept. 1956	. . . the System's credit policies since the last meeting have been appropriate (p. 8).	0
18–20 Nov. 1956	. . . credit policies have been appropriate and well executed (p. 6).	0
17 Feb. 1957	. . . the Council does not believe there are sufficient changes in the supply-demand relationships to call for a relaxation of credit restraint (p. 4).	0
12–14 May 1957	. . . the Council believes that the present degree of restraint should be maintained (p. 6).	0
15–17 Sept. 1957	. . . the same degree of restraint should be maintained (p. 5).	0
17–19 Nov. 1957	. . . it will be necessary to increase reserves if a change in policy is to be implemented. It occurs, however, at an appropriate time for the Fed usually puts funds into the market in December (p. 15).	+½
16-18 Feb. 1958	. . . moderately easier policy would be appropriate (p. 2).	+½
19 May 1958	. . . maintain the present degree of ease (p. 2).	0
15 Sept. 1958	. . . the Council expressed approval of the recent reversal of Federal Reserve policy (p. 2).	0
17 Nov. 1958	. . . current credit policies of the System are appropriate (p. 2).	0
16 Feb. 1959	. . . appropriate credit policy for the next three months would be maintenance of the present degree of restraint (p. 4).	0
27 April 1959	. . . maintenance of the current degree of restraint (p. 2).	0
14 Sept. 1959	. . . the present degree of restraint seems appropriate but . . . it might be necessary to modify credit policy if the settlement of the steel strike brought about a resurgence of inflationary pressures (p. 2).	−½
16 Nov. 1959	. . . continuance of the present degree of restraint but . . . the ultimate settlement of the steel strike might require some modification of credit policy (p. 2).	−½

Date	Excerpt	Index
16 Feb. 1960	The Council is in full accord with this [i.e. current monetary] policy (p. 2).	0
16 May 1960	... monetary credit policy had been appropriate and well executed (p. 3).	0
14 Sept. 1960	... the Council unanimously agreed that recent monetary and credit policy has been appropriate (p. 3).	0
14 Nov. 1960	... the Council concurred with the recent monetary and credit policy (p. 2).	0
20 Feb. 1961	... the Council was in accord with the recent monetary and credit policy (p. 3).	0
15 May 1961	... the current degree of ease in the money markets was appropriate (p. 4).	0
18 Sept. 1961	... continuation of the present degree of ease seems desirable (p. 4).	0
20 Nov. 1961	... current monetary and credit policy has been appropriate (p. 2).	0
19 Feb. 1962	... current monetary and credit policy has been appropriate	0
30 April 1962	... current monetary and credit policy has had a desirable impact on business activity. However, the economy has been expanding at least moderately, for over a year now and, the outlook is for a continuation of this trend. On the other hand, the deficit in the balance of payments of the United States, which has persisted for many years, continues with no definite assurance of correction. In these circumstances the Council is inclined to place relatively more weight on international considerations in view of the serious implications of a continuing balance of payments deficit, possible further withdrawals of gold, and the threat confronting the dollar (p. 3).	$-\frac{1}{2}$
17 Sept. 1962	... the Council felt that current monetary and credit policy had a favorable impact on the economy. While the members were pleased with progress that had been made in our international payments position, they did not believe that the improvement had been sufficient to warrant placing more weight on domestic considerations in the determination of monetary policy (p. 3).	$-\frac{1}{2}$
19 Nov. 1962	... the present degree of ease continues to be appropriate (p. 3).	0
18 Feb. 1963	... policy has been a constructive factor in the domestic economy and at the same time has been helpful to the balance of payments (p. 4).	0
21 May 1963	The Council believes that current monetary and credit policy has had a favorable impact on the economy (p. 3).	0
16 Sept. 1963	... the Council believes that some further tightening of monetary policy might be desirable (p. 3).	$-\frac{1}{2}$
18 Nov. 1963	... the recent monetary and credit policy has been most appropriate (p. 3).	0

(Continued)

Table A.1 Continued

Date	Excerpt	Index
17 Feb. 1964	... it was agreed that monetary and credit policy had been effective. Domestic business activity continues to rise while our balance of payments situation has been maintained since mid-1963. It was decided, however, to add ... that if the anticipated tax cut should strongly stimulate business activity and create inflationary pressures, a policy of credit restraint would be warranted (p. 4).	$-\frac{1}{2}$
22 April 1964	... there was wide agreement that the Council should support Chairman Martin in his concern about developments in the credit markets and possible emergence of inflationary pressures. Accordingly, it was decided to suggest that in view of the current volume of business activity, the additional stimulation from the tax cut, the possibility of a renewal of wage cost increases, and the probable pressure on prices, that monetary and credit policy should now move gradually in the direction of restraint (p. 4).	$-\frac{1}{2}$
21 Sept. 1964	... the Council's response ... at the April meeting was even more appropriate now than at that time (p. 4).	$-\frac{1}{2}$
16 Nov. 1964	... the Council observed that the monetary authorities had been pursuing a somewhat less easy credit policy ... The Council concluded, therefore, that credit policy is in accord with the previously expressed views of the Council ... The members of the Council continue to believe that the trend of recent wage settlements and the negotiations now taking place in the auto industry, as well as those soon to begin in steel, point to growing pressures on costs that finally may be reflected in prices (pp. 3–4).	$-\frac{1}{2}$
15 Feb. 1965	... there was a strong feeling that the [balance of payments] problem is of such importance that a comprehensive program of action was imperative. This would include not only the voluntary program to restrain temporarily the outflow of capital, but, in addition should include the following: (1) a further reduction in U.S. economic and military aid overseas; (2) an easing of barriers tending to discourage the repatriation of earnings overseas; (3) a continuation and expansion of the program to encourage exports; (4) a continuation of efforts to keep wages and other costs within productivity gains; (5) a reduction in the availability of credit. The members of the Council decided to emphasize the view that the situation required a somewhat more restrictive credit policy and, if necessary, a rise in the structure of interest rates (p. 4).	-1
17 May 1965	... monetary and credit policy has been appropriate (p. 4)	0

Date	Excerpt	Index
20 Sept. 1965	There was some feeling among the members that the Board should move in the direction of further restraint (p. 4)	−½
15 Nov. 1965	There was general agreement that the productive resources of the nation are approaching maximum utilization. In these circumstances it seems prudent to slow the rate of bank credit expansion. Failure to do so will probably result in increased upward pressure on prices (p. 3).	−½
14 Feb. 1966	... the availability of reserves should be gradually reduced to more modest proportions through open market operations and ... it also may be necessary to increase the discount rate again (p. 4).	−½
20 June 1966	... the gradually increasing restraint that has characterized credit and monetary policy in the recent past should be continued (pp. 3–4).	0
19 Sept. 1966	... the Council approves a continuation of a policy of monetary policy of monetary restraint in the critical period ahead (pp. 4–5).	0
14 Nov. 1966	... the members of the Council favor a continuation of restrictive monetary and credit policy (p. 3).	0
20 Feb. 1967	... the Council approves the easing that characterizes current monetary and credit policy (p. 4).	0
15 May 1967	[The Council repeated its statement of 20 February (p. 4).]	0
18 Sept. 1967	... most members of the Council thought monetary policy should be somewhat less expansive (p. 4).	−½
20 Nov. 1967	... the devaluation of the pound sterling ... altered the monetary and credit policy that otherwise might have been pursued. The resulting uncertainties, therefore, dictated the direction of policy, i.e., rates should be sufficiently firm to restrain any large outflow of funds (p. 5).	−1
19 Feb. 1968	... the Council would favor continuation of the somewhat less easy monetary and credit policy that has prevailed (p. 5).	0
3 June 1968	... the Council indicated its approval of current monetary and credit policy (p. 2).	0
16 Sept. 1968	... a number of members thought the reduction in the discount rate may have been premature (p. 5).	−½
18 Nov. 1968	The Council believes that a policy of monetary and credit restraint in appropriate (p. 6).	−½
18 Feb. 1969	[For excerpts for the remaining entries, see Havrilesky (1990, pp. 47–50).]	0
20 June 1969		0
16 Sept. 1969		0
18 Nov. 1969		0
6 Feb. 1970		+½
1 May 1970		+½

(*Continued*)

Table A.1 Continued

Date	Excerpt	Index
11 Sept. 1970		0
6 Nov. 1970		0
5 Feb. 1971		+½
18 June 1971		0
17 Sept. 1971		−½
5 Nov. 1971		0
4 Feb. 1972		−½
5 May 1972		−½
15 Sept. 1972		−1
3 Nov. 1972		−1
2 Feb. 1973		−1
4 May 1973		0
7 Sept. 1973		−½
2 Nov. 1973		0
1 Feb. 1974		0
3 May 1974		0
6 Sept. 1974		+1
1 Nov. 1974		+½
6 Feb. 1975		+1
1 May 1975		+1
12 Sept. 1975		+½
7 Nov. 1975		0
6 Feb. 1976		0
6 May 1976		0
10 Sept. 1976		0
5 Nov. 1976		0
4 Feb. 1977		0
6 May 1977		−1
9 Sept. 1977		−½
4 Nov. 1977		0
3 Feb. 1978		−1
5 May 1978		−1
Sept. 1978	[The *Minutes* of this meeting are not available.]	
Nov. 1978	[The *Minutes* of this meeting are not available.]	
2 Feb. 1979	[For excerpts of the remaining entries, see Havrilesky (1990, pp. 47–50).]	−½
4 May 1979		−½
7 Sept. 1979		−1
2 Nov. 1979		−1
8 Feb. 1980		−1
2 May 1989		0
5 Sept. 1980		−½
7 Nov. 1980		−½
5 Feb. 1980		−½
30 April 1981		−1
11 Sept. 1981		0
6 Nov. 1981		−½
5 Feb. 1982		−½

Date	Excerpt	Index
21 May 1982		0
17 Sept. 1982		0
5 Nov. 1982		0
4 Feb. 1983		0
6 May 1983		0
9 Sept. 1983		$+\frac{1}{2}$
4 Nov. 1983		0
3 Feb. 1984		$-\frac{1}{2}$
4 May 1984		$+\frac{1}{2}$
7 Sept. 1984		$+\frac{1}{2}$
2 Nov. 1984		0
8 Feb. 1985		0
3 May 1985		0
6 Sept. 1985		0
1 Nov. 1985	[For excerpts of the remaining entries, see Havrilesky (1993, p. 284).]	$+\frac{1}{2}$
Feb. 1986		$+\frac{1}{2}$
2 May 1986		0
12 Sept. 1986		0
14 Nov. 1986		0
6 Feb. 1987		0
1 May 1987		0
11 Sept. 1987		0
4 Dec. 1987		$-\frac{1}{2}$
5 Feb. 1988		0
6 May 1988		0

Index

Ackley, Gardner 76, 116
Ahearn, A.S. 40
Aliber, R.Z. 76
American Climax Incorporated 118
Arrighi, Giovanni 156
art of central banking 4, 27, 39, 124
ask price 29, 113
asset management 57, 98, 111

Bagehot, Walter 28
Balderston, C. Canby 68, 70, 71–2, 77
balance of payments, U.S. 142
Bank of America 127, 157
bank notes 28–9, 32
bank profit margins 29–30, 33, 113, 117
Bank Wars (1830s) 31
Bankers Trust Company 127, 157
Barro, Robert J. 103
Bazemen, M.H. 11
Bernanke, Ben S. xiv, 1
bid price 29, 30, 113
bills of exchange 28
bimetallism 31
Black, Robert P. 100
Black, Stanley W. 157
Blinder, Alan xiv, 1
Block, Fred L. 130, 156
Blough, Roger 73, 77
Board of Governors (*see* Federal
   Reserve Board)
Boddy, Raford 41, 63, 104
Bopp, Karl R. 100, 102
Bortis, Heinreich 21
Brimmer, Arthur F. 80, 82, 116, 117, 125,
   143, 146

Brinkley, Alan 64
British Empire 131
British pound sterling 144–5
Brunner, Karl 40, 103
Bruno, Michael 103
Bryan, Malcolm H. 99
Bundesbank 143, 145–50, 152
Burger, A. 3
Burns, Arthur F. 84, 87, 89
business loans 57
Business Week 95

Cagan, Phillip 3
Calleo, David P. 156
Camerer, C. 21
Capen, E.C. 11
capital market: orthodox theory 5
Carabelli, A.M. 19
Carron, Andrew S. 4, 124, 127
cartels xv, 30, 33, 133
Cash Items in Process
   of Collection 141
central banks 1, 4, 27, 16 160
Chandler, Lester V. 85
Chase Manhattan Bank 127, 157
Chemical Bank 127
Chick, Victoria 22
Clay, George H. 100, 101, 102, 127
clearinghouse currency 29
clearinghouses 3, 28, 30, 31
Coldwell, Philip E. 84, 100, 101, 102
Continental Illinois Bank 127
Coombs, Charles 144–5, 146, 147–8,
   155, 158
cost-of-living adjustments 96, 103

crop lien system 31–2, 160–1
Crotty, James 41, 63, 104

Daane, J. Dewey 83, 84, 116, 146
Dale, Edwin L. 123–4
D'Arista, Jane 33, 37
Davidson, Paul 21–2, 56
Davis, Archie K. 112, 154
Davis, Mike 62, 65
Deming, Frederick L. 116
Dequech, D. 21–2
Dewald, W.G. 40
discount rates 99, 113–15, 117
D-mark, German 152
D'Orlando, R. 21, 23
Dornbusch, Rudiger 94
Dumenil, Gerard 122
Dymski, Gary 62

Eatwell, John 20
Eichengreen, Barry 35
Eisenhower administration 76, 162
Ellsberg, D. 21
endogeneity of money, compared with
   exogeneity of money 136–42
Epstein, Gerald x–xii, 30–1, 34, 37, 41, 55,
   62–3, 104, 113–14
Eurodollar market 5, 110, 119, 122, 126,
   127, 130–56, 157
Evolution of Central Banks
   (Charles Goodhart) 35, 127
Executive Committee
   (Federal Reserve System) 56
expectations 10
expected profit, compared with actual
   profit 7, 9–10, 12–13

FAC/FACT/FACE index 51–4, 57
Fazzari, Steven M. 40, 52
Federal Advisory Council (FAC) 43, 46,
   51, 56; monetary-policy preference
   164–71
Federal Open Market Committee
   (FOMC) 43, 46, 56, 67–8, 73
Federal Reserve Act (1913) 33
Federal Reserve Bank of Atlanta 100,
   102, 127
Federal Reserve Bank of Boston 100, 102
Federal Reserve Bank of Chicago 100

Federal Reserve Bank of Cleveland
   101
Federal Reserve Bank of Dallas 100,
   101, 154
Federal Reserve Bank of Kansas City
   100, 101, 127
Federal Reserve Bank of Minneapolis
   101, 135
Federal Reserve Bank of New York 50, 56,
   66, 70, 73, 74, 100
Federal Reserve Bank of Philadelphia 99
Federal Reserve Bank of Richmond 100,
   112, 154
Federal Reserve Bank of San Francisco
   100, 102, 127
Federal Reserve Bank of St. Louis 101
Federal Reserve Board (Board of
   Governors) 33–4, 43, 46, 56
Federal Reserve Bulletin 157
Federal Reserve System: democratic
   control (1935–51) xv, 37; establishment
   (1913) 27–34, 160; independence
   ended (1969) 86; independence
   granted (1951) 37, 39, 42, 66
Federal Reserve–Treasury Accord xv, 34
Fellner, William J. 93
Ferguson, Thomas xvi, 34, 37
financial crisis (1893) 29
financial crisis (1907) 29
financial crisis (1953) 43
financial crisis (1966) 108–27
financial instability hypothesis 109–11
First Chicago Bank 127
First National Bank of Boston 127
First National City Bank (Citibank) 112,
   127, 157
Fisher, Stanley 94
fixed-exchange-rate system 130, 131,
   144, 153, 155–6, 162
fixed-interest-rate rule 34, 160, 162
Flaschel, Peter 6
Foley, Duncan K. 5
Fontana, G. 21
forward cover 145, 148
Fowler, Henry H. 116, 118, 120
Francis, Darryl R. 100, 101, 103
Fraser, Steve 64
free reserves 39, 55–6
"free-rider" problem 30, 31, 113

Friedman, Milton 3, 31, 41, 86
fundamental uncertainty 10
furnishing merchants 31

Galusha, Hugh D., Jr. 101, 135
Gardner, Richard 132
Garegnani, Pierangelo 21
General Motors 62, 63, 64, 89
General Theory (Keynes) 1, 17, 22
Gerrard, B. 19, 21
Gerstle, Gary 64
global financialization 156
gold exchange standard 28, 31, 34–5, 156;
    abolition 130, 153
Golden Age xvi, 108, 121
Goldfeld, Steven M. 85
Goldstein, Jonathan 10
Goodhart, Charles 6, 27, 30, 35, 41, 58, 127
Goodwyn, Lawrence 32, 34, 120
Gordon, David 62
Gordon, Robert 22, 40
Gorton, Gary 29
Gould, J.P. 128
government-securities market 42
Gowa, Joanna 156
Great Depression (1930s) 34
Great Inflation (1966–79) 162, 163
Greider, William 32
Greiner, Alfred 6
Guttentag, Jack 40, 109

Haberler, Gottfried 103–4
Hacking, I. 22
Halevi, Joseph 2, 10
Harrod, Roy 22
Havrilesky, Thomas 51
Hawley, James 134
Hayes, Alfred 70–1, 73, 74, 77, 78, 79, 83,
    143, 146, 150, 151
Heflin, Aubrey N. 100, 103
Helleiner, Eric 130
Herring, R. 109
Hersey, A.B. 147, 150–1, 157
Hershey, J. 12
Hester, D.D. 5
Heinemann, H. Erich 118, 121, 123
Hickman, W. Braddock 100, 101
high-powered money 3
historical time 9–10

Hofstadter, Albert 64
Holmes, A. 4, 86, 103, 149, 157
Horne, John E. 117, 119
House Banking Committee 88
House Ways and Means Committee 75

incomes policy xiv, 76–8, 80, 115, 117, 119
inflation: real xiv, 65–6; monetary xiv
information asymmetry 33, 128
Ingersoll, J.E. 16
Inland Steel Company 119
interbank lending rate 103
Interest-Rate Equalization Tax 134
interest-rate rules xv, 19, 34, 113
International Monetary Fund 130
International Union of Electrical
    Workers 67
investment multiplier 8, 21
Irons, Watrous H. 113, 154

Jackson, D.H.A. 65
Johannes, J.M. 4
Johns, Delos C. 99
Johnson administration 5, 77, 78, 80, 92,
    115, 116, 117, 118, 120, 121, 162
Johnson, Harry 40
Johnston, R.B. 132, 156

Kagel, J.H. 11
Kahneman, Daniel 22
Kaldor, Nicholas 5, 20, 56
Kalecki, Michal 41, 63
Kane, Daniel 156
Katznelson, Ira 64
Kelly, Janet 127, 157
Kennedy administration 76, 77, 115, 162
Kettl, Donald F. 85
Keynes, John Maynard xv, 1, 2, 152;
    critique of orthodox theory 6–8
Keynesian theory 1, 8–19, 29, 39, 40–1;
    see also New Keynesian theory,
    Post Keynesian theory
Khoury, Salwa S. 41, 57
Kimbrel, Monroe 100, 103
Kindleberger, Charles 4, 124
Knickerbocker Trust Company 29
Klein, Benjamin 30
Kolko, Gabriel 32, 37
Kotz, David M. 64, 122

labor market: orthodox theory 5–6
law of large numbers 11–12
leaning against the wind 38
lender of last resort xv, 27, 29
Levin, D. 11
Levy, Dominique 122
liability management 57, 98, 111
Lichenstein, Nelson 62, 64
liquidity preference 15–17
loan certificates 28–9
Lombra, Raymond 40, 93, 95
long-period method 21
long-term interest rate 22, 29
loss aversion 22
Lucas, Robert 103

McCallum, Bennet T. 104
MacLaury, Bruce K. 157
Madura, Jeff 156
Maisel, Sherman 81, 84, 115, 116, 146
Manufacturers Hanover Trust Company
    127, 157
marginal efficiency of capital 8, 21
Marine Midland Bank 127
Markowitz, Harry M. 11–12
Martin, William McChesney, Jr. 38, 49–50,
    56, 67, 69, 70, 72, 75, 86, 114, 115, 118,
    142, 146, 149, 154
Marx, Karl 7
Mayer, Thomas 93, 103
Meigs, James 40
Melton, William C. 99
Meltzer, Allan 3, 40
Michl, Thomas R. 5
Milgate, Murray 20
Miller, M. 30
Mills, Abbot Low, Jr. 68, 70
Minsky, Hyman 56, 88, 109, 127
Mitchell, George W. 78, 79, 83, 84, 93,
    116, 135, 143, 146
molybdenum 118, 128
Monetarist theory 39–40, 41, 92, 93, 103,
    104
monetary base 3, 5
money multiplier 3
Moore, Basil 4, 56, 58, 112
Moran, Michael 95
Morgan Guaranty Trust 127, 157
Morris, Frank E. 95, 102, 103

National Association of Homebuilders 86
National Bank of Commerce 29
National Development Bank 88, 103
National League of Insured Savings
    Associations 121
negotiable certificates of deposit 109,
    111–12
negotiable time deposits 112
Neoliberal Era xvi, 108, 121, 130, 151, 153
net present value 9
New Classical theory 92, 93, 104
New Deal reforms xvi, 34, 108, 161
New Economics 119–20
New Keynesian theory 94–5, 103, 104
New York Clearing House 28–9
New York Times 88, 110, 111, 123
Nixon administration 85, 87, 88, 89,
    153, 156
non sufficient reason 11

O'Donnell, Rod 19, 21–2
oil-drilling rights 11, 21
O'Hara, Phillip A. 109
Okun, Arthur M. 103
Okun's Law 94
Operation Twist 77
Organization of Petroleum Exporting
    Countries (OPEC) 95
orthodox theory 1, 2–8, 92; comparison
    with Keynesian theory 9
Owens, Jeffrey P. 157

Palley, Thomas 4
Panico, Carlo 41, 63
Pasinetti, Luigi 21
Patman, Wright 117
Patterson, Harold T. 102, 127
penalty-rate policy 50–1, 64, 98
Phillips curve 92, 104
Pivetti, Massimo 41, 63
Pollin, Robert 56, 103, 127
Populist Movement xix, 31–2
Post Keynesian theory 97, 121, 122
prime rate 79, 114, 132–4
probability theory 10–13
Proxmire, William 86, 117

Quantity Equation 2–3
quantity restraints 82–3

randomness 128
Rasche, R.H. 4
Raskin, A.H. 73
reaction functions 41
real-bills doctrine 33
real interest rate 6, 57–8
Regional Reserve banks 32
Regulation Q 79, 81–3, 100, 113, 135
Ricardo, David 8
Riefler, Winfield 50
risk 10–11, 14–15
Robertson, James Louis 68, 70, 79, 81, 83, 84–5, 87, 146
Robinson, Joan xv, 22
Rockefeller, David 118
Romer, Christina D. 41
Romer, David H. 41
Roosa, Robert V. 119
Ross, A.M. 76
Rottenstreich, Y. 12
Rousseas, Stephen W. 5, 33, 56
Rowland, Benjamin M. 156
Runde, J. 21

Sachs, Jeffrey D. 103
"safe" interest rate 7, 17
Samuelson, W.F. 11
Sardoni, Claudio 10
Sargent, Thomas J. 103
Scanlon, Charles J. 100
Schlesinger, Arthur, Jr. 31
Schomaker, P.J.H. 12
Schor, Juliet 34, 41, 55, 63
Schwartz, Anna Jacobson 3, 41
Shaikh, Anwar 8
Senate Banking Committee 88
Shepardson, Charles Noah 68–9, 70, 72, 74, 76, 81
Sherrill, Robert 81, 82
short-term interest rate 22, 29, 56, 57, 103
Shulz, G.P. 76
Skocpol, Theda 64
"sloppy" financial markets 43
Smith, Vera C. 30
social-democratic movement xix, xvi, 64, 108, 124–5, 142–3
Solomon, Robert 21, 76, 152, 158
specie certificates 28

special drawing rights 130
Sprenkle, C.M. 30
Sproul, Allan 50–1, 56, 66–7, 70
stabilization policy xiv, 33, 48–49
Steinberg, Bruce 96
Strange, Susan 132
Strauss, George 73
sub-treasuries 32
Suez Canal crisis 132
Swan, Eliot J. 102, 127

Taft–Hartley Act (1947) 64, 76, 162
Taylor, Lance 157
Teamsters union 103
Thaler, Richard H. 15, 21–2
Timberlake, Richard H. 31
time (*see* historical time)
time deposits 53, 109, 127, 128
Tobin, James 22, 128
Tobin's q 22
Torta, Raymond 40
Treasury-bill rate 43, 51–4, 57, 100
Treasury–Federal Reserve Accord (1951) 34, 161
"Treaty of Detroit" (1950) 62, 63–6, 68, 74, 153
Treiber, William F. 65, 77–8
Triffin, Robert 130
Trivoli, George 31
"true inflation" (Keynes) 22
Truman, Harry S 121
Tversky, Amos 12, 15, 22
two-tier gold market 158

U.K. banks 132–3, 151, 155
United Automobile Workers (UAW) 62, 63, 64, 67, 68, 88, 95–6, 97, 162
United Steel Workers 67, 74, 76, 97, 162

Vardaman, James Kimble, Jr. 67
velocity of money 5, 142
Verrecchia, R.E. 128
Vietnam War 131, 133–4, 142–3, 145, 162
Voluntary Foreign Credit Restraint Program 77, 78, 134

Wachovia Bank and Trust Company 112, 154
Wayne, Edward A. 112, 154

weight of arguments 11–12, 21
Weintraub, Sidney 40, 56
Weir, Margaret 64
West German central bank: *see* Bundesbank
White, Lawrence H. 29
Wicker, Elmos 40
Willet, Thomas D. 93
Williams, Alfred H. 99

"winner's curse" 11
Wojnilower, Albert M. 4, 43, 109, 124
Wolfson, Martin H. 57, 88, 109, 110, 111, 124, 125, 127
Woolley, John T. 85
Wray, L. Randall 4

Young, Allyn 72

Taylor & Francis eBooks

Helping you to choose the right eBooks for your Library

Add Routledge titles to your library's digital collection today. Taylor and Francis ebooks contains over 50,000 titles in the Humanities, Social Sciences, Behavioural Sciences, Built Environment and Law.

Choose from a range of subject packages or create your own!

Benefits for you

» Free MARC records
» COUNTER-compliant usage statistics
» Flexible purchase and pricing options
» All titles DRM-free.

Benefits for your user

» Off-site, anytime access via Athens or referring URL
» Print or copy pages or chapters
» Full content search
» Bookmark, highlight and annotate text
» Access to thousands of pages of quality research at the click of a button.

REQUEST YOUR **FREE** INSTITUTIONAL TRIAL TODAY

Free Trials Available
We offer free trials to qualifying academic, corporate and government customers.

eCollections – Choose from over 30 subject eCollections, including:

Archaeology	Language Learning
Architecture	Law
Asian Studies	Literature
Business & Management	Media & Communication
Classical Studies	Middle East Studies
Construction	Music
Creative & Media Arts	Philosophy
Criminology & Criminal Justice	Planning
Economics	Politics
Education	Psychology & Mental Health
Energy	Religion
Engineering	Security
English Language & Linguistics	Social Work
Environment & Sustainability	Sociology
Geography	Sport
Health Studies	Theatre & Performance
History	Tourism, Hospitality & Events

For more information, pricing enquiries or to order a free trial, please contact your local sales team: www.tandfebooks.com/page/sales

Routledge
Taylor & Francis Group

The home of Routledge books

www.tandfebooks.com

For Product Safety Concerns and Information please contact our EU
representative GPSR@taylorandfrancis.com Taylor & Francis Verlag GmbH,
Kaufingerstraße 24, 80331 München, Germany

Printed and bound by CPI Group (UK) Ltd, Croydon, CR0 4YY
08/05/2025
01864536-0001